KICKING WITH BOTH FEET

Frank Clark was born in Durham and played for many years for Newcastle United before transferring to Second Division Nottingham Forest in 1975. Within four years, the club were champions of Europe, thanks to the inspirational management of Brian Clough.

After retiring as a player, Clark became assistant manager at Sunderland for two years, before moving on to Orient, taking over as manager in 1983, where he stayed until 1993. He then succeeded Clough as manager of newly relegated Nottingham Forest, returning to the scene of his greatest triumphs as a player. Having gained promotion in his first season, he took them to third in the Premiership, qualifying for Europe, and was chosen by his Premier League peers as their manager of the year. Yet within eighteen months he resigned as manager in December 1996, showing how insecure the manager's role has become.

Clark moved to Manchester City a few days later, where he became the club's fifth manager of the season. He was sacked early in 1998.

He is vice-chairman of the League Managers' Association and lives in Nottinghamshire.

KICKING WITH BOTH FEET

Frank Clark

The inside story of how the game really works

HEADLINE

First published in 1999
by HEADLINE BOOK PUBLISHING

First published in paperback in 2000
by HEADLINE BOOK PUBLISHING

10 9 8 7 6 5 4 3 2 1

ISBN 0 7472 6164 4

Typeset by Palimpsest Book Production Limited,
Polmont, Stirlingshire
Printed and bound in Great Britain by
Clays Ltd, St Ives plc

HEADLINE BOOK PUBLISHING
A division of the Hodder Headline Group
338 Euston Road
London NW1 3BH

www.headline.co.uk
www.hodderheadline.com

This book is dedicated to the
memory of my parents.

Contents

Acknowledgements

I would like to thank Nick Kehoe, without whom this book would not have been written, and whose support and encouragement have been invaluable throughout.

Thanks also to all the people who have helped me during my football career with advice and encouragement, especially my father, who was my greatest critic and my greatest fan!

INTRODUCTION

Heroes and Villains

As manager of Liverpool and then Blackburn Kenny Dalglish exuded an air of infallibility. Winning two League titles with different clubs suggests the mark of genius; it's something only legends like my former boss Brian Clough are supposed to achieve. But Dalglish did it and, for a time, it seemed he could walk on water. Unfortunately, that illusion sank in the murky depths of the Tyne when he parted company with Newcastle in August 1998. He had spent millions on new players yet the team had played only two games of the new season before he went. It was a perfect example of how precarious the position of the manager has become.

Football has always been a hire-and-fire profession but the casualty rate is reaching breakneck pace because the game has changed so much in the last five years. There are a host of reasons, most of them to do with money and all of them making the manager's task more complicated. We've had the emergence of the millionaire players. How do you motivate people who are so rich they need never work again? As Pierre van Hooijdonk proved at Nottingham Forest, if they don't like the club's policy they can afford to go on strike. When my old team-mate Larry Lloyd tried something similar under Brian Clough 20 years earlier, he had to come back after a few days because he couldn't afford to pay his mortgage.

Van Hooijdonk sat it out for months until Forest's plc board decided he was too valuable an asset to have wasting away and decided to bring him back, even if it meant undermining the authority of the manager and risking the morale of the other players. A few months later Forest sacked manager Dave Bassett after a string of bad results. He claimed the player power of van Hooijdonk was a big part in his downfall.

There have been several other changes, such as the alarming tendency for the rich clubs to get richer and the poor to get poorer. Manchester United and a few other clubs are now so wealthy and so powerful they're threatening the future of the league. The Bosman ruling giving players freedom of contract is another development that has changed the game completely; and football has been embraced by the chattering classes, altering its profile and making it bigger than ever. This has led to ever more intrusive press coverage, with reporters sniffing out supposed scandals even where they don't exist. Every move a manager makes is scrutinised and he's held to account. Fans who were once content to discuss the game over a few pints at their local pub now rush to phone David Mellor on *Six-O-Six* to demand their manager be sacked once results start going the wrong way.

We've also had the lemming-like rush to flotation, turning homely, friendly clubs into ruthless, money-spinning businesses. This introduces the interests of shareholders who add a different dimension to the game. For example, Dalglish didn't really hit it off with the people of Tyneside and there was a sense of gloom about the place while he was there. When he left Newcastle, it created a sense of optimism and the share price jumped. There was no logical reason for this as no one could predict whether his successor would do any better. As it turned out, new manager Ruud Gullit was equally unsuccessful even though he spent a fortune of his own. He left a year later to make way for Bobby Robson. Nevertheless, it must have pleased Newcastle's investors at the time to see the share price jump on Dalglish's departure. Investor power is going to be a big factor in the future of club managers.

I became increasingly aware of this alarming rate of change while I was manager at Nottingham Forest. I wanted to produce a book that would reflect what was happening in the game behind the scenes and explore what the effects would be. I felt that if fans were going to understand the game fully and make valid criticism of their club's manager, as they're entitled to do, then they ought to be aware of the pressure-cooker conditions in which he works. I wasn't trying to create sympathy for myself or my fellow managers. It's a great privilege to run a football club and no one is looking for sympathy. It is, however, important for fans, especially those who've become shareholders, to understand how their clubs are being run.

I felt that if the fans could walk a few miles in the manager's shoes then it would be a good start. As it turned out, they would have had to walk pretty fast to keep up with the chain of events that unfolded once the book got started. I was about to experience the incredible ups and downs all managers encounter if they stick around long enough. I had taken over the reins from Brian Clough after Forest had been relegated in 1993. I began with some incredible highs, winning promotion at the first attempt then finishing third in the Premiership, earning the Manager of the Year award in the process. The golden period continued the following season as Forest outpaced the likes of Manchester United and Arsenal to become England's last surviving representative in European competitions. We got to the quarter-finals of the UEFA Cup. It seemed I could do no wrong and soon I was even being touted in the press as a candidate for the England job. Journalists wrote of my astute dealings in the transfer market, buying, for example, Stan Collymore when no one else would take the risk and nurturing him into the England squad. They also spoke of my tactical skills which enabled me to get the best out of my journeymen players at Forest.

Such a honeymoon period couldn't last of course. The following season turned out to be a nightmare and we couldn't seem to win a game. Suddenly I changed in people's eyes from tactical genius to football ignoramus; those same reporters who praised me as a master of the transfer market now began to slaughter me for buying badly when new players like Kevin Campbell weren't instant successes. Then, like Kenny Dalglish, I quickly experienced the wrath of the hitherto worshipping fans. As my position weakened, I clashed with club directors absorbed in financial wheeler dealing while the club was being taken over by big businessmen. The ground was being cut from under me and I knew I had to go.

I parted company with Forest only to take up the challenge again at Manchester City. The main difference there was that this time, like Dalglish, it only took me a year to go from hero to villain. In my first six months, I was hailed as a messiah as I saved the club from relegation and restored some of its pride. In the second six months, our results slumped and so I quickly reverted to villain. Again, like countless managers before me, I faced another ignominious departure.

So, I went from European glory and prospective England manager to the indignity of the sack in just a few years. From success to failure; hero to villain. How can it happen? What does it mean? It means of course that there is only a hair's breadth of difference between winning and losing. If you fall on the wrong side, even if it's only for a few months, you're unlikely to survive.

The book I began in the heady days of European competition had to be constantly revised to keep up to date, not only with the changes in the game but the changes in my career. The result I think is a book that takes the reader on a journey through the world of football to look at the way the game is played, structured and organised from a manager's point of view. I've tried to cover every important aspect of modern football.

There's a chapter on Manchester United and BSkyB television and the threat they pose to the game. I've looked at the effect of money and shown how so much time can be taken up negotiating multi-clause contracts with prima donna stars who want you to arrange everything from reflooring their houses to finding jobs for their wives. I've looked at the rush to turn clubs into limited companies and how it can lead to power struggles behind the scenes with directors. These can destroy a manager as they did with me at Forest.

I've tried to explain some of football's conundrums, such as why so many gifted players don't live up to their promise; why so many star players from George Best to Alan Shearer can be overlooked as youngsters by their local clubs; why so many small clubs can pull off the so-called shock cup results and beat glamorous opposition; why we've had to smash the power of schools football to help young players develop properly.

Specific subjects like Manchester City had to be tackled, of course. If sacking managers were a way to success then City would be European champions by now. Unfortunately for them, it isn't and they aren't! Instead, they've had to serve their time in the lower divisions. I accept my responsibility for City's lack of success during my year at the club, but the overall difficulties went much further than anything a manager could put right. I've tried to describe the problems that plagued the club for years and prevented it from fulfilling its potential. I've tried to be as fair and honest as possible without dodging the issues.

I wouldn't want anyone to think this is a negative read. The whole theme of the book is positive, looking at our game and seeing how we can make it better. And I hope I can also give people a valuable insight into some of the great characters I've had the privilege of working with, such as Brian Clough, Stuart Pearce, Stan Collymore and Georgi Kinkladze.

I've had more than 30 years in football and most of

those years contribute something valuable to this book. I've played more than 500 top-flight league games with Newcastle and Nottingham Forest and won a European Cup medal. I'm vice-chairman of the League Managers' Association and I've managed clubs in every division. I know what it's like to scrimp at a club like Orient. We were so hard up I had to drive the team bus and we were obliged to pay hotel bills up front because our credit rating was so low. At the other extreme, there's the glory of working with some of the country's top internationals and marching through Europe with Nottingham Forest. I've experienced the pain of being sacked at Sunderland only months after helping them get promotion.

Football clubs are full of drama, with incredible highs and unbearable lows for all concerned. Most managers are professional and competent, but try as we might it's unlikely we'll be able to build a team from nothing that will frighten rich clubs like Manchester United. Football being football, however, we'll continue to be sacked for failing to do just that.

If you stick with this book, you will end up knowing a lot more about the world of football. You'll understand more why the game has developed into what it is today and where it's likely to go in the future. But take care, the further in you go the more likely you are to understand the problems faced by the manager at your club. Of course, that doesn't necessarily mean you won't join the chorus on the terraces calling for him to be sacked when things go wrong, but it will certainly make you think twice about applying for his job.

CHAPTER 1

Every Boy's Theatre of Dreams

As a raw 16-year-old his ability was frightening. I watched with a mounting sense of excitement, thinking perhaps that I had found a star of the future. It's the kind of feeling that makes you anxiously check the handful of spectators scattered around the touchline, just to make sure there are no others scouts watching who might snatch away your special discovery. You can never be sure.

Meanwhile, this prodigy gathered the ball on the halfway line and set off, gliding past defenders before curling the ball inside the near post from 20 yards. It was like looking at the next George Best. Surely this boy would play for England.

His name? Danny Cairstow. Danny who? Exactly! The last I heard of him, he was working on a building site in Sunderland. Sadly, Danny never made it as a professional. He turned out to be another of those thousands of supremely talented youngsters who quicken the heartbeat of coaches but fall by the wayside on their way to the top. One of those players we thought might be the next Bobby Charlton, Kevin Keegan, Paul Gascoigne, Alan Shearer, Michael Owen or whoever. Nearly all failed and are no doubt even now wondering about what might have been.

Football may be every boy's theatre of dreams, but very few wake up to enjoy it as reality. There are lots of talented young boys around and it really is very difficult to predict who will make the grade. Strange though it may seem, when players like Paul Scholes or Robbie Fowler were 16-year-olds there would have been hundreds of boys of the same age up and down the country who looked equally promising.

If you find that difficult to believe, then ask yourself why Newcastle paid £15 million for Alan Shearer when they could have had him for nothing ten years earlier. He was a Newcastle fan and stood on the terraces as a boy hero-worshipping the Toon Army's idol of the day, Kevin Keegan. Shearer dreamed of joining his local club but somehow he slipped through the net, even though he went for trials. Instead, he ended up at the other end of the country with Southampton. The Newcastle accountants haven't stopped crying since.

The scouts who missed out on Shearer may take some comfort from the experience of the semi-professional clubs of Northern Ireland who overlooked an even more spec-tacular star. The Irish could see the skinny youngster seeking a trial had ability, but felt he was too small and fragile to withstand the rigours of the game. Thankfully, he had other ideas and got himself a trial at Manchester United. They took a chance on him and their faith was repaid a million times over. The boy's name, of course, was George Best.

This kind of thing happens all the time because of the difficulty of predicting which 16-year-olds will be winners five or six years into the future. It's not for the want of trying. Scouts and coaches may have agonised for months over whether to sign the spindly legged 16-year-old Steve McManaman or choose from a host of more robust players. Elsewhere coaches will have had endless arguments about whether to pick the rough and ready 16-year-old Stuart Pearce or select from a list of more cultured alternatives. Only time would tell whether or not they had made the right decisions.

The coaches who overcame their reservations about the skinny McManaman and chose him over the stronger-looking lads obviously made the right decision, skin and bone though he is. Those who preferred a more cultured alternative to the raw energy of the young Stuart Pearce made a spectacularly wrong decision, for we all know what he went on to achieve with his never-say-die attitude.

The Reebok advert which showed famous players in alternative lives where they don't make it as footballers, because they didn't choose the right boots when they were boys, was nearer the truth than it realised. There really are thousands of people throughout the country eking out a living in mundane jobs who could have made it to the top. You may well see them some time, propping up a bar and telling anybody who will listen about how they nearly made it. In one respect at least, they may be right: they might have had enough talent. But sadly for them, talent isn't everything, as Danny Cairstow and thousands like him have found out to their cost. All the 16-year-olds taken on by professional clubs are extremely talented. But the key to success is the way they develop, physically, mentally and emotionally, between the ages of 16 and 20. Some youngsters just don't seem to progress at all.

It could be simply that they don't have the strength to withstand the physical demands of the modern game, which can be very hard. It could be that they can't apply themselves mentally and show the dedication and determination necessary to succeed. Some youngsters show very little hunger; it's as if they expect it all to fall into place naturally. This is an attitude that probably every parent of a teenager studying for GCSE exams will recognise, but as an approach to professional football it just won't work, because the competition is fierce. It could be that players do work hard but find that their ability remains static and so they get left behind by others who do manage to progress. Or they may retain their skill as individuals but fail to make sufficient progress in working properly for the team.

Lifestyle and personality are important. We've all heard stories about players letting a bit of early success go to their heads and then going off the rails. They get too fond of parties and night clubs, drinking and, in extreme cases, drugs. It does happen, of course, but it isn't as common as you might think. No more common probably than the opposite extreme: the introvert who's just too shy to really fit in and so ends up lacking the confidence to make the most of himself. Talent is no good if you lack the nerve to perform in front of thousands of screaming fans.

It nearly affected the career of one of the most talented players I've ever worked with, the former Nottingham Forest and England striker Tony Woodcock. He was a terribly shy introvert. Even Brian Clough, who was as good a motivator as any manager you're ever likely to come across, struggled to bring him out of his shell. For a while it began to look as though Tony wouldn't make it and Clough considered selling him. Graham Taylor was trying to sign him for Lincoln, which might have meant Woodcock was lost to top-flight football forever.

Fortunately for both Woodcock and Forest, the deal fell through. Tony still had time to run on his contract, remained at Forest and so gained extra time to mature and develop his confidence. It worked out for him. Again, luck played a part. Forest only had a small squad of players and when a series of injuries depleted it even further, Clough was forced to play Woodcock in the first team. He took to it surprisingly well, better than anyone could have predicted. That extra little bit of time had given him the chance to overcome his shyness. In fact he seemed to go from one extreme to the other. He went on to play for England and then surprised everyone by following Kevin Keegan to Germany to build a successful career there. Soon the lad who was almost too shy to speak to his team-mates had grown in confidence so much that he was giving television interviews in German and handling the demands of the world's press.

Sadly, it doesn't always work out that way, which brings me back to Danny Cairstow. That's not his real name, of course, for he was a lovely lad and I would hate to embarrass him. I watched Danny when I was assistant manager at Sunderland. He was a gifted winger and there's no doubt in my mind that he could easily have held his own in the Premier League and possibly played for England. I would have signed him as an apprentice without hesitation. Unfortunately, he'd also been spotted by several of the bigger clubs. They competed for his signature and he eventually joined one of them.

But like Tony Woodcock, Danny was a painfully shy lad. His ability was obvious yet he just couldn't settle. He was away from home for the first time. That can be difficult for the most confident of people but for an introverted 16-year-old it was a major problem. Danny got round it by getting on the first bus home every chance he got. That just cut him off even further from the rest of the apprentices. As they developed friendships among themselves, Danny became more and more of an outsider. It was a vicious circle. The more isolated he felt, the more he went home and the more time he spent at home, the more isolated he became. In spite of this he remained popular with his young colleagues, who could see his tremendous ability.

That ability nearly got him into the first team at the age of just 17. Again, injuries had taken their toll on the first-team squad and the manager, one of the biggest names in the game with League titles to his credit, considered playing Danny. The manager had no doubt about his ability but wondered how his temperament would cope with such sudden exposure to the limelight. The press picked up on the story and ran pieces about how one 17-year-old wonderkid was going to be thrown in at the deep end at the injury-stricken club. It was the first and unfortunately the last big press coverage Danny got.

In the end, the manager thought the pressure would be too much for him at that time. He didn't want to risk Danny and picked someone else. You might have expected Danny to feel crushed, but he didn't. He admitted to me years later that he just felt relieved, rather like a young student might feel having been told he doesn't have to sit that dreaded maths exam after all. Instead of watching the match he went home for the weekend, ostensibly to overcome his disappointment but in reality to celebrate not having to submit to such exposure.

When his apprenticeship was over, the club were keen to sign him in the hope that he would mature and grow in confidence. It was no good. He turned them down. He wanted to return to his home town, which was the only place he felt comfortable. His uncle had offered him a job with his building firm and Danny arranged to join the local non-league team and play for a £20 appearance fee. If you can imagine someone like Michael Owen making that kind of decision then you'll have some idea of the sense of loss felt by everyone who could see Danny's potential.

It seems a terrible waste but it suited Danny, and although I haven't spoken to him for years, I don't think he has any regrets. He was back with people who made him feel at ease, he had a good job and the appearance money meant he was better off than most of his contemporaries. Who's to say he was wrong?

Seeing the problems of people like Tony Woodcock who eventually made it and Danny who didn't, it's obvious that young players not only need football coaching but also a lot of back-up and moral support. That's why it's vital to have a consistent youth policy at a club. We've all seen examples of how first-team players suddenly find themselves out of favour when a new manager arrives. The same sort of thing can happen at youth level. A youngster who impresses one coach may not impress another. I'm sure many youngsters can be affected this way, because some clubs will change their youth coaches when they change their manager.

A typical example is what happened when Graeme

Souness took over at Southampton. Within four days of his arrival he sacked the youth and reserve team coaches, Ray Graydon, Lew Chatterley and Dennis Rofe. They were highly regarded in the game yet Souness got rid of them to bring in his own people.

Who knows how many good youngsters Southampton may have missed because of the upheaval? Continuity is vital at that level. Young players and their parents need to know who they are dealing with and feel confident about the future. It is impossible to say whether the changes meant that Southampton missed out on the next Alan Shearer or Matt Le Tissier, but it's unlikely the instability at the club helped their cause very much. Then to compound the problem, Souness himself resigned just 12 months later, saying he couldn't take the club any further on the resources available.

The irony is that the new manager, Dave Jones, very quickly parted company with the men Souness had brought in, so the whole silly merry-go-round had to start all over again. No rational, civilised business would behave that way. Goodness knows how many players clubs miss because of it, or how many young careers are damaged by it. It would be much better if a club's youth policy was totally independent of the first team set-up. That way young players' careers would not be affected by the ever more frequent comings and goings of managers.

There are great rewards to be gained by taking the long-term approach, as Alex Ferguson has proved at Manchester United. United's great wealth means they can afford to pay huge transfer fees like the £12 million for Dwight Yorke. It's ironic therefore that their current success is based on a crop of home-grown youngsters. Many people thought Ferguson had gone mad when he started offloading quality players like Mark Hughes, Keith Gillespie, Paul Ince, Andrei Kanchelskis and Lee Sharpe. Then they saw the players coming through the youth scheme and it all made sense. David Beckham, Paul Scholes, Nicky Butt, Phil and Gary Neville and, of course, Ryan Giggs.

They are the most exciting crop of players to emerge at one club in a generation, but would they still have come through if the club's momentum had been torn apart by the sacking of the manager? It's impossible to say for certain, but it seems unlikely that they would all have progressed as well as they have.

United went through a series of managers after Sir Matt Busby retired in the late 1960s. They included some of the biggest names in the game – Dave Sexton, Tommy Docherty, Ron Atkinson. Most were dismissed within a few years for failing to deliver the League title which the club seemed to think it had a divine right to win. Ferguson, despite failing to produce the goods in his first seven years in charge, broke that pattern and kept his job.

He repaid the club's faith in spectacular fashion and there must be a lesson here for every other club hungry for success. It's clear that United won that first Championship in 26 years not by chopping and changing managers but by sticking with one person and giving him time to build a winning side. The extra bonus in creating that stability was that it enabled those young players to emerge, saving the club a fortune in transfer fees and making United more successful than ever.

As we've seen, between the ages of 16 and 20 there can be any number of reasons for failure; but there's only really one for success – unswerving dedication. It means very few make it. And by contrast it means that some who aren't the most talented in the world do go on to succeed. They manage to get a good career out of the game by squeezing the absolute maximum out of themselves. There are many players like this. I should know, I was one of them.

I was probably very unusual as a schoolboy player. Most kids want to be professional footballers but their parents want them to go to university instead. In my house it was the other way round. My parents wanted me to be a footballer while I wanted to go to university. This, of course, was back in the Fifties when the maximum wage was still in force. There weren't huge sums of money to be made as there are now.

I considered football to be a very precarious career. This was quite a widely held opinion at that time, when injuries considered relatively simple nowadays were enough to put a player out of the game. I didn't want to be a failed pro at 19 with nothing to fall back on. I thought that if I got an education I would have a choice.

As a teenager I thought I could combine being a footballer with going to university, so I signed for Sunderland as an amateur while I studied for my O-Levels, or GCSEs as they are called now. I used to have to travel down there two nights a week for training. It meant having to catch two buses and a train. I did it for a year but at 15 it was just too much so I asked them to release me. Allan Brown was the manager at the time and fortunately in those days there were still a lot of honourable people in the game, so they agreed to let me go. Nowadays a lot of clubs would want money before they would let you leave.

I carried on with my schoolwork, but suffered a blow when I didn't get good enough A-Level results to go to university. I was a bit disillusioned but still not convinced that becoming a professional footballer was a good idea. I decided to hedge my bets by signing for Newcastle as a part-timer. At the same time I got a job as a laboratory technician at the Royal Victoria Hospital in Newcastle.

I quite enjoyed it but then I broke my leg playing for Newcastle reserves against Liverpool at Anfield. It was a major fracture and I was out for 10 months. During that time I realised that it had to be one or the other. You couldn't succeed as a professional player while trying to hold down a job outside the game.

The other major factor was that while I was recovering from the injury, the game introduced its biggest change in a generation, and we're still feeling the repercussions now. The maximum wage for players was abolished. It was a change brought about partly by the work of a certain Jimmy Hill, one of the top players of his day but better known now as a television pundit. Many of today's players might sneer at his analysis of their performances, but without him they might not be nearly so well off.

With the promise of earning some real money, football suddenly seemed a better prospect as a full-time career. My job as a lab technician was beginning to pall and so I decided to leave and join Newcastle full-time. It was difficult to get into the Newcastle side and I really had to work at it. Like everyone who ends up as a professional I had been outstanding as a schoolboy, but obviously this was a totally different league.

When Newcastle were trying to decide whether or not to sign me as a young player, they asked one of their most experienced coaches to do an assessment. He wrote: *'Well, what can I say about the fellah Clark? He's not all that skilful, he doesn't like receiving the ball and he can't wait to get rid of it when he does get it. But on the other hand, whenever there's any problem, whenever the ball has to be cleared or a last-minute tackle has to be made then he always seems to be the one there doing just enough to clear the danger.'*

I knew I wasn't overblessed with ability and quickly realised that I had to make the most of the little I had or I would never survive. I made sure I played in a way that maximised my strengths and minimised my limitations. I concentrated on doing these simple things well. It worked. As an approach it was never going to make me Footballer of the Year but it was enough to keep me in the Newcastle first team for 12 years. It was also good enough for Brian Clough to sign me for Nottingham Forest at the age of 32, when most players are going out of the game.

In a way, I 'thought' myself towards being a better player than I had any right to be, given my limited ability. I worked out all the angles, played the percentages. I always wanted to win and was prepared to do whatever was necessary for victory. People watching me play used to say they could almost feel the concentration coming out of my head. If I had had the ability of a Paul Gascoigne it might have been different. Players like him can have an off-day and still win you the match with one touch of brilliance. I didn't have that leeway. I couldn't afford to be below my best and get away with it. There was no margin for error.

If young players were to learn anything from my experience, it would be how to get the best out of yourself and go on to have a successful career. Unfortunately, that's a lesson many find hard to grasp. Most big clubs will have more than 20 apprentices. They may not appreciate it at the time but it's an idyllic lifestyle. The days when they were expected to sweep the terraces and clean out the toilets are long gone. Some clubs don't make them do anything at all but I always liked them to do a few little jobs, if only to give them a taste of what real life is like.

At most clubs the apprentices arrive at the ground at about nine o'clock and help the youth coach put out the kit and boots, etc. Then they go and train, get some coaching and play in five-a-sides or whatever. They have at least one day off, possibly two, every week for their schooling. This is very important because probably only about one in 10 apprentices at the bigger clubs achieves success at the top level. Perhaps about another three will go on to make a successful career in the lower divisions. But that still means that over half don't make it at all. That's a very high failure rate and so we owe it to youngsters to make sure they have something to fall back on when the dreaded day comes and we have to tell them they aren't wanted. That's always the worst day of any manager's year.

I try to make it as gentle as possible but there's no nice way to destroy a young boy's dreams. It usually comes at the end of their apprenticeship when they're approaching 18. I have to take them into my office and tell them I don't think they've made sufficient progress to be offered a contract as a full-time professional. I've seen some boys cry and that's always a salutary reminder of how young and fragile they are, for all their youthful swagger. Some of the boys are half-expecting to be disappointed but that doesn't make it any easier for them or for me.

I say to them quite genuinely that I hope they prove us wrong and go on to have great success elsewhere. There's always the odd one who does. Look at David Platt, who was released by Manchester United and had to slip down the divisions with Crewe, but then managed to resurface with Aston Villa. Within a few years he was making a fortune in Italy and went on to play for England more than 50 times.

So there are always going to be the ones who get away. With me it was Warren Barton. He was an apprentice at Orient when I was manager there but when he reached 18 I decided to let him go. In this case, however, I can plead mitigating circumstances. Orient were in a terrible financial state at the time and the board told me I could only take on one apprentice as a full-time pro, no matter how good the others were. I wanted two. One was called Kevin Nugent and he was a very good prospect. The other was Warren Barton.

I was certain that Nugent would make it but I wasn't nearly so sure about Barton. He was very small when he was 18 and it was difficult to tell if he would be strong enough. I would have liked to give him another year to see how he shaped up because he had a bit of something about him and he was a great lad. Unfortunately, Orient couldn't afford to let me do that. I had to choose one or the other and I chose Nugent because he seemed the safer bet.

Warren was naturally disappointed but he showed great strength of character. He ended up playing non-league football with Maidstone. When they forced their way into the Football League, Warren came with them and he went from strength to strength. I was absolutely delighted for him because he's a great character, but he's the only one I released who went on to do anything. In the end Nugent wasn't anything like as successful as Warren but he did play more than 150 games for Orient before being sold on to Plymouth for £275,000, so he was hardly a failure.

He too had a good career but he remained in the lower divisions.

Examples like Warren Barton and David Platt are rare and for most youngsters there's no way back. It's such a hell of a blow being rejected that it's almost impossible to recover. It would take enormous determination and strength of character, and without wishing to be cruel, if they had that kind of determination they probably wouldn't have failed in the first place. I tell them that if they can't get another league club then they should get a job and try to join a non-league team. That way they still have an involvement in the game and there's always a chance of finding a way back. Some go along that path but many find it a difficult thing to do. It's a totally different way of life from everything they've been used to and they prefer to stop playing altogether.

We offer them all the help we can. If we think they have a chance of making it at a lower level then we try to get them fixed up with another club. If not, we give them every help we can in finding a job outside football. We try to tell them in plenty of time. Their apprenticeships usually expire in May but we try to make our decisions by March so the lads have time to sort out their futures. They're allowed to leave straightaway if they want with their contracts paid up, or they can stay until the end and they're treated just the same as everyone else. You just hope the education and training they've been receiving during their apprenticeships will hold them in good stead. The lads might find it small comfort at the time but they will probably appreciate it later in life.

Sometimes in the past as I watched young lads walk out of my office with their young lives shattered, I wished that I could give them more time to develop and prove themselves. Thankfully, changes in the game are now making that possible.

It's already commonplace to see clubs guaranteeing very promising 15-year-olds an extra year or two on top of their apprenticeships. They do this as an inducement for them to sign because they can't offer them money up front at that age, it's against FA rules. It gives the youngster an extra year or so to prove himself, which is obviously a good thing. It does have its down side, though. Sometimes you know by the time they're 18 that they're never going to make it but you're committed to them. At that point you might talk to them and their parents and explain that there is no real hope of any future success. It's in everyone's interest for you to pay up their contract and let them leave early so they can get on with a different career. But very few of them see the logic of this. They prefer to see out the contract and carry on playing in the hope they might turn things round. You know very well it won't happen and they're only deceiving themselves but there's nothing you can do about it.

Developing young players is vitally important for all clubs, as investing in youth can save millions of pounds in the long run. It's obviously crucial that you have the right people to do the coaching and make sure the boys are happy and properly looked after. The system will never be perfect, of course, and we will all continue to make mistakes.

In spite of our best efforts, we still sign boys who fail to make the grade, and will always run the risk of rejecting the boy who turns out to be tomorrow's superstar. All we can do is try to reduce the margin of error on both sides of the coin. You can be sure everyone will be working as hard as they can to get it right. No one wants the embarrassment of a spectacular failure. I still feel a pang of regret over turning down Warren Barton, but then I think: 'Well, it could have been worse. I could have been the man who turned down Alan Shearer.'

CHAPTER 2

The Poverty Trap

They are two of the most talented players of their generation; both stars at their clubs, both England internationals. The transfer fees of the two of them combined have already topped £25 million, yet I could have bought them both for next to nothing. Years later I watched them battling against each other with fascination and a huge feeling of what might have been. Stan Collymore picked up the ball for Liverpool and set off on another one of those powerful runs of his. I never tire of seeing him and when he's in that kind of mood he can terrify defenders. Not this time, though. Graeme Le Saux, playing for Blackburn at the time, casually nicked the ball off his foot and the danger was gone. It was very classy defending.

Imagine putting the two of them together at a tiny, unfashionable club and building a side around them. I nearly did just that, at Leyton Orient. They were both young lads at the time and reaching a point where their clubs were beginning to think they wouldn't make it at the top level. I was manager at Orient and always on the look-out for players being given free transfers. That was all I could afford, because the club was spiralling ever further into the poverty trap. I used to watch eight reserve games a week searching for talent. There were a lot of afternoon games in the reserves league, the Football Combination, so it was usually possible to watch two matches a day.

The games involved the big London clubs – Spurs, Arsenal, Chelsea and so on. I was looking for players who weren't going to make it with them but who still had a bit of something that might flourish if they came and played first-team football with us. I had to concentrate on the London clubs because there was no point watching promising players from outside the city. We wouldn't have been able to pay them enough to cope with the extra cost of living in London.

I took two players from Chelsea. A lad called Kevin Hales was my first and probably best ever signing. We got him on a free, paid him £200 a week and he went on to play more than 450 games for Orient. Terry Howard was another. He came on a free and played 250 games.

We were reasonably successful but it's very difficult to achieve anything on those terms. The problem was that we weren't just competing for the free transfer players, but for what was left of the free transfers after the other, slightly richer, clubs had taken their pick. Unlike them we couldn't afford to pay signing-on fees so it made it very difficult to get anyone. We missed out on some superb players for the want of literally just a few pounds.

A classic example was Colin Clarke, who went on to have a wonderful career. He played for Northern Ireland 38 times and took part in their World Cup campaigns. He even became their all-time leading goalscorer, surpassing illustrious names like George Best and Derek Dougan. I wanted to sign Colin when he was given a free transfer by Peterborough. I even managed to get him to waive a signing-on fee and everything looked promising. But then we hit a stumbling block. Colin wanted £220 a week; hardly excessive even in those days, but the Orient board would only let me offer £200 a week. He wouldn't go any lower, the board wouldn't go any higher . . . and I'm in the middle tearing my hair out with frustration.

Just a mere £20, but it represented a gap that couldn't be breached. Neither side would move, so Colin turned us down. He went on to great success at Oxford and was later transferred to Southampton for about £800,000. Imagine how many £20s a week we could have got out of that. It was so frustrating but worse was to come.

I had watched Stan Collymore with great interest when he played for Crystal Palace reserves. He had everything going for him but his temperament. For whatever reason, Palace decided he wasn't right for them and they were prepared to let him go. I would have taken him like a shot but there was no way we could raise the £100,000 that Palace wanted. It was a bargain but they might as well have been asking for a hundred million because there was no way Orient could pay it. I had to stand by as Collymore eventually signed for Southend and turned out to be the best bit of business they ever did, partly because of me. I never lost interest in Stan and he was one of the first players I signed when I became manager of Nottingham Forest.

By this time, however, he had re-established himself as a top-flight player and I had to pay a more realistic market rate of £2.5 million. What a terrific bonus for Southend! They got a good season out of him and well over £2 million profit. That money could have been Orient's, but they just weren't able to stretch themselves.

It was a similar story with Le Saux. I had watched him several times playing for Chelsea reserves and he had always impressed me. For some reason, however, the club at one point felt he wasn't going to make it and were open to offers. They only wanted a nominal fee, but again, for Orient there was no such thing as a nominal fee. Any fee at all was too much. We couldn't sign him. He stayed at Chelsea, managed to recover his form and went on to have a hugely successful career.

Top managers like Alex Ferguson and Kenny Dalglish will tell you of the terrible pressures they face as men at the top of their profession. They're right, of course, but they need to manage a small club to understand what pressure, frustration and desperation are really like. I have found that no matter how bad the pressures become at a big club like Forest or Manchester City, they're nothing like as bad as they are at a small club like Orient. My time there was desperate – it was a constant battle just to survive, let alone win matches.

I went there in 1981 as assistant manager to Ken Knighton. At the time we were both still reeling from a gruelling experience in charge of Sunderland. That was our first taste of management and our first taste of what it was like to fight with hard-headed directors over money. Our first season at Sunderland, 1979–80, was tremendous. We won promotion at the first attempt back into the old

First Division. We had some good young players, a terrific staff and a real chance of being successful. Then before we knew what was happening, we were sacked. We had fallen foul of the club's new chairman.

Imagine a clichéd, identikit picture of the hard, self-made millionaire and you'll have a good idea of what Tom Cowie was like. He had started out in business selling second-hand motorbikes on a bit of waste ground just after the war. By the time he took over as Sunderland's chairman he had turned it into a multi-million pound car dealership. He very quickly clashed with me and Ken and we felt he was seeking to undermine us at every opportunity. The main argument was about money and who ran the club. He and Ken had some real battles. One highly public dispute began when Ken wanted to take the players to stay at a hotel on Christmas night before a big game on Boxing Day. Cowie said the club couldn't afford it.

Ken knew a hotel that would let us stay just for the linen charge of a tenner a room. However, he didn't tell Cowie that. Instead, he tried to gain a little political capital. He contacted a friend of his on the local paper and leaked a story that he was having to pay for the players to stay at the hotel because the chairman was too mean. He hoped to shame Cowie into picking up the bill, but it was a big mistake and the whole thing backfired.

Cowie went along with it and just said: 'Ken, that's a great idea. If you want to pay for the hotel then you go ahead and do it.' It was silly. For the want of a bit of common sense on both sides, they ended up having a big row played out in the pages of the press. The two men became increasingly hostile to each other and at the first opportunity he got, Cowie sacked us. It was a humiliating experience. The chief executive stood over us as we emptied our desks. The club stopped paying us immediately and our cars were taken away.

We each had about 15 months of our contracts to run, yet they offered us a pitiful settlement figure. We refused and said we would take the dispute to an industrial tribunal. The club decided to fight it.

The whole thing dragged on for four months with them refusing to pay up our contracts. Then the day before the hearing, they paid up in full, probably fearing they would lose the case, or that the publicity would be unwelcome. Maybe they hoped we'd be forced into submission. I had seen that happen to several managers and was determined it would not happen to me. Ken and I were out of work from April to August 1981 but fortunately we both had enough money to get by until we got a settlement.

Cowie's period in charge was without doubt a disaster for Sunderland. He seemed to treat the club as a rich man's plaything and the fans suffered because of him. He appointed Alan Durban and when that didn't work out he took on Lawrie McMenemy on a huge salary that helped nearly bankrupt the club. For all the power Cowie wielded, he didn't really put much money into the club and by the time he left Sunderland were almost in the Third Division.

By then Ken and I had moved on to Orient. Ken doubled my wages, which I thought was great until I discovered he would have had to treble them to compensate for the extra cost of housing in the south. Those apparently mundane considerations matter at that level. It was a hard existence and totally lacking in any of the glamour that people associate with football clubs.

I was supposed to be the assistant manager but it wasn't like being an assistant at a big club. It was more like being a general dogsbody. There was always something that had to be done yet there was never anyone to do it, so I ended up having to fill in. If we travelled to a game by train, quite a luxury, I had to look after the skip carrying all the kit. I would push it across the railway platform and make sure it was loaded safely.

If we travelled by road then I would double as minibus driver. We didn't have our own, so I had to go and hire one from a firm in Walthamstow, north-east London. It meant driving over there in the morning to get the bus, then driving back to pick up the team and the kit before heading off to the match. After the game I would drive back to the Orient ground and unload the kit and players before returning the bus to the hire company. It all had to be done in one day because it made it that bit cheaper.

Every penny had to be accounted for. The club secretary was forbidden to spend more than five pounds without permission from the directors. Our credit rating was virtually zero. The bus company always wanted money up front. Hotels wouldn't let us have an account because they knew it would take us too long to pay. We used to take our credit cards with us so we could get 28 days' free credit.

Our dwindling gates of two or three thousand just weren't enough to cover our costs. In that kind of world, the directors aren't too interested in results; survival becomes all that counts. You have spells where different people with a bit of money come in every so often and take over. They inject a bit of cash and things can go well for a while, until they run out of money or patience and decide enough is enough. They pull out, taking their money with them, and suddenly it's calamity time again until someone else takes over.

It was during one of these reshuffles in 1983 that I became manager of the club. Brian Winston was the chairman who had brought me and Ken Knighton to Orient, and he had reached a point where he couldn't put any more money in to keep it afloat.

A paper merchant called Neville Ovenden took over. He had enough money to just about keep the club going, but not enough to put any extra capital in so we could begin to progress. It was decided that a much tighter regime was needed. When we had arrived a few years earlier, the club wasn't very wealthy by any means but there was a bit of cash about. They still had some players on First Division contracts, which was one of the reasons they had got into difficulties in the first place. All that was to stop.

Under the new system, the outgoing chairman Brian Winston would take over as chief executive and deal with the day-to-day running of the club. Money, especially for salaries, would be kept even tighter. It was felt that Ken Knighton wouldn't be able to accept this. He had always been strong-willed and confrontational.

Ken was sacked and I was offered the job as manager. It was a difficult situation for me. With a wife and two children, I couldn't afford to walk out on principle – the moral high ground can come with a very high price. If the same situation had occurred at Sunderland I would have had no choice. The way they had behaved, even if they had offered me Ken's job I would have had to say no, starvation or not. At Orient it was different. When Ken got the sack he walked out of the chairman's office with a cheque in his pocket for the rest of his contract. If someone has to be dismissed then that is the right way to do it and it made it easier for me to take his place. Ken certainly didn't hold it against me.

The other factor was that, unlike at Sunderland, I sympathised with the directors' need to do something about the dire financial situation of the club. We couldn't spend money we didn't have, no matter how many Stan Collymores we missed.

It was still an uneasy time, though. Ken was very disillusioned and ended up going out of the game altogether. He started selling insurance, like a lot of ex-professionals at that time, and he managed Dagenham on a part-time basis but found that a very difficult adjustment to make, as I'm sure many of us would. Soon afterwards he was offered a job with the telecommunications giant Plessey in their sales department. He didn't know anything about electronics but he was always a very good salesman. He now lives in Bristol and has a wonderful lifestyle. As the years unfolded afterwards at Orient, there were times when I wondered if he hadn't got the better end of the deal.

The conflicting attitudes of Sunderland and Orient influenced my thinking on the way the game should be run and the way managers should be treated. It was around this time that the need for a League Managers' Association was being discussed. People like Graham Taylor, Howard Wilkinson, Lawrie McMenemy and me were the inspiration behind it. We felt football managers would have more power and influence if we had our own professional organisation. Progress was slow but we eventually got it off the ground in 1992.

Howard Wilkinson became the first chairman and I went on to become the chief executive. With the help of my fellow managers I set about trying to introduce changes which would improve both the standing and reputation of the profession, but also provide better conditions and job security. One of the most important was registration of contracts. Most managers accept job insecurity as an occupational hazard but even so, there had to be a better way of dealing with dismissal than the way Ken Knighton and I were treated at Sunderland. Through the LMA we managed to get the Premier League and later the Football League to adopt a proper system of honouring contracts. It means that if someone is sacked then his contract has to be settled within 30 days or the club can't appoint a new manager. It's only fair to the people involved, and it's right for the image of the game if it's to be taken seriously as a professionally run industry.

The LMA also introduced other benefits for members. We hired solicitors and accountants to advise managers who suddenly found themselves in difficulties, whether with their clubs or otherwise. Kenny Dalglish used some of these services in his dispute with Newcastle in 1998. We also provided basic things like health insurance schemes. Many of these things have been taken for granted in other professions but are only now becoming available to football managers.

In my first year as manager of Orient we finished in the top half of what is now the Second Division. My reward for that was to be told that I would have to cut the squad back even further. I had to disband the reserve team and operate with just 15 or 16 pros. I just about managed to keep the youth team going but it meant I had to do it myself with help from the club physio. There was no one else. Not surprisingly, we were relegated the following season, in 1985. To be fair, the directors could have used that as an excuse to sack me but they didn't. They stuck with me and we survived for another couple of years.

Then one morning I walked into work to be told by the chairman: 'Unless you find £10,000 within a month, the club will go under.' I had to sell one of my best players, Keith Houchen, to Hull City. We managed to get £15,000, which gave us a bit of breathing space, but only for a while. With that sort of policy you constantly descend further and further into the vicious circle. If you sell your best players, you lose matches; if you lose matches, you get smaller crowds. That in turn means even less money and so you have to sell yet more players. So it goes on.

For the next few years we operated on a budget to lose £20,000 a year and the directors made up the shortfall between them. Then it got to the stage where they couldn't even afford to do that and there was a crisis looming. At that point I had had enough and was ready to pack it in. It gets to you eventually. I had had enough of scrimping and saving, and watching talented young players slip through my fingers for the want of only modest fees.

We were about a week away from receivership with no hope in sight when suddenly a guardian angel turned up. His name was Tony Wood. He was a lifelong Orient fan and a successful businessman. What's more, he was a down-to-earth person with a lot of common sense.

We had first come across him a year or so earlier when he appeared in the vice-president's lounge as a guest of somebody or other. No one knew him because he spent most of his time in Rwanda, where he ran a successful coffee business. He approached the chairman Neville Ovenden after a match and out of the blue gave him a cheque, saying he wanted to make a donation to the club. Neville thanked him politely but didn't have his glasses on at the time and didn't realise where he had put the decimal point. When he looked at it later he could hardly believe his eyes. This stranger had just given him £10,000.

Straightaway the board thought: 'Wow, we've got to cultivate this man. He could be our saviour.' Ten thousand pounds was the difference between survival and going under for a club like Orient. It would pay the wages bill for a few weeks. Tony soon went back to Rwanda but he would turn up at games from time to time and made a few more donations. He didn't seem to want anything in return, which is most unusual in football. Now, as we were faced with the threat of going under, Neville Ovenden approached Tony to see if he would be prepared to help. Without any hesitation he agreed to bale us out.

He bought 76 per cent of the shares, which gave him complete control, but surprisingly he didn't want to wield absolute power. He seemed to have no ego at all – quite incredible for a club chairman and in complete contrast to Tom Cowie at Sunderland. Tony just wanted Orient to prosper. His business in Rwanda meant he couldn't be involved in the day-to-day running of the club, and so instead he asked me to run it for him. I was still unsure about him and still looking to get away, so I asked him what his plans were for the club.

He said he felt we could run it as a successful, but homely, friendly little club which could hold its own in what is now the First Division. He had no silly aspirations about going off and winning the Premier League title. He wanted to make steady progress and to develop a thriving youth policy so we could find our own players. It all sounded great to me and I told him I thought we could do it. I felt it was reasonable to assume we could go from the Third to the First Division within five years. I estimated it would cost him £1 million. He just said, fine, let's have a go. He was prepared to subsidise us up to £200,000 a year. It was almost too good to be true. I was still at the same club but it was like a fresh start to me.

For the next two years I took control of everything; the playing and the business side. We were reasonably successful. In 1989 we got promoted back into what is now the Second Division and were holding our own. Then I realised it was impossible to do everything. It was just too time-consuming. I had to decide whether to run the team or the club. I chose the club because it provided the fresher challenge.

I became managing director and concentrated on the business side of things. I brought Peter Eustace in to run the team and the whole thing worked very well for a while. The youth scheme was working well and produced some excellent players, most notably Chris Bart-Williams, who was later sold to Sheffield Wednesday.

I'm sure it could have worked out for us but for one thing: the Taylor inquiry into the Hillsborough disaster in which 96 fans were killed. The tragedy forced everyone connected with the game to face up to the issue of ground safety. Lord Taylor's report was completely justified and led to some much-needed improvements to our stadiums. In the short term, though, it threw our calculations at Orient completely off course. We had originally reckoned on having to spend £20,000 a year on the upkeep of the stadium. The Taylor recommendations meant we had to spend £150,000 a year just to stay in business.

It wasn't money we begrudged but it meant there was less to spend on the team and although we got close, we couldn't quite make it into the First Division. If we had been able to make that jump, the extra revenue would have enabled us to stay within budget and our plan would have worked. Tony Wood might even have been able to get some of his money back. But it wasn't to be.

The failure put some pressure on my relationship with Peter Eustace. We had developed the joint approach to management which was common in Europe and is becoming more fashionable over here. He dealt with the playing side and I looked after the finance, the contracts and the administration.

I thought it worked well, but I'm not sure Peter would agree. He certainly had a problem with it. He didn't want to let go of the financial side of the contracts and seemed to dislike it if I was negotiating with a player and he wasn't directly involved. He also found it difficult to cope with the amount of power I wielded at the club. I had been there a long time and was managing director, but he didn't like it. He also felt that I was earning a lot more money than he was. In fact, I wasn't earning all that much more, but it annoyed him to think I might be.

We had numerous arguments, mainly about players' wages. Peter felt we were relying too heavily on young players and needed some experienced pros to give us more balance. I agreed entirely but felt we couldn't afford them. It might throw the whole financial structure out of balance, especially if it didn't work out and we weren't successful. While I was in charge I agreed to only one such signing: Chris Turner, who was supposedly going to solve our goalkeeping problems for the next five years. We signed him from Manchester United so we had to pay high wages, but he was the only one.

Turner's signing also coincided with us reaching a point where Tony Wood couldn't really afford to put any more in. I spoke to him and said the time had come when he really ought to be thinking of taking some money back. The club owed him £1.4 million in a loan account for which he was charging no interest and for which there was no set date for repayment. It was extremely generous of him but I felt it was too big a debt for the club to feel comfortable with, given its limited earnings and potential. We agreed that from then on he would take half the profit from every player we sold, so we could get the debt down to something more reasonable. We sold Bart-Williams to Sheffield Wednesday for an initial fee of £275,000 with the promise of much more if he did well and played a certain number of games for them.

In spite of the differences with Peter Eustace everything was going reasonably well, but then in 1993 I got the chance to go to Nottingham Forest. There was no way I was going to turn down the chance to return to the club where I'd had my greatest success as a player. I hoped that Tony Wood would understand, but I'm not sure he did because he ended up feeling very bitter about it. I never had a contract at Orient and I thought I had an understanding with Tony that if ever a top club came in for me then I would go. He doesn't seem to see it that way and I think he feels that I left him in the lurch. It certainly all went downhill at the club after I left.

I managed to get them £25,000 compensation from

Forest. It was money that would otherwise have gone to me, but I wanted it to go to Orient. I also took Forest down there for a pre-season friendly and we didn't take a penny. That would have earned them another £25,000.

After I left, Peter had some horrendous rows with the directors over money. It wasn't all his fault. When I was there I was able to act as a buffer between them and filter out the excesses from both sides. I understood Peter's problems and was sympathetic to them, but I also understood the directors' point of view that money was limited.

The whole thing fell apart. Tony's money was drying up and the team weren't being successful enough to make up the shortfall. Within two years of my leaving, the club had run up an overdraft of £750,000. That was in addition to the money they owed Tony Wood. He never managed to get his money back. The club ended up making at least another half a million on the Bart-Williams deal but it was all wasted. It was the same with the other players they sold including Kevin Nugent, who as I said earlier went for £275,000.

Then suddenly there was civil war in Rwanda and Tony's business was badly hit. He couldn't sustain the club any more and in the end he virtually had to give it away to the snooker and boxing promoter Barry Hearn, best known for his association with Steve Davis. Orient owed Tony an awful lot of money but he got very little of it back. I still feel sad about it and on the last few occasions I've spoken to Tony, he's been very bitter. I don't really have a relationship with him any more and he's now back in Rwanda trying to rebuild his business. He stayed on the board at Orient but had no control and very little input.

It was all very sad. I had some wonderful times at Orient as well as all the bad. There are some advantages to being at a small club. Everyone knows each other well and there can be a wonderful friendliness and camaraderie. There has to be, really, or you would never survive. Despite the disappointment of missing out on so many players, you do get the satisfaction of seeing some come through and make it at the top level. It's easier for them at a club like Orient where they have a much better chance of getting in the first team.

The other good thing, of course, is that occasionally you get the chance to tweak the noses of the big boys. One of my greatest moments at Orient was when we took on Tottenham in the League Cup in 1985–86. Orient were in the old Fourth Division. Tottenham were the aristocratic thoroughbreds with some of the best players in the country, Glenn Hoddle, Ossie Ardiles, Chris Waddle and Steve Perryman. However, Orient cut them down to size and beat them by two goals to nil. It was one of the greatest victories in the club's history and for the fans, so long accustomed to living in the shadows of their more illustrious London neighbours, success at last was sweet. It was also short-lived, unfortunately, as Tottenham won the second leg 4–0.

As at all levels of football, the margin between success and failure in the lower divisions is very small. We nearly made it but just couldn't go that extra mile. If only we had been able to make that final jump into the First Division we would have earned the extra revenue to complete the financial cycle. Unfortunately, it didn't work out that way. Nor does it work out for most of the other small clubs scraping out an existence in the lower divisions. It may, as they say, be tough at the top, but it's an awful lot tougher at the bottom.

CHAPTER 3

Stepping into
Brian Clough's Shoes

_____

If Roy of the Rovers really existed, the chances are he would have teamed up with Brian Clough in the late Seventies. For what Clough achieved with his Nottingham Forest team at that time was as incredible as any comic book story. I was part of it and even I can't believe it really happened. Roy's exploits with Melchester Rovers seem far more realistic.

In 1977, a lacklustre Nottingham Forest were plying their trade in the old Second Division. There was nothing to suggest they would ever do anything else and little was expected of them. At that time, if you had wanted to be certified as clinically insane you could have taken a deep breath and made the following prediction: *'Forest will win promotion within a few months, win the League the following year, win the European Cup the year after that and then*

*win it again a year later just to prove it wasn't a fluke. Oh,
and they'll win two League Cups as well! They'll do all this
with tremendous style, with a team made up of misfits and
rejects.'*

I'm afraid the men in white coats would have taken you
away before you had even finished the first sentence. They
would have been a bit premature, of course, because that is
precisely what happened. The likes of the mighty Liverpool
and Manchester United had to stand aside while a bunch
of journeymen put together by the genius of Brian Clough
raced to the top of the league. Soon it was the turn of
aristocrats like Barcelona and Ajax of Amsterdam to play
second fiddle as Forest set about conquering Europe.

None of the experts gave us a chance and kept waiting,
game after game, for our bubble to burst. They were still
waiting as we beat Malmo 1–0 to win the biggest club prize
of all. Holding aloft that European Cup in the Olympic
Stadium in Munich was the pinnacle of my career.

The buzz and excitement around Nottingham then was
just unbelievable. I had four incredible years at Forest
in an era when Brian Clough was undoubtedly at the
height of his powers. It came at a time when I thought
my career was effectively over. I had just been released
by Newcastle United after playing for them for 12 years. I
had enjoyed a wonderful career with them and had a UEFA
Cup winner's medal.

I was given a free transfer and at the age of 32 didn't
have too many options on where to go next. Darlington,
Hartlepool and Doncaster were showing some interest,
but with all due respect, they weren't the most attractive
propositions. Winning European Cups was the last thing
on my mind; earning enough to pay the bills was the

more immediate concern. Then Brian Clough arrived on the scene.

I was having talks with Doncaster when a journalist friend phoned and told me Forest were interested. Brian had put him up to it. He didn't dare ring himself because he knew Doncaster wouldn't have let him near me until after I had signed for them. I'm not sure what appealed to Brian most – my ability, or the fact that I wasn't going to cost him anything. I would like to think it was the former, though I suspect it was more to do with the latter. Whatever the case, Forest seemed a much better proposition than anything else on offer and I had no hesitation in signing for them.

I already knew Brian quite well but nothing could have prepared me for working for him. Nor could anything have prepared me for the whirlwind events of the next four years. I hoped I would be able to help Forest win promotion within a few seasons and become established in the First Division before I finally bowed out of the game. My expectations were no higher than that. In the event, what actually happened was breathtaking.

I won more honours in that brief spell than in the rest of my career put together. What Forest achieved was almost superhuman and I don't think it will ever be equalled, certainly not by a club with such limited resources. Those achievements, of course, were all down to Clough. He was recognised, quite rightly, as the most outstanding manager of his generation, possibly any generation.

A comparison with another top manager like Alex Ferguson may put the achievement in perspective. After 12 years in charge of the richest club in the country, Manchester United, Ferguson was still waiting to win his first European Cup. After five years in charge of a poor club like Nottingham Forest, Clough had won the European Cup twice. This is not a criticism of Ferguson, whose achievements are tremendous. It just highlights how Clough was in a league of his own.

What makes him even more remarkable is that he achieved all this on a shoestring budget. His transformation of Forest was very different to the transformation worked by Kenny Dalglish at Blackburn or by Kevin Keegan at Newcastle. There was no benefactor with a bottomless pit of money bankrolling Clough. Every penny he spent he first had to earn. He had to balance the books, even when it meant selling his star players like Garry Birtles and Peter Davenport to Manchester United.

He couldn't go out and buy success, which is effectively what Dalglish and Keegan did. He had to be far more imaginative. He took what our winger at the time, John Robertson, described as a rag, tag and bobtail bunch of misfits and made them world beaters. Some people have claimed it was because he frightened people, but it wasn't really to do with fear. He just had this incredible personality and charisma. When he walked into the room, the electricity went up immediately. There were all kinds of different characters in the side and they all needed handling in different ways, yet Brian managed to get the maximum out of all of them. It sometimes meant turning conventional wisdom on its head.

Robertson himself was a classic example. He was a very skilful tramp going nowhere fast until Brian got hold of him. He was overweight, too fond of cigarettes and in danger of drifting out of the game. He was perhaps lacking a bit in confidence because he had been working with coaches who concentrated on pointing out his weaknesses and making him correct them. Brian took exactly the opposite approach. He told John to forget about his failings and concentrate on the things he was good at, such as going past defenders in the tightest of places and delivering quality crosses. That simple change of attitude worked wonders and turned Robertson into a Scottish international.

Kenny Burns was another player who had a total transformation under Brian. He had a reputation as a trouble-maker and was close to being thrown out of the game before he joined Forest from Birmingham City. In fact, he was supposedly so bad that Forest were warned off buying him. Burns was bought as an attacker but as soon as he arrived at Forest he was converted to a centre-back. That was a complete surprise to him and everyone else, but it worked wonders. The nearly-man striker blossomed into a world-class defender and went on to play for Scotland. The way he blocked Kevin Keegan out of the game was one of the main reasons Forest were able to win their second European Cup final against Hamburg in 1980.

The supposed troublemaker side of Kenny never really surfaced. Maybe that was down to the shock he had waiting for him after one particular match. Kenny, it seems, had made a careless pass during the game, so in typically unpredictable style, Clough decided to fine him £50. Kenny couldn't believe it. Players are used to being disciplined for bad behaviour on or off the pitch, but this was something different. From his reputation you might have expected Kenny to blow up, but he didn't. He took it and he never really caused any trouble.

Brian had the measure of the rest of the team, too. There was Peter Shilton, arguably the best goalkeeper in the world at the time. He'd done and seen it all, but Brian was still able to fire his enthusiasm. He also made sure Shilton didn't get ideas above his station. Every Friday morning we used to have a team meeting in the club's guest room. It was customary to have a drink, mostly soft drinks although you could have a half of lager if you wanted.

One Friday, Brian had the TV commentator Brian Moore in to see him for some reason. He brought him along to the team meeting to introduce him to us. As soon as Clough walked into the room, he told Shilton to get Moore and everybody else a drink. It was his way of letting Shilton know that even though he was probably the best goalkeeper in the world, he was still just one of the lads. Peter complied without a murmur.

Martin O'Neill presented Brian with a different challenge. Martin was a wonderfully articulate character who would argue black was white with anyone and had an answer for everything. Brian would often get on his back and wind him up. He gave Martin very little credit for what he did. He would understate his role and tell him all he had to do was to ferret about on the right and then get the ball to Robertson on the other flank – Robbo would do the skilful stuff and create the goals. It worked very well. Martin scored a lot of goals, most of which were created by Robertson. But when the brickbats started flying, Martin would always answer back. He and Clough had many arguments. In terms of the quality of the discussion they would usually end in a draw, but of course Brian was the boss so in reality he always won, though Martin could never accept that.

The arguments arose partly because both of them always wanted to win and neither would let the other have the last word. With hindsight, however, I think Martin would agree that it was also a ploy on Brian's part to get him going. For the main part it worked. As Martin has said since, Brian could make you desperate for his approval.

By the time we won the Championship there were several internationals in the side but there were also a lot of journeyman professionals. I don't mean that in a derogatory sense – I was one of them. Brian certainly got the best out of me. He left me alone most of the time but he made me feel very relaxed and comfortable, and I gained more confidence.

I think my problem was that I had been at Newcastle for too long. I had got into a rut there without realising it. I found that I was fighting everyone's battles for them. If a kid had a problem, I would try to sort it out for them. Looking back, I think I might have become a nuisance to the club.

When I got to Forest everything changed. It was partly because I was at the end of my career, most people were writing me off and anything that happened from then on was a bonus. But it was also because I had complete faith in the management of Brian Clough and his assistant Peter Taylor. I didn't feel I had to get involved to sort things out. For the first time in my career I became very relaxed about myself and less intense. I remember thinking: 'Don't worry, just take it easy and look after yourself. Don't get uptight. If there are any problems, they'll take care of them. That's their job.' It made such a difference and I became a far better player.

I was also helped, of course, by the fact that I was surrounded by such good players. John Robertson was an ideal winger for me to play behind at left-back. Brian had seen how our two very different styles would combine perfectly. I was never very comfortable on the ball – I was good at winning it but then I couldn't wait to get rid of it. Robertson on the other hand couldn't get enough of the ball but was too lazy to chase after it. So as soon as I gained possession I would lay it off to him and he'd be away doing what he was good at, turning defences inside out.

Playing in front of the best goalkeeper in the world also helped. Peter Shilton filled everyone with an enormous amount of confidence. As did my colleagues in defence, Larry Lloyd, Kenny Burns and Viv Anderson. They were too good and too mean to give anything away.

Many people have Brian Clough's success down to him being some sort of tactical genius, but I don't think it was that, really. In all the time I was with him I can't remember once when he did anything special to deal with a particular threat posed by the opposition. He just had one way of playing and he stuck to it through thick and thin. In fact, he never really bothered about the opposition at all. He was of the school of thought that says this is the way we play and if we do it well enough, we'll be successful. He had a great knowledge of the basics of the game and he never made things over-complicated. He never deviated from a straightforward 4–4–2 formation. He made us pass the ball and try to keep it on the ground. Those Forest sides always had a lovely balance, with two wide men, and he made us play with discipline. There was no arguing with referees. That was it.

There were slight changes over the years, of course. Initially we were a very attacking team and you had to get the ball forward as quickly as possible. But once we got into Europe, Brian developed a more counter-attacking style. He very quickly learned that if you play in a gung-ho fashion against Continental sides, you're likely to get punished severely. He developed a more cat-and-mouse approach, but it was still 4–4–2. The only time he really deviated from that was in the second European Cup final when he played Birtles up front on his own.

Some pundits commented afterwards that it was a clever tactical change to enable Forest to soak up pressure from Hamburg and then hit them on the break. That was nonsense. The reality was that Brian didn't have much choice. Trevor Francis was injured and there was no one else to play. He only had a small squad, even in those glory days.

It was the shortage of players that brought out one of Brian's other great skills. He had an amazing knack of putting square pegs in round holes. There were times when someone was injured or lost form and I would wonder what Brian would do. I used to think, well, he's going to have to change the way we play. He can't expect so-and-so to go and play in that position. But that was exactly what he expected. His reasoning was that although the replacement might not be all that effective in that position, the other ten remain in their usual places. They know what's happening and they can still perform and feel comfortable within the usual system.

It worked more often than not. I even benefited from it when Brian Clough pulled off what was perhaps his greatest achievement of all – he got me to score my first and only league goal at the age of 35. I had played over 500 professional games but had never managed to find the net, but then I rarely got into the opposition half so it wasn't that surprising. Then one day I found myself on the bench as a sub in an away match at Ipswich. Suddenly Brian pulled off our centre-forward Peter Withe and sent me on. I would have expected him to change the team around and put me in my usual position as full-back, but no. Brian decided he didn't want to change the rest of the team because they were all playing so well, and I was sent on as a striker. The opposition half was such unfamiliar territory I almost needed a map. Then a chance came along and I put it away. It was a nice feeling, so nice that I fancied doing it again. After the match I took a lot of stick from the other lads because they said I kept bombing towards goal and wouldn't pass when I should have done. Well, it was only once in over 500 games, and my goal did clinch victory.

While I was playing for Brian, he took me by surprise one day by saying he thought I should eventually succeed him as manager. It was like being given the royal seal of approval. I didn't take him seriously at the time but I suppose I should have known better. Brian was seldom wrong, and even when he was, no one would dare tell him. He had turned the club into his own personal kingdom and he reigned supreme.

I had been away from the club for more than 12 years when Brian finally retired and the job became available. I kept an eye on the situation while I was at Orient and stayed in touch with the Forest chairman Fred Reacher, although I never thought anything would come of it. I had more or less resigned myself to doing what I was doing at Orient.

Then Reacher phoned me and asked if I would be interested in the manager's job. We met at a hotel to discuss it. Nobody knew about it. I was a real outsider

– my former team-mate Martin O'Neill was the red-hot favourite to take over. Reacher had certainly spoken to him and I think Fred had an idea that Martin and I could work together in some way. I didn't fancy that and I don't think Martin did either. I didn't think our personalities would allow us to make it work. Martin is very dogmatic and I could see us having too many arguments.

As it turned out, the issue never arose because Martin pulled out of the running and Fred Reacher phoned me a few days after I'd met him in the hotel to say the job was mine if I wanted it. I don't know what happened between him and Martin, but I wasn't bothered about that. All that mattered was that I was being offered the job and I wanted to make the most of it. I believe it helped that I had played at Forest and knew the set-up. I think the chairman wanted continuity.

Once I accepted, things moved very quickly and everything suddenly became very cloak and dagger. Reacher smuggled me out of the ground past waiting reporters and took me to his house. It was the same night as Brian's last game in charge and Reacher didn't want my appointment to attract any attention away from such a great occasion.

It was 11 May 1993 and Forest were playing neighbours Notts County for the privilege of becoming Nottinghamshire County Cup winners. Thousands invaded the pitch to crowd around the players' tunnel to cheer him one last time. Any disappointment at relegation was perhaps tempered by the knowledge that had it not been for Clough, the club wouldn't have been anywhere near the Premier League in the first place. Nor would it have a modern stadium fit for the future or a glorious past littered with League titles, European Cups and League Cups.

The next day, my appointment was made public and I came out to meet the press and the television cameras. There was obviously a lot of interest in how I might change things and how I would rebuild the team to win promotion. But journalists later told me they were also interested to see how my methods of dealing with the media might differ from Brian's. He had always liked to keep them on their toes so they never quite knew what was going to happen. Television reporters told of Clough's eccentric sense of humour. He'd been known to take the mickey or kiss them just before an interview – anything to throw them off balance. On some occasions he would grab hold of them in the place where men most definitely do not want other men to grab hold of them. All with a mischievous grin and always in a way that made it difficult for the reporter to concentrate.

Fortunately for the reporters, they had nothing like that to fear from me. I never particularly relished meeting the press and tended to keep it more businesslike. Where Brian was likely to make controversial comments that made the headlines, I was more careful and measured in what I said. Apparently most reporters regarded it as a trade-off. The quotes may not be as lively with Frank Clark, but at least you didn't have to worry about being grabbed.

One of the questions I constantly faced was how I would cope with the problem of following such a legendary figure. The truth is I didn't find it daunting at all. It obviously helped that I had played under Brian and knew his methods, but really I just had faith in my ability to do the job. I was convinced that if I did it right, all the other things would become irrelevant. Who I was following, who was offered the job first, how far down the batting order I was; all those things wouldn't matter.

When Howard Wilkinson took over at Leeds, one of the first things he did was take down all the pictures of the club's glory days under Don Revie – Howard thought it was unhealthy to have people harping back to a golden age. People asked if I thought of doing something similar to remove the shadow of Brian Clough. But what would have been the point? During his 18 years at Forest he had totally transformed the club so that his hallmark was everywhere. To erase his memory I would have had to do a lot more than remove a few pictures; I would have had to knock down the entire ground. It had been completely rebuilt under his management and transformed into a magnificent stadium standing proudly by the banks of the Trent. Many fans thought God had put the river there so Brian could avoid the rush-hour traffic and walk along the water to get to work. Well, I couldn't walk on water but I could walk on the pitch.

I looked at the ground and the stands and the trophy room and I just saw it as a great opportunity. The tremendous achievements of the previous manager were an inspiration to me, not a millstone. I looked at all the silverware: the European Cups, the League Cups, the League Championship trophy. I looked at the photographs of the team that had won them. I couldn't possibly throw those pictures away; I was on most of them.

In a way I suppose it helped that the club had been relegated. It took some of the pressure away. Obviously it's easier to take over at a club after it has suffered a relative failure, but things weren't as bad as they seemed. To outsiders it appeared to be in disarray, on the slippery slope down. I could see more than that. I could see the potential it had and I thought I could turn it around.

The internal organisation had become a little ragged during that traumatic relegation year. That was made perfectly clear to me that first night when I sat in Fred Reacher's living room after being smuggled out of the ground. Before setting off for the match, he presented me with my first task as Forest's new manager.

I had to stop ten multi-million-pound players walking out of the club, most of them on free transfers. Through some oversight their contracts had not been renewed and were about to run out in the next few days. Under FA rules, if they weren't offered equally good deals before the old ones elapsed, they could walk out on free transfers. From the players' point of view that could be a fantastic opportunity to earn a fortune with a new club, as with no transfer fee to pay, the new club could afford to give the players very high wages. From Forest's point of view, however, it was a potential disaster. Not only could the club lose most of its first team squad, it could miss out on millions of pounds in transfer fees. It could cause irreparable damage. I had to come up with some sort of holding deal to avert the crisis. Obviously, it was extremely difficult as I didn't know most of the players. I didn't want to sign someone on high wages and then find I didn't really want them; on the other hand, I didn't want to let a good player walk away for free. And I had 48 hours to sort it all out.

After 12 years of scrimping at Orient, arriving at Forest was something of a culture shock. I remember staring several times at the ten contracts. Could footballers really earn that much? I hardly recognised some of the players concerned. It frightened me to death to see the kind of money they were getting.

When Reacher returned from the match, we stayed up until three in the morning discussing those contracts. Then I went over them in detail with my assistant Alan Hill, who was already at the club and knew the players better than I did. We managed to come up with holding deals that would prevent them leaving on free transfers. That did not mean they would stay, however. There was still a lot of negotiating to be done. There was also a lot of negotiating to be done with players who were still under contract but unhappy at the club because it meant them playing in the First Division.

That relegation year had understandably produced an air of depression around the place. But I knew there was also a legacy of good things – good players and good habits. The basic structure that Brian had put in place was still there and I tried to build on that. I knew that the building would have to be done very quickly. Football club directors are not noted for patience and nor are the fans, especially at a place like Forest where they've grown accustomed to success, stylish football and regular trips to Wembley.

To be fair to Brian, that was the only real problem he left me, the incredibly high level of expectation. Having tasted the glory he brought them, the supporters expected it to happen again. I could hardly blame Brian for that. Nor could I complain about the way he sank into the background after leaving the club. If he had come back every few weeks, it might have been difficult for me. He contacted me a few times and I went round to his house for tea occasionally, but basically he kept a low profile. That allowed me the space to establish myself. I shall always be grateful for that.

I felt it was particularly important as I wasn't first choice as manager for many supporters and I knew it might be difficult to win them over if things didn't go well. I would have a brief honeymoon period but all too soon people would start judging me. I had no illusions about it. If I wasn't successful very quickly, I would be sacked. But nobody forces you to do the job. You've got to accept the insecurity. If that worries you then you should get out.

I pared the job right down to what really matters. I told myself, if the first team is winning games, you're all right; if not, you've got problems. It doesn't matter how nice a fellah you are, how good an accountant or administrator you are. It doesn't matter how good your youth policy is or how well the reserves are doing, how good you are with the media or at your relations with the community. If the first team aren't winning, you've got problems; if they are winning, then everything falls into place. I know that's a sweeping generalisation but it's true in the main. Whether people like you or dislike you is irrelevant.

So it was to the first team that I turned my thoughts on my first day in charge. The task for the season was simple to recognise – it was to bounce straight back into the Premier League. That was the club's rightful home and where the fans expected to be. It was also where the money was. Relegation to the First Division was going to lose Forest at least £1 million in reduced gates and lost television revenue. I needed to start planning for the season ahead.

My first few months in charge were to turn into a whirlwind of transfer wheeler-dealing. More than £10 million was to change hands as star players came and went. That, too, was something of a culture shock – I had never spent more than £50,000 on a player during my time at Orient. Long discussions with Alan Hill identified one of the main priorities as a first-class goalscorer. This was to set me up for a stormy and colourful relationship with a young man destined to become Britain's costliest player, Stan Collymore.

But before I went chasing new stars, I first had to try to hold onto the ones I had already got. Four internationals, Stuart Pearce, Nigel Clough, Roy Keane and Gary Charles, seemed desperate to get away. They were the backbone of the team and I was equally desperate to hold onto them. It didn't go very well for me. Roy Keane was the first to resolve his situation. He had already made up his mind to leave before I even arrived and there was no stopping him. He left for Manchester United.

Most players change clubs to get a better deal and earn more money, but sometimes there is much more to it. Nigel Clough was a classic example. Having been unable to hold onto Keane, I was even more determined to keep Nigel. I felt I could build a team around him. He was out of contract and free to go, so it was always going to be an uphill struggle to persuade him to stay at a club which had been relegated.

There were a few points in my favour, however. Nigel had been a Forest hero for nearly eight years and, of course, because of his father he was steeped in the tradition of the club. He was Forest's second-highest goalscorer of all time. You have to go back to the turn of the century to find a player with a better record, a Mr A.G. Morris who knocked in 217 goals. Nigel had scored 130 and might have as many more to come, I felt, if he could be persuaded to stay.

He had all the worries of the other top internationals, though. He didn't want to drop a division and was concerned about the effect it might have on his international career. He even consulted the England manager at the time, Graham Taylor, to find out what difference it would make.

Within two days of my appointment we came up with a package to put to Nigel. He at least agreed to consider it. Unfortunately, there were forces working against us which had nothing to do with football. The shadow of Brian Clough was looming large. Back in April, an article had appeared in the *Sunday People* quoting Forest director Chris Wootton accusing Brian of having such a bad drink problem that it was affecting his health and his managerial ability. It was suggested he should step down for the good of the club. Brian strenuously denied the allegations. A few days later, Fred Reacher announced that Brian had decided to retire at the end of the season. The announcement of the retirement and the allegations about drink were not connected, but the timing was unfortunate and to many people there did seem to be a link. The Clough family were understandably outraged that Brian's reign should come to an end under such a cloud.

It was bound to have an effect on Nigel. It would be difficult for him to stay at Forest while people he regarded as his father's critics remained. I must admit I had mixed feelings about what he should do under the circumstances. If I had been his independent adviser, I would have urged him to go. He had been at Forest a long time and after all that had happened it was probably best for him to leave and make a fresh start. Liverpool were showing a lot of interest in him and they seemed the ideal club for a player of his style. But of course, as manager of Nottingham Forest I did everything possible to persuade him to stay.

It came to nothing, though. In the end the allure of Liverpool and the bad feeling created by the manner of his father's retirement meant it was inevitable that Nigel would go. He signed for Liverpool on 10 June. The two clubs haggled over the fee, Liverpool offering £1.5 million while we wanted £2.5 million. The fee was eventually settled by an FA tribunal, which split the difference.

Gary Charles was another very fine player I tried hard to keep, but again I found myself fighting against forces that had nothing to do with football. He had had a very troubled time in the city during the previous few years. He had been involved in a crash in which a young motorcyclist was killed. Gary wasn't to blame but it brought him a lot of unwanted publicity, on top of all the problems anyone would face in such a situation. Then in a separate incident he was fined for speeding. Taken altogether it didn't endear him to the supporters and they gave him a bit of stick. He wanted to get away, not from the club but from the city. I did all I could to persuade him to stay but he was adamant he wanted a fresh start. He was out of contract so there was nothing I could do about it. In the end he went only 15 miles up the road to Derby County, but it got him out of Nottingham and that was mainly what he wanted.

So far I didn't have a lot to show for my efforts. Three of the big four had gone and things weren't looking good. I was concerned about the effect the departures might have on morale at the club. Fortunately there was still one player who hadn't yet made up his mind – the club's very own Roy of the Rovers whose reputation with the fans was matched only by that of Brian Clough himself. Stuart Pearce was still considering his options. If only I could persuade him to stay, things would look a lot brighter.

CHAPTER 4

Psycho Therapy From Stuart Pearce

Minutes before an important European match, my captain Stuart Pearce is in the dressing room shaking his fists and screaming at the rest of the players. He's been listening to his punk rock music and he's all psyched up. Sitting in front of him is an array of different nationalities: Dutch, Norwegian, Italian, Scottish, Welsh, Irish. Pearce is shouting at them all, explaining why we're better than the French opposition and why we're going to win.

He punches the air. '*Because we're English!*' he screams. '*Because we're English!*' The factual inaccuracy of the statement doesn't seem to occur to Stuart. I'm not sure if it occurred to his Norwegian, Dutch, Italian, Scottish, Welsh and Irish team-mates, but if it did, none of them seemed in much of a hurry to point out his mistake. In fact, from the nervous looks on their faces, a few

of them might have been considering changing national-
ity.

There is no doubt that Stuart Pearce is the most influential player I have ever worked with in over 35 years in the
game. He's not only a great player, he's also a great leader,
on and off the field. I sensed this as soon as I arrived at
Nottingham Forest. Good leaders in football are rare, so I
knew it was vital to keep him.

Equally I knew it wouldn't be easy. With other star players like Roy Keane and Nigel Clough already jumping ship
to join glamour clubs Manchester United and Liverpool,
the temptation for Stuart to follow suit must have been
enormous. But their departure made Stuart even more
important to us. I wanted to hold onto him not just because
he was a world-class player, but because I knew it would do
wonders for the club's credibility if he stayed. It would be a
vote of confidence in me as a manager and in the future of
the club. His presence and commitment to Forest would
make it easier to attract other top players to Nottingham.

Stuart's a very straightforward man and he likes you to be
straight with him. I had to do some real negotiating to get
him to sign. It wasn't just about money. I had to convince
him that his England career wouldn't suffer because he
would be out of the Premier League. England were still
trying to qualify for the 1994 World Cup in America at
that time. I told him I couldn't see the manager Graham
Taylor discarding him at such a crucial period just because
he was playing in the First Division. We would know by the
following October whether England had qualified or not.

If they did, then I was sure Taylor would want to keep
Pearce for the duration of the tournament; if they didn't,
then Taylor would be sacked and a new manager would be

appointed to build for the future. I couldn't see the new manager, whoever he was, being interested in a 31-year-old full-back so Stuart would probably be out anyway. Stuart seemed to accept that view and I think he appreciated my honesty, although as it turned out I was only half right.

Stuart certainly did keep his place in the England set-up. That much was true, but when Graham Taylor was sacked after England failed to qualify for the World Cup it wasn't the end of Stuart's England career as we both thought it would be. It was only the beginning of the most exciting chapter. The new manager, Terry Venables, kept him on, as a squad member initially to make use of his vast experience. But when his replacement at left-back, Graeme Le Saux, sustained a long-term injury, Stuart was back in what many people still regarded as his rightful place in the team. And, of course, he returned as football was coming home to England for the European Championships. He was to play a major part in the tournament as we restored some pride in ourselves as a footballing nation.

Everyone in Nottingham had grown accustomed to Pearce's passion, commitment and determination, but perhaps the rest of the nation didn't fully appreciate him until those Euro 96 Championships. The most enduring image of the whole tournament must surely be Stuart's emotional reaction after he scored in the penalty shoot-out against Spain. It was a magical moment that had been six years in the making.

It went all the way back to Italia 90 when Pearce was involved in the penalty shoot-out against West Germany in the semi-final of the World Cup. He had had a marvellous tournament and was at the height of his powers. The score in the shoot-out was 3–3 when he stepped up to take England's fourth penalty. The tension was incredible. His shot was quite well hit but the goalkeeper managed to block it. Pearce turned away, totally crestfallen. A few moments later Chris Waddle hit his shot over the bar and England were out of the World Cup. Pearce looked inconsolable.

He returned home to a mixed reception from the fans. On the positive side there were sacks of letters from fans all over the country commiserating with him for the miss. They didn't blame him for England's exit and all wished him well. It was a different story on the terraces, however, as might be expected. During most games, it wouldn't be long before the opposition fans would start chanting, 'Pearce lost the World Cup, Pearce lost the World Cup.' Not as vehement as the chanting aimed at David Beckham after the 1998 World Cup, but hard to take nevertheless.

True to character, though, Pearce came bouncing back to score more goals for Forest that season than he had ever done before. He went on to say the devastating experience of the penalty miss even helped to make him a better player, stronger and more mentally resilient. Then in that match against Spain in the quarter-final of Euro 96, he got the chance to put the record straight. When you're in the game, you tend to get a bit cynical and hard-nosed about it all. Moments of real emotion are rare, but that day was such an occasion. The expression on his face after he scored was just amazing – six years of regret, frustration and anger released all at once. It took incredible courage to stand up there and take it. He had gone through agonies after missing the last time. No one would have blamed him if he had wanted to duck out of the responsibility this time.

Those European Championships were a tremendous

bonus for Stuart, who was 34 at the time. Apart from anything else, that one goal and his subsequent jubilant reaction increased his marketability ten-fold. Suddenly everyone wanted to speak to him and his face began staring out from advertising hoardings all over the country. Television companies wanted to make documentaries and videos about him. He even began acting in television commercials. One involved a comedy routine with Chris Waddle and Gareth Southgate, the other two who had missed crucial penalties. I think most people would agree that Stuart was a far better footballer than actor, but I don't suppose they would begrudge him the extra attention. He had earned it.

He also earned himself a stay of execution on his England career. At the end of the tournament he announced his retirement, understandably thinking he was too old to figure in the plans of yet another new England manager, Glenn Hoddle. He was wrong. Hoddle phoned him up to persuade him to change his mind. He didn't guarantee him a place in the team but asked him to stay on and give the younger players the benefit of his vast experience. Stuart didn't need asking twice. The next thing you know, he's playing in the qualifying matches for the 1998 World Cup. He then retired again only to be recalled once more to the England team by Kevin Keegan at the age of 37. He played against Luxembourg and Poland in the Euro 2000 qualifiers. There can't be many players who've survived five England managers, but then there aren't many players like Stuart Pearce.

The kind of power and passion Stuart displayed so graphically during the Euro 96 campaign was something Forest fans had come to take for granted over the years.

It had made him into something of a cult figure. He had spent the best eight years of his career at the City Ground. During that time he had enjoyed several trips to Wembley on Forest's various Cup outings, played for England more than 50 times and been appointed captain of his country by Graham Taylor. Pearce certainly saw Forest as being largely instrumental in helping him achieve that success and felt an enormous loyalty to the club. Years before, Manchester United had shown an interest in him but he chose to stay at Forest. He had also rejected approaches from Glasgow Rangers. Although he was ambitious, he felt he could be successful at Forest, which of course he was. Moreover, he had a marvellous, unique relationship with the fans.

It was a relationship he enjoyed. At the start of a match he would acknowledge the crowd with his fists clenched and arms outstretched. He looked like some latter-day Roman gladiator and would then proceed to play like one. His fearsome tackling earned him the nickname 'Psycho' – colourful, but it hardly did justice to his skill. He may have gone in where others feared to tread, but the tackles were well-timed and he usually emerged with the ball. His full-blooded commitment became a feature of Forest matches, so much so that a Pearce tackle could please the crowd as much as a defence-splitting pass from someone like Nigel Clough. Quite an achievement in a side renowned for stylish, passing football.

I was able to use all this in my campaign to keep Stuart at Forest when I arrived. I threw in everything I could think of. The fact that he was a local hero, only Brian Clough and Robin Hood were ahead of him. I pointed out his wonderful lifestyle in Nottingham. He and his wife like horses and had a smallholding. I didn't think he would want to give that up. But he also wanted reassuring that the club was still ambitious. I told him the directors would allow me to spend every penny we raised on the transfer market to buy new players.

At the time I was chasing Colin Cooper and Stan Collymore. Both were playing in London, so I had seen a lot of them during my time at Orient. I regarded Colin, who was playing for Millwall, as the best central defender in the First Division. He wasn't very big but he got up very well and had a welcome habit of scoring vital goals just when they were most needed. He was also a good leader and organiser. Stan Collymore, of course, was a raw but tremendously exciting striker I had been watching with interest for many years.

I ended up having to pay more than I wanted for both Cooper and Collymore because both were still under contract. But if you want real quality and they're tied up in that way then you have to pay over the odds. Cooper was the first to sign for £1.75 million in June. As soon as he put pen to paper I phoned the Southend manager Barry Fry and told him I would pay the full asking price for Collymore. I signed Stan the next day for £2.2 million.

I think Stuart was relieved to at last see some positive action on the transfer front and the arrival of Cooper and Collymore did a lot to ease his mind about the club's hunger for success. Negotiations with Stuart lasted over six weeks. I was working on the other two deals at the same time. They all came to fruition together and all three players signed for Forest within the space of a week. It was a huge boost for me and the club. Suddenly there was a new buzz about the place. For the first time people began to think, well, maybe there's something to this fellow Clark after all. Season ticket sales, which had been very sluggish, picked up dramatically. Everyone was looking forward to the new season.

Stuart was a huge help to me in my first few months and I often had cause to be grateful for his leadership qualities and unswerving professionalism, as had my predecessor Brian Clough. Brian actually joked that Stuart virtually did his job for him, he just didn't get the salary for it! It is vital that the manager and team captain get on well and show a united front to the rest of the club. It is particularly important when you are a new manager at the club and the captain is someone as well-respected and influential as Pearce. The last thing you would need is someone of that stature undermining your authority. But there was none of that at all.

I introduced a lot of new training methods and new ideas when I arrived. Stuart just adapted to them straight away and got on with it. There was no prima donna business of 'I'm Stuart Pearce and I've played for England 50 times.' He just did it. He sometimes came up to me afterwards and said he wasn't sure about some things, but that was all right. Any disagreements we had were in private and I respected that. In public he still got on with it. And, of course, if he's prepared to get on with it, you can be sure the rest of the players will follow.

Stuart has that effect on people. I'm not saying they all like him, but they all respect him, not just at his club but at every club in the country. Howard Wilkinson admitted he always hoped Stuart would be missing when his teams played Forest. He feared his ability to influence a game by inspiring other players. Bobby Robson described him as fiercely competitive and awesome in the tackle. He had this advice for any winger thinking of playing against him: Don't! Go and play on the other side of the field.

There were certainly a lot of wingers taking Bobby's advice. None of them liked taking him on, that was patently obvious every week. They got nervous when they got the ball and he was around, even seasoned pros – a couple of clatterings and they liked to keep away. It's more difficult to frighten people these days because of changes in the law. The hard men can't come and kick you like they used to, but you still have to get past them with the ball and that can take a lot of nerve. Stuart was certainly very intimidating and most people paid him a healthy respect. The only person I've seen who looked as though he enjoyed playing against him was a young lad called Paul Hall from Portsmouth. We played them in the First Division and he caused Stuart all sorts of problems. He obviously didn't know who he was. Ignorance is bliss.

Stuart is very single-minded when he's out there on the pitch. You never see him laughing and joking with the opposition during the match, even if the game's stopped for any length of time. There's never any social chit-chat, he gives everyone the hard stare. In that respect he reminds me of Jack Charlton years ago. I remember playing for Newcastle against Leeds one day when the game was stopped for quite a long period because someone got injured. I thought I would go and have a chat with Jack. I didn't know him very well but we were both Geordies from the same part of the world. I went up to him and made some sort of pleasant remark, hoping to engage him in conversation. He just turned round and said: 'F— off.' Then he walked away. It seems funny now but it showed how seriously he took everything, and that attitude can be quite intimidating. Stuart is the same. He once said he couldn't understand how players like Dwight Yorke can go out on the pitch with a big smile on their faces looking as though they're having a great time. I know what he means. You are out there to win and it's too important to laugh about. That doesn't mean you're miserable, just that the actual playing of the game is too important to simply enjoy. What you enjoy are the rewards of the game, the preparation and the build-up and the warm glow afterwards if you do well.

I think Stuart and I worked well as a partnership in motivating the Forest players. Our approaches complemented each other. I try to motivate people by giving them a framework where they can go and make the most of their ability and be successful. I like to build up their confidence and self-belief. Stuart's more of a fist-shaking motivator and in Europe that's a major factor. He's very good at that, but it's on the pitch that he can be inspirational. He lifts the other players – sometimes he frightens them a little bit, but he always gets them going. He has this refusal to accept defeat and a constant determination to go and do something.

Fortunately, we won a lot more games than we lost while I was at Forest, but not that many of them were by comfortable margins. There were an awful lot of nailbiters. There were several times in games like these when just by the force of his personality, Stuart took the rest of the players forward to go and win it.

He also gets the crowd going. Sometimes a game can go off the boil and the atmosphere goes a bit flat. The fans need something to warm them up. Then Stuart launches into one of those rampaging runs of his and suddenly there's a buzz of excitement about the place. The anticipation mounts and the place is alive again. He might end up scoring or the ball may end up in the back of the stand, but the sense of excitement is still restored. It has a galvanising effect on the whole ground and the crowd is back chanting in full voice again. That in turn helps to urge on the players that little bit more.

There were some people, mainly journalists and those outside the game, who wondered at the wisdom of my giving Stuart a lucrative four-year contract at the age of 31. I had no qualms about it at all. I played until I was nearly 37 and I wasn't nearly as good as him. I knew there was no reason why he shouldn't play on well into his thirties as well. He's an excellent professional and looks after himself properly.

More and more players carry on playing these days and I think we'll see more of it. We have more knowledge about how they should look after themselves, in every area from better training techniques to the right kinds of food to eat. We're also much better at treating injuries. A lot of players are coming back after injuries which would have put them out of the game 20 years ago. Brian Clough had to retire early after damaging his cruciate ligaments, yet operations to rectify that are commonplace nowadays. Paul Gascoigne suffered a similar injury to Clough playing for Tottenham against Forest in the 1991 FA Cup final and he was back within a year, a little slower but still a formidable player. Roy Keane made a similar recovery from an injury that would have ended his career were it not for the advances in medical science. The future looks good for professionals who are prepared to work hard and look after themselves, and Stuart Pearce certainly comes into that category.

It isn't only a case of keeping in good physical shape. Players need to increase their knowledge of the game to compensate for the slight loss of pace and energy. Stuart did that and I would like to think that he learned a little while playing for me. No one is so good that they can't learn something, and I think we managed to improve him in some small respects.

Stuart's game changed towards the end of my stay at Forest. He began to show me, through the way he played but also the occasional little things he said, that he didn't fancy playing left-back any more. He obviously couldn't go on as many rampaging runs in his thirties as he did when he was 25. He saw himself as the third centre-back of a 3–5–2 formation, the way he had by then started playing for England. I could understand that, because it's easier to play that way when you're getting older and losing a bit of pace. It's only 15 yards further infield but it makes an enormous difference. He was beginning to struggle against wingers of real quality.

This was particularly noticeable when we played Manchester United at the start of the 1996–97 season. We played 4–4–2 that day which meant Pearce found himself up against Karel Poborsky. I think he's quite an ordinary player but Stuart didn't want to go out there and play left-back against him. It was a problem for us. He was such an influential player that he had to be in the team. The answer, of course, was to play 3–5–2. I actually wanted to be able to do that anyway because a lot of Premier League clubs had started playing that way and it can create problems for you if you stick rigidly to the old system.

We tried it a few times and not surprisingly Stuart was

magnificent as the third centre-back. He could obviously do it in his sleep and so that was fine. He learned to read the game a lot better and his positional sense improved enormously. He became a slightly different player but no less effective, so much so that when his four-year contract was nearly up I had no hesitation in offering him another three-year deal. He was 34 at the time yet I knew I could have sold him for £2 million if I had wanted. People would have been buying his personality, character and leadership qualities. As it was, I had no intention of selling him because I wanted to keep all those qualities at Forest. I told him he should try to play for as long as possible. He would know when the time came to stop, when he felt he could no longer do himself justice.

Six months after I left Forest, Stuart did what many thought would never happen; he too left the club. Ironically, he found himself in the same position he was in when I had joined Forest four years earlier. Forest had just been relegated to Division One in 1997 and he was frightened it would affect his chances of playing for England in the next World Cup. He felt he needed Premier League football. It was amazing that a player of his age should even be in contention for an England place, but that was the measure of his ability and influence.

What makes Stuart's achievements all the more remarkable is the fact that he came into the professional game at a very late age. He was rejected by the big clubs when he was 16 because he was considered too small. Other players might have moped about and packed the game in. He just got on with his training, got himself a trade as an electrician and tried to rebuild his career. He stuck at it and finally got his big break at the age of 21.

The Coventry manager at the time, Bobby Gould, went along with his wife to see a non-league match between Stuart's team Wealdstone and Bath (Bobby's obviously a man who knows how to treat a woman to the high life). Despite the mundane surroundings, however, the couple were immediately impressed by what they saw. Bobby joked afterwards that Stuart sent the opposition right-winger flying so high he landed in Mrs Gould's lap. It was a fair tackle as well! Bobby signed him the next morning for £25,000. It must rank as one of football's all-time best bargains.

Stuart did well for Coventry but even at that stage there was little to suggest he would mature into such a great player. When he joined Forest he was just the makeweight in a £450,000 deal designed to bring the England Under-21 international Ian Butterworth to Nottingham. Brian Clough described Stuart modestly as 'a good defender who uses the ball well and has the ability to get down the line.' Perfectly true but hardly effusive. Yet a few years later Clough was naming Pearce in his team of all-time greats, and praising him for virtually carrying the club on his own and saving them from relegation. He went on to say that Pearce had put more into Forest in terms of courage and commitment than any other player.

No one could ever accuse Pearce of having had it too easy. After his early rejection he had to do it the hard way. I mentioned earlier that he had a special relationship with the Forest fans. This was due mainly, of course, to the fact that he was such a great player and competitor, but there was perhaps another underlying factor. I think the fans found it easier to identify with him than with most other players. Like them, he had had to work in the real world when he failed to make it initially as a footballer. In fact, he continued to work in the real world even after he had made it in the game.

While at Wealdstone, he served his apprenticeship as an electrician and worked for Brent Council. He continued his trade at Coventry and even when he arrived at Forest he wouldn't give up the day job. He set up his own one-man electrician's business in Nottingham. He still had it when he received his first call-up to the England team from Bobby Robson. Stuart felt it was important for players to plan for life after football. He even had a business card, which said, *'All Work Guaranteed.'* Well, anyone knowing Stuart's professionalism would know that, but who on earth would argue with him if they weren't satisfied?

Of course, as his career began to really take off, the electrician's business had to go, but the experience had helped to establish him as a man of the people. The supporters felt he was closer to their world than some gifted superstar who had breezed his way easily to the top. It was easier to identify with the down-to-earth, self-made qualities of Pearce than, for example, the gifted but seemingly lazy approach of a Bryan Roy or Stan Collymore.

Stuart has been a great professional and an example to everybody. He once said he wouldn't have any regrets about his career because he knows he made the most of every ounce of ability he had been given. You can't ask for any more from anyone.

CHAPTER 5

Fairytale on Tyneside

My European Cup-winning experience with Brian Clough wasn't the only inspiration I could call upon as I prepared Nottingham Forest for the new season. In 1969, my first club, Newcastle United, had also conjured up an unlikely piece of magic to produce a fairytale year in which we won the Inter Cities Fairs Cup, the forerunner of what's now called the UEFA Cup. That European campaign was an amazing time for Newcastle. The fans were ecstatic, they had never seen anything like it before. It was the biggest thing the club had won since the days of Jackie Milburn and the three FA Cups back in the early Fifties. Newcastle haven't done anything to equal it since, despite the tens of millions they've spent.

Our incredible cup run was all the more enjoyable for being totally unexpected. In all fairness, we had no right even to be in the competition. We earned our place only through a bizarre set of circumstances that kept out some of the top teams, and it led the press to launch a frenzied attack on us. In 1968, Newcastle had finished only tenth in the league, way below the usual level needed to qualify for European competition. This is how the table looked at the end of the season:

1. Manchester City
2. Manchester United
3. Liverpool
4. Leeds United
5. Everton
6. Chelsea
7. Tottenham Hotspur
8. West Bromwich Albion
9. Arsenal
10. Newcastle United

There were three Inter Cities Fairs Cup places on offer to English clubs that season. As league champions, Manchester City would obviously go into the more prestigious European Cup, so the qualifiers would normally be the next three highest placed teams: Manchester United, Liverpool and Leeds United. Fortunately for us, it was more complicated than that. Our first lucky break came when Sir Matt Busby fulfilled his lifelong ambition and won the European Cup with Manchester United. It meant that they would also qualify for the European Cup the following season and so forfeit their place in the Inter Cities Fairs Cup. That meant the three qualifying teams should now be Liverpool, Leeds and Everton. However, Leeds had won the Fairs Cup the previous season and so qualified automatically. Their place could therefore go to the next highest team in the league. That meant the qualifiers would now be Liverpool, Everton and Chelsea; Newcastle should have had no chance.

This is where the bizarre rules of the Inter Cities Fairs Cup came to our rescue. At that time, you couldn't have two teams from the same city in the competition. Everton were furious to find that they could not take part simply because they were from the same city as Liverpool. They had to stand aside and give their place to a team below them. That would have been Tottenham, but they couldn't enter either because they were from London which was already represented by Chelsea. Spurs therefore had to cede their place to West Bromwich Albion, but here we were lucky again. Albion didn't want the place because they had won the FA Cup that season and so would be going into the European Cup Winners' Cup. The baton would be passed on to the team below them.

We still weren't home and dry, though. There was still one team above us, but God must have been a Newcastle fan that season because who did he place above us? Arsenal, who like their north London rivals, Tottenham, couldn't take part because of Chelsea's participation. Through an amazing series of coincidences, Newcastle had made it. The clubs above us who had lost out were understandably angry and disappointed. The press, especially the London-based papers, were furious. They were outraged that the big glamour clubs like Tottenham and Arsenal had to stand aside for the sake of a bunch of also-rans from Newcastle. Their comments were typically over the top, but even we could see the reasons for their anger. Newcastle weren't exactly high-flyers at the time.

Our manager was Joe Harvey. He was appointed in 1962

and I was one of his first signings when he took me from the local amateur side, Crook Town. He was a sergeant major-like figure and he absolutely terrified me in those early years. Harvey was from the old school of managers. He always wore a suit and tie and very rarely took us for training. He left that to the coaches. His main qualities were that he had a good eye for a player and he was good at motivating people. He did this mainly through discipline and fear but it worked. Newcastle had been in the doldrums before he took over, languishing in the old second division and dreaming of their former glories with Jackie Milburn. The fans desperately wanted to return to the top flight but relegation to the Third Division seemed more likely when Joe took over. He very quickly turned things round. He saved them from the drop in his first year, stabilised things in the second and then won the Second Division championship in the third year, 1965.

Promotion brought a sense of euphoria back to the banks of the Tyne but things were to remain tough. We struggled in the First Division, finishing 15th and 20th in our first two years. Finishing 10th in 1968 was our highlight of the decade so far. We could see why the press weren't on our side. We had almost been relegated the season before. The papers ran campaigns to try to get UEFA to change the rules about not having more than one team from the same city. When that failed, they turned their wrath back on us. They described us as talentless journeymen, lacking in skill and finesse. They said our predictable, unsophisticated style would not be good enough to compete against Europe's best and we would shame the nation.

We let it all wash over us. To be honest, we did feel a little embarrassed to be taking part but we were determined to make the most of it. And, in a way, the criticism of the press worked in our favour. It helped to motivate us to show them that we were better than they suggested, yet at the same time their comments took away any pressure there might otherwise have been. We hadn't expected to qualify and no one thought we would last very long. We didn't think so either. None of the players thought we could win it. It meant we went into the games feeling very relaxed because we had nothing to lose. European football was completely new to us and we saw our trips as great adventures; enjoyable, but not to be taken too seriously. As it turned out, we had a secret weapon. In fact, it was so secret we weren't aware of it ourselves until the tournament got under way. It was none other than the direct, journeyman approach to the game which had been so roundly slated by the press.

We didn't think of it as long-ball football, but that's what it would be called today. It was completely new to our more sophisticated opponents and took them by surprise. The focal point of the team was Wyn Davies, our Welsh international centre-forward. He was big, brave and very good at getting on the end of long balls hit from the wings or from deep out of defence. He got most of the glory that year and rightly so because the Continental teams just couldn't cope with him. Alongside him was Bryan 'Pop' Robson who snapped up a lot of the balls knocked down by big Wyn. We had Jimmy Scott on the right wing and Jackie Sinclair on the left. They both got the ball across to Wyn as early as possible. The central midfielders did the same. We had people like Scotsman Tommy Gibb and Benny Arentoft from Denmark. They weren't the best passers of a ball but they were great athletes who could run all day. As they lacked real creative skill, they too concentrated on getting the ball forward early to Wyn Davies.

In defence, we had me at left-back, David Craig at right-back with Bobby Moncur and Ollie Burton in the middle. None of us was overblessed with passing ability but we were solid as a unit and very hard to get past. Like the rest of the team, we tried to get the ball upfield early for the front two.

The Dutch masters Feyenoord were the first team to feel the full force of our simplistic approach. They were a wonderful side technically. They went on to win the Dutch league the season that we played them and then the European Cup the following year. However, they were unused to aerial bombardment and had no answer for it. We took them on in the first leg in front of 46,348 fans at St James' Park. Until that night, everyone thought we were just making up the numbers in the competition. That all changed when we played them off the park. We hammered them 4–0 and still managed to hit the woodwork three times. Davies was winning everything in the air and Feyenoord didn't know what to do about him. He scored along with Scott, Robson and Gibb.

We were very confident going into the second leg – a 4–0 lead takes some overcoming, even for a side as good as Feyenoord. As it turned out, it was fortunate we had such a good cushion. They tore us apart with a level of skill we could only dream about. We had to make lots of last-ditch tackles and resort to desperate boot-it-anywhere kind of clearances. The 2,000 Newcastle fans that travelled to Holland to support us had a nervous night waiting for the final whistle. In the end, we managed to keep Feyenoord down to only two goals. It meant we went through 4–2 on aggregate.

That away tie showed us just how good Continental teams could be but it still didn't worry us. We didn't expect to progress much further and remained relaxed. We were also taken with the travel arrangements for European football. Nowadays, it's all very pressurised. Teams tend to fly out the day before the match and return within hours of the final whistle. In the Sixties we used to fly out on the Sunday so we would have plenty of time to acclimatise and relax before the game on Wednesday. After the game, we would have a night on the town before returning the following day. It was a great break for us and it was even better for the press. It was like a four-day holiday to many of them. It didn't make them any more friendly to us, however, and they still gave us no chance against our next opponents, Sporting Lisbon. We were in good spirits, though, having scored four goals in each of our previous league matches against Nottingham Forest and Ipswich.

Sporting Lisbon's ground was truly magnificent and, with its own hotel complex, it was unlike anything we had seen in England. The city too was beautiful and it all added to the sense of adventure we felt at being in a competition when really we had no right to be there. It seemed every game was a bonus and we were able to perform without getting too tense. We surprised everyone by taking the lead from a goal by Jim Scott. We then got pushed back and had to defend furiously as Sporting surged forward again and again for the equaliser. We held out until the dying seconds when a speculative long-range shot from Morais finally beat our keeper, Willie McFaul, who'd had a wonderful game. It was disappointing to concede so late but we consoled ourselves that 1–1 was a tremendous result away from home and we had every chance of going one better back at Newcastle.

The European bandwagon was beginning to roll and 54,000 people turned up at St James's Park three weeks later to watch the home leg. Again, it was Davies's prowess in the air that created the breakthrough. We got a free kick just outside the Lisbon penalty area. Gibb floated it in and Davies rose above the defenders to knock it down to Robson. He volleyed it in from waist height. It was a particularly satisfying goal because it was a move that had been practised on the training ground over and over again. It turned out to be the only goal of the game but it was enough. We were through to the next round.

The holiday atmosphere continued when we came up against our next opponents, Real Zaragoza of Spain. The Northeast was covered in snow when we flew out from Newcastle on New Year's Eve. We were able to celebrate the New Year in the Spanish sunshine. Zaragoza had a very impressive record in the Fairs Cup. They had reached the finals twice and had won it in 1964. They beat us 3–2, but we were satisfied with that and those away goals were to prove crucial. Again, they were down to our supremacy in the air. The Zaragoza centre-half, Santamaria, was one of the best and most experienced defenders in Europe, but he couldn't deal with the bustling physical approach of Davies. Davies caused the Spaniards all sorts of problems and scored one of the goals. Robson got the other. There was a crowd of 56,000 for the return leg, bringing in record gate receipts of £20,000. The supporters didn't have long to wait to get their money's worth. Robson put us in the lead after only 90 seconds with a fierce

Judging youngsters is a lottery. Newcastle overlooked Alan Shearer as a schoolboy. Ten years later, they paid £15 million to correct their mistake. (*Empics*)

Despite his spectacular talent, many clubs thought George Best was too small to make it and declined to sign him. (*Colorsport*)

Colin Clarke is Northern Ireland's leading goalscorer, even ahead of George Best. He wanted just £20 a week more than Orient could afford so we couldn't sign him. (*Colorsport*)

At Orient I had a tough but great apprenticeship, which included everything from driving the team bus to looking after the kit. This picture was taken shortly before I moved to Forest and with me are chairman Tony Wood (cap) and director Derek Weinrabe. (*Empics*)

Clough bought Peter Shilton when he was one of the best goalkeepers in the world, then made him serve drinks for TV commentator Brian Moore so that he kept his feet on the ground. (*Colorsport*)

Playing in the 1979 European Cup final. Victory in the Olympic Stadium in Munich was the high point of my career. (*Empics*)

When I took over at Forest, some people thought I should erase Clough's memory by removing the photos of the club's glory days. But I couldn't do that. I was in most of them. (*Popperfoto*)

There can't be many managers who could see their side relegated yet still get a standing ovation from the fans, but then there aren't many managers like Brian Clough. (*Empics*)

Stuart Pearce progressed the hard way from non-league football. He was still working part time as an electrician when he got his first call-up for England. (*Nottingham Evening News*)

My first game in charge at Forest and I'm left in no doubt about Pearce's formidable character. He is the most influential player I ever worked with. (*Colorsport*)

Football fans are wonderful when they're on their own, but when they get together in a group they can shed individual responsibility in favour of mob rule. (*Colorsport*)

Shortly before Alex Ferguson won his first Championship, Manchester United fans wanted him sacked. If that can happen to him, what chance do the rest of us have? (*Empics*)

Success can be fleeting so you have to enjoy it while you can. Here I am savouring one of those moments – manager of the month for September 1994 – with Stan Collymore and Bryan Roy. (*Empics*)

Football takes everything to extremes and managers are either heroes or villains. Kenny Dalglish was considered a messiah at Liverpool and Blackburn, but a disaster at Newcastle. (*Empics*)

Having reduced the power of schools football, professional coaches can now work with youngsters like these. It should help us produce technical players who can compete with the Continentals. (*Colorsport*)

Unlikely heroes: against all the odds my first club Newcastle United won the 1969 Inter Cities Fairs Cup. The Hungarian goalkeeper cannot stop Jimmy Scott scoring our third goal in the first leg of the final at St James' Park against Ujpest Dozsa. (*Popperfoto*)

30-yard shot into the top right-hand corner. Gibb added another with a diving header from a corner. We were looking comfortable, but then Zaragoza pulled one back and that made for a very tense finish. They had to score only one more to go through. For much of the second half they made us look second best. We lacked their skill but we made up for it with effort and determination. Despite their domination, the game ended 2–1 to us. That made it 3–3 on aggregate and so we went through because we had scored more away goals.

The weather we had escaped over the New Year was to play a big part in helping us through the next round. Our opponents were Vitória de Setúbal from Portugal. They were in great form and had scored 17 goals in the previous three rounds. We shouldn't really have had a chance against them but this was a charmed year for Newcastle and it seemed fate was holding our hand. It was a bitterly cold March evening when we played the first leg at Newcastle. The snow was thick on the ground and I'm convinced the game would not have gone ahead if it had been an ordinary league fixture. Because of the complications it would have caused to postpone it, the match went ahead. The decision played right into our hands, suggesting yet again that our names had somehow already been written on the cup.

The Portuguese team just weren't used to those conditions and they couldn't cope. They had three players from the former Portuguese colonies in Africa. They had never even seen snow before and spent most of the match shivering near the touchline wearing gloves and goodness knows what to keep warm. Vitória couldn't produce anything like the form they had shown earlier in the competition. We hammered them 5–1, with a goal each from Gibb, Davies and Foggon and two from Robson. Then we went over there and they showed us what a fantastic side they really were. Davies still caused them problems and managed to score, but they beat us 3–1 in a bruising match. We went through because of the big lead we had from the first leg. The snow won it for us really.

Six weeks after our victory against Setúbal, we came up against a top-class team from nearer home. Glasgow Rangers were living in the shadow of their European Cup-winning neighbours Celtic in those days but they were still a formidable side. We weren't afraid, however, because we could feel ourselves growing in strength and confidence. Our European success was rubbing off on our league form. By the time we came up against Rangers, we had 12 league games still to play. We went on a great run and lost only two of them. We finished eighth, our highest position since being promoted. We were starting to feel that we really did belong in the top flight. Bryan Robson was emerging as a striker of real quality. He hit more than 30 goals that season, the first Newcastle striker to do so since the Fifties. We really were seeing the beginning of a purple patch for the club.

We met Rangers in the semi-finals for what turned out to be something of a replay of the Battle of Bannockburn. We drew 0–0 up there, largely thanks to a fantastic display from goalkeeper Willie McFaul who stopped a penalty as well as pulling off a string of fine saves. We won the second leg 2–0 at St James's Park with goals from Gibb and Sinclair. We had made it to the final, but our achievement was overshadowed by the antics of the Scottish fans. Hundreds of them invaded the pitch after Jackie Sinclair scored. It turned into a running battle with police, with bottles and beer cans being thrown. The referee took us off the pitch for 17 minutes until order was restored.

In spite of our success, the press remained hostile. They gave us little credit and still criticised us for our lack of skill and finesse. They didn't seem to realise it was our direct, no-nonsense approach that was proving so effective. We didn't care. We couldn't really believe we had got that far, but having done so, we had come to fear no one. Our next opponents were Ujpest Dozsa from Hungary. They had knocked out the holders Leeds to reach the finals. Afterwards the Leeds manager, Don Revie, described them as the best team in Europe. He gave us no chance in the final. Neither did the press. Six of the Dozsa players were part of the Hungarian World Cup team.

In those days, even the final of the competition was played over two legs. More than 60,000 turned up for the first leg at St James's, bringing in what was then a staggering £42,000 in gate receipts. As well as everything else, the tournament had turned into a massive money-spinner for the club. The critics sat back to watch the game, confidently predicting that the Newcastle bubble was about to burst. It never did. We won 3–0. Our centre-back Bobby Moncur got two goals and Jimmy Scott scored the other. No one could believe it. The crowd went mad, we were ecstatic and the press were apoplectic because they were left with egg on their faces. It wasn't over yet, however, we still had to go to Hungary. We knew we would face an onslaught.

On their own ground, Ujpest Dozsa were magnificent. It was like chasing shadows as they tore us apart again and again. At half time, we were 2–0 down. We were on the ropes and it was hard to see how we could hold on to our slender one-goal aggregate lead. We sat in the dressing room with our chins on the floor. We could all sense that we were going out. Then came one of the great managerial quotes of all time. Our manager Joe Harvey wasn't into tactics at all; but he did sometimes have a knack of stating the obvious. He looked at us and said, 'Don't worry, lads. Don't panic. It's going to be all right.' A ray of hope shot through our dejected hearts. Had Joe come up with a cunning plan? We waited for him to continue, desperate for a lifeline. He looked at us and then said in all seriousness, 'All you have to do is go out and get a goal.'

We all looked at him, expecting him to go on to tell us how we might go about doing that. He said nothing. He had no idea at all. We all looked at each other and raised our eyes to the heavens thinking, 'Wow, thanks boss. Thanks for nothing.' Joe just repeated his advice, 'All you have to do is go out there and get a goal.' He let the words sink into our brains. He was trying to point out that if we could just sneak a goal then the match would effectively be over. Because away goals counted double in the event of a draw, if we could just score one then Dozsa would have to score five to beat us. That would be a tall order, even for them. Although we still had no notion of how we were going to get the ball off them let alone score a goal, the idea somehow gave us a lift. Then something happened that finally convinced me that fate really had put our name on the cup that year.

Bobby Moncur had been a wonderful player for Newcastle but he had scored only one goal in his long career with them. Then he scored two in our first leg match against Dozsa at St James's Park. That was incredible in itself and there could be no way in the real world that he would score again, but by now we were beginning to think that we weren't really performing in the real world any more. Moncur confirmed it that night in Hungary. Five minutes into the second half, five minutes after Joe Harvey told us to go and score a goal, Bobby Moncur did precisely that. He scored from a corner. The effect was incredible – the game was as good as over. Joe had been right. Dozsa now had to score five if they were going to win. You could tell straightaway that they didn't think they could do it. You could see their players deflate as if someone had stuck a pin in them. They just weren't the same team after that. We grew in confidence, came back into the game and actually went on to win 3–2 on the night.

Benny Arentoft got the second goal and then, as if to emphasise the fairytale quality of our cup run, a young sub called Alan Foggon came on to score the third and winning goal. Foggon had come through the youth team and had the long, unkempt hairstyle of the day. Joe Harvey had once introduced him as a local Georgie lad: 'He likes a pint, he'll go far.' He certainly made a good start that night. It was a dream for him and no less of a thrill for the rest of the team. No one, including ourselves, could believe what had happened. We had beaten a side described by Don Revie as the best in Europe by 6–2 on aggregate. Bobby Moncur, who had hardly scored a goal in his life, had got three of them. We had won the Inter Cities Fairs Cup.

The whole thing had a rags-to-riches quality about it. We had been written off at the start by the press as a bunch of provincial no-hopers. By any sensible criteria, we should never have even been in the competition. Everton, Tottenham and Arsenal had much better claims. It was only good luck and bizarre UEFA rules that got us there.

Nevertheless, having got there we were determined to make the most of it. The reaction of the Newcastle fans was just unbelievable. When we flew back from Hungary the next day, we took an open-top bus from the airport through the city. The streets were lined with people cheering us on. No one had seen anything like it since the days of Jackie Milburn. When we arrived at the ground there were 60,000 people waiting inside to welcome us. Goodness knows how many more were locked outside. And this was on a Thursday afternoon. It was just fantastic.

The victory did wonders for my standing with the fans with whom I had always had a mixed relationship. Because I had a couple of A-Levels and could speak reasonably well, the club often sent me on public relations missions, attending supporters' club meetings or doing charity work. I felt I was popular as an individual with the fans at these events, but they seemed far less happy with me on the field. Many of them didn't like my style which wasn't over-skilful and they gave me a lot of stick. That all changed after our Inter Cities Fairs Cup victory. It was as if they had decided I must be able to play after all. It also helped when Sir Alf Ramsey picked me for the Football League team to play Ireland the following season. Pop Robson was also selected. I'm sure the Fairs Cup run played a big part in Ramsey's thinking. Unfortunately, it was the nearest I got to international football.

The Fairs Cup victory was also a tremendous springboard for the club. We were very successful over the next few years, nearly always finishing in the top half of the table. We earned the money to buy new players, including the record £180,000 spent on Malcolm Macdonald who went on to be one of the all-time great heroes on Tyneside.

My career continued to flourish there and I became club captain in my final year, the 1974–75 season. Looking back, I think the Joe Harvey era was one of the most successful Newcastle ever experienced, certainly over the last 40 years. I don't think he ever got the credit he deserved. He certainly never got the acclaim granted to Kevin Keegan who, in all honesty, had far more resources yet achieved far less.

Joe Harvey and I were both sacked on the same day at the end of the season in 1975. Joe moved upstairs to make way for new manager Gordon Lee and I left the club to team up with Brian Clough. We had both had wonderful careers at Newcastle and I remain very fond of the place. I'm still the president of the London branch of the Newcastle United supporters' club.

I had 13 great years on Tyneside but that Fairs Cup run in 1969 was definitely the highlight. That season had a huge impact on my career and influenced my thinking on the game. It gave me first-hand experience of how a group of good but unspectacular professionals, playing with good discipline and good team spirit, could be a match for the most talented sides in the world. It was a force I tried to harness at every club I managed, and it was something I knew could help Forest fight their way back into the top flight.

CHAPTER 6

Winning Over the Fans

I don't know which team you support and I don't know where you sit at the ground, but I know all the people who sit beside you. They're the same people who fill every ground in the country. They're good people, fine people, conscientious at work, polite to their bosses, patient with their kids and kind to the in-laws. They are only human, however, and the frustrations of being a civilised human being build up throughout the week. The stress has to go somewhere, so it goes to football. These civilised people attend matches and undergo a personality transformation when they walk through the turnstiles. They fall into a few different categories and they're easy to recognise. I'm sure you know them already.

The Warrior: Mild-mannered throughout the week, but on match day he's a gladiator protecting his players. When the opposition commits a foul he's on his feet, shaking his fists and screaming abuse. With the courage of a dog on a leash, he wishes he could get at the culprit. He keeps up this peacock display of aggression throughout the game, although he sometimes has to leave early to pick his daughter up from ballet class.

The Heckler: Spends the entire 90 minutes slagging off one of his own team. Picks on the same player every week. When that player is missing it completely spoils his enjoyment until he finds someone else to abuse.

The Moaner: Isn't content with criticising one player and needs to shower his contempt on the whole team. 'Why do we pay to watch this rubbish?' is his favourite cry. Thinks it's very witty to add: 'They should be paying us instead.' Likes to feel sorry for himself. Everything's unfair. The team doesn't try, the manager doesn't care, the tea is too cold, etc.

The TV Pundit: Spends too much time listening to Alan Hansen and wants to show everyone how well he understands the game. Complains loudly that no one is finding space or tracking back. Likes telling everyone if the team's playing 4–4–2 or 3–5–2. Can't understand why the stupid manager doesn't follow his advice and play such-and-such instead of so-and-so.

Dad and Lad: One of the most heart-warming images in the game. Father gets a bit petulant when he can't concentrate on the game because he has to answer endless questions from his son about what's going on. Son gets petulant when father won't queue to buy him a greasy hamburger at half-time.

The Tribesmen: All lads together using football as a form of tribal identity. An essential part of the footballing experience. Their songs and chants create the atmosphere and they're often more entertaining than the game. Sing as one and think as one. More supportive than all the other categories put together, but sadly under threat from rising ticket prices. No wonder they long for the days of the terraces.

I'm sure you'll recognise most of these people and I don't wish to denigrate them by poking a little gentle fun their way. I have every respect for them, they've given me my living for the last 35 years. During that time, though, I've learned to be philosophical about the differing reactions you can get from them.

When you meet and talk to football fans individually they are marvellous. It's when they're in a group at the match that you get problems. They obviously come to watch a match for enjoyment, but it's more than that. They have tremendous loyalty to their club, and football almost becomes like a substitute religion. It really is tribal and so you get the whole gamut of emotions associated with crowd mentality. There can be a wonderful camaraderie born out of the joy in a common cause; or there can be the ugly cruelty that comes when people shed individual responsibility in favour of mob rule.

It means that otherwise reasonable people can behave at a football match in a way which would amaze them if they saw a video recording of it afterwards. The anger and aggressive gestures can be terrible, but going to a match gives people the chance to release all the tensions and frustrations built up over the week. I don't think we understand fully, yet, how important this is. No doubt some psychologist will one day do a learned paper on it.

In the meantime, everyone in the game has to try to understand the fans and accept them, for they are ultimately the masters. There would be no game without them and they are unfailingly loyal to their club – and we must remember that it is *their* club. Players and managers are transient, we work then we leave. When we go, we have to transfer our loyalties. But the supporters remain loyal and we have to respect that. The important thing is that they come to the game and pay their money. If they do that they're entitled to express their opinions, even if we don't like those opinions. I wish they were fairer, a bit less dogmatic and a bit more open-minded. I wish they were a bit more tolerant of players, but the important thing is that they pay their money.

I've had many brushes with fans over the years; some good, some not so good. One of the most chilling was on a warm September evening during my first season in charge of Forest. It came not on a football field but on the M1 as the team were returning home from a match. As the Forest coach sped along the motorway, a bus carrying a group of football fans drove up the slip road to take the Mansfield turn-off. For a time the two coaches were side by side and suddenly the Forest players were subjected to a torrent of abuse, insults and aggressive, obscene gestures.

The hatred on those faces and the stuff that was coming out of that coach were horrendous. What made it all the harder to take was that these people weren't from Manchester, Liverpool or Newcastle, they were our own supporters. Nottingham Forest fans! I'll never forget the faces on the coach that day. It's still my most abiding memory of the season.

What had we done to warrant such a reaction? We had been beaten 1–0 by a very ordinary Barnsley side. It had been a dire game in which nothing had gone right. We had played dreadfully and expected to be criticised, but nothing prepared us for the anger and hatred we encountered.

I could understand that the awful performance at Barnsley was all the harder to bear because it followed a very poor start to the season. In the first six games we had only taken eight points out of a possible 18 and were near the bottom of the First Division. The fans had become spoiled during the Brian Clough years. They saw Forest as a big club. They saw that I had spent millions of pounds and they wanted instant results. The faces on the coach were a reminder, if indeed a reminder were necessary, of just how unforgiving the fans could be if their expectations weren't met.

But I didn't need the anger of the crowd to tell me that things were not working. There were several reasons, some of them obvious. There had been more than the usual crop of injuries to key players, and new players like Cooper and Collymore obviously needed a little time to settle in. At one point there were ten first-team players injured. However, the problems were much more fundamental than that and I had recognised them right at the start of the season, even though the team were unbeaten after the first three games.

We drew 1–1 away at Southend and then drew with the same score at home to Derby. A few days later we took on Grimsby at the City Ground and romped home winners by five goals to three. The fans went home reasonably happy having seen eight goals. They might have expected me to be reasonably happy too, having picked up my first league win as Forest manager in front of a crowd of more than 23,000. But I was far from happy. I couldn't let the result cloud my judgement of our performance that day.

We may have won 5–3 but it was awful. Players were

just careering forward without any thought for the state of the game or about winning the game. They were indulging themselves, playing to enjoy themselves, not to win. They wouldn't or couldn't accept the responsibility of playing the way I wanted. The midfield was just bombing on willy-nilly. We scored five but it could just as easily have been ten. They scored three but could just as easily have had ten themselves. There's no way you can ever win anything playing like that. I knew then that we weren't good enough.

It can be tempting to think that when you're winning everything is fine and when you're losing everything is wrong. Many fans tend to think that way, but it's a dangerous mindset. It feels a lot better to play badly and win than it does to play well and lose, but as a manager you have to be objective because although it is possible to get a victory while playing badly, you won't do it too often.

My assessment was borne out as the team's patchy form showed little sign of improving through September and into October. We won only three of our next 10 league matches and picked up 11 points out of a possible 30. We were hovering perilously close to the bottom of the table and relegation seemed a far more realistic proposition than the much-hoped-for promotion at the first attempt.

The fans were getting restless and quick to shout their disapproval. I could cope with that and knew a few wins would quickly change their outlook. What concerned me more was the increasing realisation that I didn't have the full backing of all my players. If that was the case, it was hardly surprising that they weren't prepared to accept the responsibility of playing the way I wanted. There was an atmosphere in the dressing room and I felt that some of the players weren't convinced about what I was trying to do.

I thought it best to meet the problem head-on and have a no-holds-barred meeting. I took the players to a hotel, booked a room and locked them in for the day. We gave them fish and chips and as much wine as they could drink and had a major talking session. Things were understandably tense to begin with but as the wine began to flow, so did the complaints. They were mainly about the new training methods I had introduced. Under Brian Clough, Forest had been comparatively relaxed about physical training. Former striker Lee Chapman once even blamed this approach for the fact that the team often started the season quite badly and then picked up after Christmas when they had played several games to sharpen them up. He thought it might have been one of the reasons why Forest failed to win the League during the 1980s but seemed to make endless trips to Wembley for various Cup finals. Most Cup matches, of course, are played in the second half of the season.

When I arrived I was determined to improve the levels of fitness and brought in a new trainer called Pete Edwards. He was a body-builder, marathon runner and a keen exponent of martial arts with a black belt second dan in karate. He treated fitness training as a form of religion. He had worked with top Italian clubs like Lazio and Parma and studied their methods. I had used him when I was manager at Leyton Orient and believed he could do a lot for the Forest players. I knew it would be a gamble bringing him in. He's a bolshy bugger and he gets up people's noses, but I was prepared to risk that.

It was revolutionary. It meant the players had to train

harder than ever before and some of them didn't like it. Then, of course, the results weren't going our way at the start of the season. They put two and two together and came up with the wrong conclusion. We got lots of rumblings from them that the training was to blame for our poor form, but that's the same in every organisation. If you introduce change then people get nervous. They need to see how it works and benefits them before they'll accept it.

At the hotel, the players had their say and then I had mine. By the end of the day, most of them were prepared to go along with it and give it a chance to work. A few were still hostile but I dealt with them. Some of them left the club and I managed to isolate the others. I knew that would work for me in the short term, but ultimately I knew we would have to start winning matches if the squad were to be totally convinced that the harder training was helping them.

All that remained to be seen, but at least the meeting had cleared the air and there was a greater sense of optimism about the dressing room – an optimism that was about to be severely tested. The mood of the fans, so graphically illustrated on that coach on the motorway, wasn't getting any better. The hostility was now being directed against individual players during the match. One of the first victims was goalkeeper Mark Crossley. He wasn't playing badly but became a scapegoat for a defence that was leaking too many goals. The fans weren't prepared to make allowances for the fact that so many first-team players were missing. In many cases, because of the injury crisis, we had to throw in teenagers who weren't yet ready for top-flight football. The supporters started to taunt Crossley and boo him when he had the ball.

I had to act before things got out of hand. Crossley wasn't playing badly and he didn't seem to be too upset by the taunts of the crowd, but I felt he needed to be taken out of the firing line for a while for his own good. I didn't want things to get any worse and put him under even greater pressure. I was perfectly happy with his performances but I bought Newcastle's reserve goalkeeper Tommy Wright so that Crossley could be rested until the situation improved. Wright was immediately thrown in for a baptism of fire away at Bolton Wanderers. Forest played dreadfully. If we could have defended even half competently we would have won easily, thanks to two goals by Stan Collymore and another by David Phillips. But on the day we couldn't defend competently. We lost 4–3.

Much of the pressure that day fell on youth team centre-half Steve Blatherwick. I knew he wasn't ready for football at that level but I had no choice, as no one else was fit. It was a traumatic experience for Blatherwick and may well have been detrimental to his development. It was his last game for the first team and it took him two years to fight his way back into contention again.

After driving out Crossley, the fans needed new scape-goats. They turned their attentions to the new right-back Des Lyttle and reserve-team striker Lee Glover – both young players, both yet to establish themselves in the first team, both given a torrid time by the supporters. It got so bad that I had to appeal to the fans to be more tolerant. I tried to point out in newspaper interviews that their actions were counter-productive. By jeering the team and booing individual players, they were making it more likely that things would get worse. Their actions were irrational because they were contributing to the very failure they wanted to avoid.

My appeals were ignored, of course, and when you look again at the reasons why some people attend matches, it's easy to see why. As we've seen, people don't come to football just to watch an entertaining game. They come to release frustrations. During a bad patch in a game, the need to release those frustrations is more pressing than the need to do the more sensible thing, which would be to encourage rather than intimidate players who are struggling. It's unlikely that this will ever change.

And so the abuse continued. Lee Glover even had to suffer the curious indignity of being booed by his own fans immediately after he'd scored a goal. That was against Millwall, but then that was a curious game and was to be a major turning point in the season. I thought we played quite well.

If the fans had heard me say that on the night they might have feared I had gone mad, or that I was in a state of denial, trying to ignore the fact that Forest had been beaten 3–1 by Millwall in front of their own supporters. The fans' reaction to the result was predictably very hostile, but I was trying to see beyond the result to assess the performance. And just as I had refused to be misled by the 5–3 victory over Grimsby, so now I wasn't going to get too despondent about the defeat by Millwall. I felt we had played quite well in certain areas. Obviously we defended badly and we failed to take our chances but overall it was a good performance. There was more discipline and we got nearer to the way I wanted to play.

As it turned out, we went on from that Millwall game and never looked back. We thrashed Birmingham 3–0 on their own ground and it all started to fall into place. Ironically, that victory was set up by two goals from Lee Glover, the player who had been jeered when he scored against Millwall. This time the jeers were replaced by cheers – fans can have very short memories.

After Birmingham, Forest went 12 games and three months without being beaten in the league. We jumped from 16th place to sixth and at last began to look like the real promotion contenders we were supposed to be. So what happened during that game against Millwall that signalled a change in fortunes? Several things. The wine, fish and chips and brainstorming session at the Griffin Hotel had obviously had an effect. The team spirit was better and the players were more disciplined. There were also a few changes in personnel. A young Norwegian arrived at the club and Stuart Pearce got injured, forcing two players to switch positions with spectacular results.

Lars Bohinen was best known to English fans as the man who scored the goal for Norway which helped knock England out of the 1994 World Cup, but Forest fans didn't seem to hold that against him. He wore Stuart Pearce's shirt when he played his first game for Forest against Birmingham, but he played in his usual position in midfield. He quickly became a favourite with the crowd and was to have a major impact.

Meanwhile I was assessing the abilities of the players I already had. Steve Stone was only 21 but had already broken his leg three times. He had managed to work his way back to fitness and was looking to establish himself as a first-team regular. I had no doubt he would make it and put him straight into the team because I loved his attitude. He was very positive. He was good at running forward and I played him initially as a central midfielder, but I didn't think he had enough quality at that time to do it. His composure on the ball wasn't very good, nor was his knowledge of when and when not to run. He got into scoring positions but he didn't score.

Shortly after the start of the season I bought David Phillips from Norwich. He was playing wide on the right and was doing very well. Then after Pearce got injured in the Millwall game, I decided to play Phillips in Pearce's place at left-back, switch Stone out into Phillips' place on the right and bring Bohinen in to fill the gap left by Stone. It worked and we won comfortably at Birmingham.

Pearce was fit enough to play in our next game, away at Wolves. Phillips had done well and I didn't want to drop him, and although we had played well against Birmingham I still wasn't happy with the balance. I've always been keen on having a central midfielder acting as an anchorman, someone who plays in front of the defenders. It's a difficult role to play because you have to have a lot of discipline and you have to understand the game. I thought Phillips would be ideal for it because of his vast experience.

Thankfully, he took to it brilliantly and it made us much stronger in defence. At the same time, Stone was taking to playing wide on the right and Bohinen was settling in well in the centre of midfield, and so the whole thing dropped into place and we never looked back. We raced back up the table and picked up two Premier League scalps in the Coca-Cola Cup, first beating West Ham 2–1 at home and then winning 2–1 away at Manchester City. The whole team was buzzing. Stan Collymore was scoring the kind of goals which would eventually make him Britain's costliest player, while Stuart Pearce was discovering that being 31 didn't mean having to slow down or compromise. He was as effective as ever.

It wasn't just a case of bringing in new players; the way we played had to develop as well. Under Brian Clough, Forest had developed a reputation for playing stylish football, based on keeping the ball on the ground and accurate passing. They were patient in their approach play and prepared to wait for the chance to score. It was a system I understood and was comfortable with, having played under Clough and enjoyed great success.

But clearly something had gone wrong the season before or the side wouldn't have been relegated. They had become a very frustrating side to watch, and not just because they were losing. They lacked an out-and-out goalscorer and it seemed that for many players neat passing had become an end in itself. Fans got used to watching intricate moves progress steadily upfield only to peter out as they approached the opposition goalmouth. Everyone seemed to want to pass and nobody seemed to want to take the risk of shooting at goal. It was purist, no-risk football which lacked passion and bite and, more importantly, wasn't producing results.

When I arrived I was often asked, mainly by journalists, if I would change the system. I think some of them were worried I might abandon the attractive Forest approach and opt for the long ball game. That would have been totally inappropriate and I had no intention of going down that path.

I don't have a single philosophy about how the game should be played. I'm a pragmatist. If you strip the game down to its basics, the simplest way to play is what's wrongly called the long ball game, the way John Beck makes his teams play and the way Wimbledon were criticised for playing in their early days. You take all the decisions away from the players and they're told how to react in every situation. For example, Beck would tell his wingers to get to a certain point then cross the ball no matter what. He's fined players because they've looked up before they crossed it. It didn't matter if there was anyone there or not. In turn, the front players knew they had to get in the box because they knew the ball was coming.

The reason for this is very simple. Making decisions about how and where to play the ball is one of the hardest things in the game. Contrary to what intellectual snobs may think, it requires a great deal of intelligence. Not the kind of intelligence that makes someone speak articulately or work out mathematical equations, but the kind that enables people to see a pattern in the midst of a frenzied, high-speed chaos. The more footballing intelligence a player has, the more angles and openings he will be able to see, and the more he will surprise and delight us with a pass which opens a defence we all thought was shut tight.

He will have the speed of mind and body which enables him to do this despite the fact that hard, determined footballing Neanderthals are snapping at his heels trying to stop him. People like Michel Platini, Glenn Hoddle and Liam Brady could do this supremely well, but unfortunately not everyone has their talent and vision. Many players are great athletes but lack that decision-making ability. With them, the long ball approach is the easiest way to play because the responsibility for decision-making is taken away from them. It compensates for their lack of skill and makes the most of their athleticism. If you have very ordinary players, that system can help you be successful in the short term. I don't decry it. I know how to play that way, but I don't think it would have worked at Forest.

I developed a style there which suited the players I had inherited. They were all skilful and steeped in the Clough philosophy of passing football. I would have been foolish to have gone in and said: 'You're not going to pass it now. You're going to push and pressurise and lash it into the box where we've got two big players who are going to head it in.' It comes back to pragmatism. You've got to work with what you've got. The club had a basic philosophy and everyone was comfortable with it. I tried to make subtle changes and instil a bit more steel, not just in defence but throughout the team. I tried to be more positive. I wanted to get the players to take on responsibilities they had been shunning the season before. If you have good players and you're positive then you will be successful.

It worked. We moved steadily towards the top of the table and within striking distance of achieving my main objective, promotion at the first attempt. The slow start to the season meant we had little chance of actually winning the First Division championship. With only five games left to play, Crystal Palace had established a virtually unassailable 12-point lead at the top, but there was still the second automatic promotion place to play for. I was determined to get it and so avoid having to take part in the lottery of the play-offs for the third promotion slot.

By the end of March we had forced our way up to that second place. We were still there at the end of April when we travelled to play Peterborough. Victory there would ensure that no one could catch us and we would be promoted automatically; defeat would mean the possibility of the play-offs looming ever larger.

We went there full of confidence and full of determination, but that was all shattered when we went 2–0 down within ten minutes of the game starting. If we were ever going to face a test of character, resolve and fitness, this was it. Thankfully, we showed tremendous spirit and I was so pleased that I had been able to persuade Stuart Pearce to stay with us.

There was just no way he was going to accept defeat. He urged the team on constantly and kept bombing down the left wing. The constant pressure paid off and eventually Stan Collymore pulled one back for us. As the game went on, time was running out and we desperately needed the equaliser. We won a corner which led to an unsightly goalmouth scramble. The Peterborough defenders were trying to clear the ball by booting it as far away as possible. Suddenly, among the mêlée, Stuart appeared, thrusting his face forward among the flailing boots to head home the equaliser. It wasn't pretty, it wasn't classic, stylish football, but it was a fantastic moment. Somehow Stuart emerged unscathed, although it wouldn't have mattered to him if he had been kicked black and blue. He would have regarded it as a fair exchange for having scored the equaliser. Stan Collymore then went on to make sure by scoring the winner a few minutes before the end. That 3–2 victory secured our place in the Premier League. It was a tremendous achievement to come back from 2–0 down and said a lot for the spirit and determination within the team.

Stan Collymore's winner in the last few minutes of the game gave it a kind of fairy-tale quality. But I took deep satisfaction in the knowledge that the real reason for the inspired fightback was much more basic. It wasn't just skill and determination which helped us win, it was our high level of fitness. It enabled us to keep going at full speed throughout the whole game.

My thoughts went back to that day of fish and chips and wine at the hotel and the complaints about the trainer who was getting on everyone's nerves. After our successful season, and particularly after the fightback at Peterborough, I felt my decision to introduce the new trainer had been vindicated. I remember thinking: 'Well, he's still the trainer and he still gets up people's noses, but they accept it because they can see it works.'

It was a truly wonderful day. I felt I had not only won over the players but I had also won over the fans. The same people who had been shouting abuse at me from that coach were now chanting my name: 'Frank Clark's Red and White Army.' It was a great moment. After a shaky start it had turned out to be a wonderful season, but I didn't want to spend too much time reflecting on it. I don't think the fans did either. Most of them regarded relegation as an aberration, a nuisance that should never have happened in the first place. Unlike with many other clubs, promotion to the Premiership was not an exciting adventure into new and unfamiliar territory. It was a return to their rightful home.

So within minutes of winning promotion, all thoughts were turning towards next season when Forest would no longer have to worry about Crewe, Grimsby or Huddersfield. They would be back where they belonged playing the likes of Manchester United, Liverpool and Arsenal. The fans went home happy to enjoy their summer holidays and watch the World Cup on television. I went home to plan my strategy for the return to the big time, and to go chasing across Europe for a very special player.

CHAPTER 7

Manager of the Year

Watching Alex Ferguson celebrate his fifth Premier League title win and the glorious treble with Manchester United in 1999, it seemed strange to think that anyone should ever have wanted him sacked. Yet thousands of people did. Little more than a year before the first title win, the *Manchester Evening News* was running a poll on whether he should be dismissed. Never mind that he'd already proved with Aberdeen that he was a first-class manager. For thousands of fans that wasn't enough and they wanted him out.

Football club directors are not known for their loyalty to managers in distress, but to their eternal credit the United board ignored the cries for blood and stuck by Ferguson. It was the best decision they ever made in their lives. The man so many fans wanted sacrificed emerged as one of the club's greatest managers, arguably eclipsing even the great Sir Matt Busby in his overall achievement.

If a manager with the track record of Ferguson can be put under that kind of threat, what hope is there for the rest of us? It begs the question: what makes a good manager and how do we recognise it when we see it? The reality, of course, is that with the divide between success and failure balanced on a knife edge, all managers will experience terrible blows if they stick around long enough. No one is immune. Not Ferguson and not even Kenny Dalglish. Dalglish could do no wrong at Liverpool and Blackburn, but as soon as he lost key players like Shearer and Asprilla at Newcastle he started to struggle and the fans started to get restless. The fact that no side could lose players of that calibre and not struggle is irrelevant to the supporters and the pressure starts to mount. Finally, Dalglish was forced out after only two games of the 1998–99 season.

All you can do is be philosophical and enjoy the good times when they come. For me there was a glorious purple patch between 1994 and 1996. Within five games of being promoted we had stormed to the top of the Premier League, looking down on the very same Manchester United, Liverpool and Arsenal we had dreamed of playing a few months earlier. We didn't stay there for long, of course, but it paved the way for a great season. I had no illusions – I knew there was no way we could win the Championship with our limited resources. But I saw no reason why we shouldn't mount a serious challenge for a European place.

I had spent the summer taking stock and planning my strategy for the coming campaign. I felt we had a good squad of players who had grown in stature during the promotion season. We could have done with a lot more strength in depth but I felt it was even more important to inject some quality to meet the extra demands of the Premiership. There was no way we could do both, given the way transfer fees were spiralling. My chairman Fred Reacher managed to scrape £2.5 million together, a lot of money for a club like Forest but no longer an enormous amount when it comes to buying top-class players.

I then got a phone call from an agent in Italy asking if I was interested in finding new players. I told him I was looking for a left-sided attacker to give us some more options. He said: 'You mean someone like Bryan Roy?'

I laughed and said: 'Yes, but let's be realistic.' But the agent insisted Roy might be available at a price we could afford and had made it known that he'd like to come to England. This was just before the huge influx of foreign players and so Bryan's arrival caused quite a stir. He began to pay back some of his £2.5 million fee in the very first game of the season away at Ipswich, scoring the goal in our 1–0 victory. We were on our way.

The signing of Bryan Roy also produced a very welcome bonus. A journeyman pro whom I once criticised because he 'walked too much for a footballer' was shocked into producing the best football of his life.

I had always found Ian Woan a frustrating player. He had joined Forest under Brian Clough from non-league club Runcorn. He was a typical non-league player. He had more than enough ability to be a professional but he was too laid-back. That's why he dropped into non-league in the first place. Then Bryan Roy arrived and things began to change. It was like Woan said to himself: 'Well, he's not having my place,' which is exactly the response you want.

He began to concentrate more and do what we wanted him to do. Before I arrived Ian had been pinned to the left touchline – Clough always liked wide players to go up and down the line. I felt Ian could contribute more. He was one of the best passers of the ball we had, but it's difficult when you're stuck on the touchline because you don't have as many possibilities.

I encouraged him to move inside more, get into the box and find more scoring positions. He improved enormously and did very well. His attitude and commitment were spot-on. Within two years, Woan was being hailed as a potential England player and on many occasions was even outshining Bryan Roy in the Forest line-up. He grabbed the headlines in the memorable fifth-round FA Cup tie against Tottenham I mentioned earlier, when he scored two spectacular free-kicks, one from an almost impossible angle near the touchline. Even Stuart Pearce, who missed the game through injury, had to admit he'd been outshone. Not bad going for a former non-league player who 'walked too much for a footballer'.

Woan's transformation enabled me to play Roy up front alongside Collymore. It worked out perfectly. Bryan felt happier there and he looked even more dangerous. We were very lucky with injuries for the first few months and went 11 games unbeaten. That run came to an end when we lost 2–0 to Blackburn. Then inevitably a few players took a few knocks and we stuttered through November and December. Things looked up again in the New Year. On 21 February we went to Arsenal and got beaten 1–0, but it was the last time we lost that season.

I was lucky enough to be able to pick virtually the same team every week. That was a tremendous advantage and we finished very strongly. During the last three months, Collymore and Roy were absolutely flying and because they were doing so well it enabled everyone else to develop their game. We ended up in third place behind Blackburn and Manchester United, but ahead of Liverpool and the high-spending Newcastle. It was a tremendous achievement and earned us a place in Europe.

The winning ways continued at the start of the following season and we went 12 games unbeaten. Added to the 13 games undefeated from the previous season it created a new Premier League record of 25 games without losing. Ironically it was the second unbeaten record the club had set. Under Brian Clough Forest went an incredible 42 games undefeated between November 1977 and December 1978.

Our record-breaking effort in the Premier League ended emphatically at Blackburn as we were thrashed 7–0. Sometimes you lose a match and you spend forever wondering what went wrong and how you could have done things differently, but I never spent a minute worrying about that Blackburn result. It was a one-off. Blackburn had eight shots at goal and scored seven times. Incredible, but it just wasn't our day and nothing went right for us.

It was nice to set the record. It was even nicer to be voted Manager of the Year by the other Premiership managers for finishing third in the league. The halcyon days continued in 1995–96 when we reached the quarter-finals of the UEFA Cup and the FA Cup, and finished a creditable ninth in the Premier League. Hopes were high for the following season and things certainly looked very promising after the opening match when we won 3–0 away at Coventry. Kevin

Campbell, signed from Arsenal, was magnificent and got a hat-trick.

Then, before we really knew what hit us, it all blew up in our faces. We got a real kick in the next game at home to Sunderland the following Wednesday. We didn't play too well but then we didn't play all that badly either, yet we ended up losing 4–1. That happens sometimes and although we were bitterly disappointed, we didn't worry about it too much.

We couldn't, because we had to prepare for the game against the multi-national Middlesbrough, complete with newly acquired Italian striker Ravanelli and the Brazilian stars Juninho and Emerson. What I would have given to be able to afford just one of those star names. It was a terrific game and ended up a draw. Then we went to Southampton and although again we weren't at our best, we were winning 2–1 until we conceded with the last kick of game from Matt Le Tissier. It meant we only had five points from four games and we began to get a bit nervous. We lost Campbell in that game when he pulled a hamstring. He would be out for ten weeks, which was a major blow.

The next disaster was Leicester at home. We drew 0–0 in a mediocre performance, but that was the least of our problems. One of our most influential players, Steve Stone, by now an England international, stumbled as he ran towards the ball. There was no other player near him but his legs suddenly gave way and he keeled over. It's hard to believe such an innocuous-looking stumble could have had such a devastating effect. He had torn the ligaments in his knee and would be out for the rest of the season.

From there on, things just got worse. We lost Pearce for

a few games and then Chris Bart-Williams with a long-term injury. I had bought Bart-Williams from Sheffield Wednesday for £2 million in 1995, but my association with him went back to the late 1980s when he signed for me as an apprentice at Orient. He was a very important and versatile player. The injury to him and the others meant that suddenly half the first team was missing, and in many ways the most influential half. The results continued to go downhill and before we knew it we were snowballing out of control. Sometimes we played well but missed our chances or couldn't get a break. Other times we played dreadfully and were lucky not to get beaten more heavily.

Once the downward spiral begins it's very hard to break out of. Confidence, such a fleeting thing at the best of times, just disappears. Players who had been strutting through Europe six months earlier, scoring from every little titbit of a chance that came their way, suddenly found they couldn't find the net under any circumstances. Ian Woan had got 14 goals the previous season, many from the kind of spectacular long-range curving efforts that only Brazilians are supposed to be able to achieve. Now he hardly managed a shot.

Bryan Roy had spent his first season teasing and taunting every defence in the country. He scored 15 goals for us and probably made as many more. But now he, too, looked just a shadow of his former self. It would be unfair to single out any particular player, however. Most people were performing below par. In those circumstances you have to remain positive and keep working with the players. We changed the emphasis in training just to break up the routine. We broke the game down a bit, did more functional work. We spent a lot of time trying to convince the players that they were better than the results were showing. I felt that all we needed was a few wins to trigger us off. Unfortunately, those wins seemed to be nowhere in sight.

As the performances dip on the field, you find your problems increase off it. A panic-stricken sense of doom descends on the fans and certain parts of the media. Immediately it's all relegation talk. Then, of course, the flak starts flying at the manager. I accept that. We bathe in the glory when things are going well so we have to accept the criticism when things are going badly. Even so, some of the comments you get are quite ridiculous. One fan wrote in slating me for not having a replacement for Steve Stone in the reserves. I had to reply saying where would I get someone good enough to replace Stone who was prepared to play in our reserves every week?

Another big criticism was of the number of team changes being made. Some of them were forced on us by the number of injuries we had, others were an attempt to make the best of the players we had available. But people's perception of team changes depends solely on whether or not you win. The previous season when I changed the team and we won, I was hailed as a tactical genius and a potential England manager. Now we tended to lose and so I was branded as a failure who had lost his way. When we were winning I was thought to have the Midas touch in the transfer market, because signings like Collymore, Cooper and Roy were very successful. As we started losing I became the man who bought donkeys, because of the supposed failure of people like Kevin Campbell, Andrea Silenzi and Dean Saunders.

The truth, of course, is in between; I never was that

tactical genius, but then neither was I that failure. It comes back to the knife-edge difference between success and failure, especially when measured over a short space of time. Clubs like Forest have to work with small squads and the loss of a few key players can be crucial. If you can avoid injuries, as we did when we finished third, then everything is fine. If the injuries pile up then you have problems. If you don't believe me then ask Kenny Dalglish about the problems of replacing Alan Shearer.

Transfer dealings are always going to be a lottery, especially for clubs like Forest who work on tight budgets and consequently have to take risks. It's easy to identify good players. It's even easy to identify players who are virtually guaranteed to perform well. Alan Shearer and Roy Keane are two good examples. They have not only the talent but also the character to shine wherever they go, under any circumstances. The problem is that everyone else recognises that too and so the value of those players skyrockets.

Kevin Keegan didn't risk £15 million on Alan Shearer just because he was a talented player. He also knew he was buying consistency and dependability. Shearer is as near as football gets to Bank of England certainty – that's why he costs so much. If I could have afforded £15 million I would have bought him myself.

Lower budgets mean you not only have to buy less talented players but also less certain ones. Sometimes it works, sometimes it doesn't. In 1993 many top teams were interested in Stan Collymore, a player with enough talent to rival Shearer but nothing like the temperament or dependability. I took a risk on him and paid out a club record fee. It worked. He was brilliant for us and everyone applauded it as a good buy. When he went to Liverpool I took a different kind of risk with one of the players I bought to replace him, Andrea Silenzi, who was the first Italian to play in the Premier League. The question over Silenzi was simply would he settle and be able to perform in England? The answer turned out to be that he couldn't. Simple as that. He had a few injuries, a few problems with his family and in the end he just couldn't produce any real form. Eventually he returned home, but not before I was slated as someone who couldn't buy strikers.

Sometimes it's a matter of timing. When Manchester United bought Andy Cole for £7 million he was soon considered by many to be an expensive flop. Very little allowance was made for the injuries and health problems he suffered during those first few years. He was helped, however, by the fact that United have a huge squad of players and so Alex Ferguson could afford to rest him and not put him under too much pressure. The club was still doing well without Cole so Ferguson didn't come under fire for wasting money. Then, having put his problems behind him, Cole came good and rediscovered the form he had showed at Newcastle. Ferguson was rightly praised as a canny manager who could bide his time with a player and coax him back to form.

I had a similar, though less rewarding experience with Kevin Campbell, the other striker I bought to help replace Collymore. I knew Kevin was a very fine player but like Cole he was dogged by injury during his first couple of seasons. Unlike Ferguson, however, I didn't have enough quality players to enable me to give Kevin the time and rest he needed. Too often he had to be patched up and sent out to play. He couldn't do himself justice, he was seen as a flop and I took flak for failing in the transfer market.

Campbell was fully fit and fresh at the start of the 1997–98 season and hit tremendous form. He played a huge part in Forest's promotion success and at last looked like the player I knew he could be when I bought him. But by then I had moved on and Campbell's resurgence was too late to vindicate my decision to buy him. From my point of view the timing was wrong, but then timing is very important in how a manager is judged.

When Alex Ferguson was facing that newspaper poll he was perceived as a failure. A few years later he was perceived as a huge success. When I was voted Manager of the Year I was perceived as a success. A few months later I was seen as a failure. Neither I nor Alex Ferguson underwent any personal transformation during those years, no sudden loss or gain of ability. We didn't change, the circumstances did – and with them the results and people's perceptions. These changing perceptions mean that sometimes people get the sack even though they're good managers. Sometimes circumstances can simply conspire against you and this is a very unforgiving profession. It's possible to make a rod for your own back by achieving success early on and not being able to sustain it.

That certainly played a part in the sacking of Howard Wilkinson at Leeds. He won promotion and the League Championship within four years. A wonderful achievement that makes Alex Ferguson's performance at United look pedestrian, but perhaps it was too much too soon. When the results dipped, the fans turned against him and he was sacked. The club chairman Bill Fotherby explained his decision with typical Yorkshire bluntness: 'I had lost confidence in Howard. Maybe he has been here a little too long. We must have success at this club and we have not been getting it. I have felt for a while now that the fans have not accepted Howard and that the time has come to change managers.'

So that was that. Wilkinson was sacked because the fans wanted him out. And, of course, they always see the negative side. It never seemed to occur to them that had it not been for Wilkinson, they would not have even been in a position to compete for another trophy. They would still be where he found them, in the First Division. Nor did they make any allowance for the fact that the club's difficulties coincided with long-term injuries to key players like Yeboah, Dorigo, Pemberton, Deane and so on.

As Fotherby's statement makes clear, the fans have a major say. When the chairman goes out for dinner on a Saturday night he doesn't want people coming up and abusing him, saying the team is rubbish and the manager should be sacked. Like all human beings, they want to be liked. They can weaken under the barrage of criticism.

Once the fans start getting on the manager's back, it inevitably filters through to the players and confidence can suffer. From there it can be a downward spiral and the demise of the manager can become like a self-fulfilling prophecy. People lose confidence in him because they feel he's a bad manager and so he effectively becomes a bad manager because people have lost confidence in him. Once that point is reached, there's little that can be done except for the manager to leave.

A new manager can, of course, give a club a lift. The new man will enjoy a honeymoon period when he's given more time and a bit more tolerance while he tries to pull things round. That extra breathing space can make a difference, but experience shows that probably 80 per cent of changes have no effect whatsoever, either short term or long term. I would say that, of course, so don't just take my word for it. Consider research done by academics at Hull University. They studied results all the way back to the 1970s and found that, on average, struggling clubs who keep faith with their managers tend to do better than those who chop and change.

As a manager, you quickly come to terms with the logic of the game, however twisted it may seem. You have to accept it and try not to let it affect your thinking. You couldn't do your job properly if you thought every day at work would be your last. The irony is that while every manager knows that short-term success is everything, he still has to make long-term plans for the good of the club. When Wilkinson arrived at Leeds, he instigated a ten-year plan to rebuild the club in every way and put a lot of effort into improving the youth set-up. He did well by today's standards in getting eight years in the job, but always in the back of his mind he would know that he might not be around long enough to see the fruition of that plan. Being the true professional that he is, Wilkinson would have carried on regardless, making sure everything possible was being done to secure the long-term good of the club. The value of his work emerged in spectacular fashion only two years after he'd gone. When Wilkinson's replacement George Graham left Leeds for Tottenham, David O'Leary took over. He was delighted to find that he'd inherited several superb young players from Wilkinson's youth policy who were ready to break into the first team. Youngsters like Harry Kewell, Alan Maybury, Ian Harte, Alan Smith and Jonathan Woodgate quickly established themselves and enabled Leeds to compete with clubs who'd spent a fortune on foreign stars. The performances of those youngsters were a great tribute to Wilkinson's foresight and hard work, but he got little credit for or benefit from them.

The problem is, winning is so important in football that it sometimes prevents people, fans and directors alike, from thinking straight. They lose all sense of proportion when it comes to judging a manager's performance. On the face of it, it may seem straightforward. The good managers are the ones who win things. But in reality that doesn't tell you nearly as much as you might think. The winners are usually the ones with the most money. No one would sack the manager of a small pharmaceuticals company because he failed to make it as successful as ICI. Yet the equivalent happens all the time in football and everyone thinks it's perfectly acceptable.

Many clubs are becoming public companies and the property of hard-headed businessmen, so it might be hoped that some sanity will come into the game. The early signs, however, are not good. Shortly before Howard Wilkinson was sacked by Leeds in 1996, the club was taken over by the Caspian group. I don't know what they think about football but they are certainly not a charity and they didn't buy the club as a philanthropic gesture. They are there to make money. This kind of ownership places yet another kind of pressure on managers because if the team is doing badly, the share price can go down.

When Caspian took over, there were discussions on the financial pages saying that the quickest way for the club to raise the share price was to sack the manager and appoint someone more high-profile. We will probably never know whether such considerations had any bearing on Wilkinson's dismissal, but I am sure that the stock market and share prices will have an increasingly menacing role in the future of managers. The trouble is that people expect too much and when we fail to deliver the impossible, they use us as whipping boys.

That may be partly our own fault. In the past we have imbued ourselves with a false sense of importance and it's now rebounding on us. People want us to be superhuman figures who can do anything. That is clearly not the case. As in all professions, there are a few outstanding managers, a lot of good ones and a few poor ones. But even if we all really were superhuman, it would not alter the reality of the way football is organised. No matter how good we all are, there can only be one League Champion, one FA Cup winner. In fact, of all the 92 league clubs only about a dozen can expect to win something. So where does that leave the rest of us? As Wilkinson found out, facing the sack.

I believe the pressures now facing managers running multi-million-pound businesses should and eventually will lead to a change in the way the job is organised. At the moment, most managers simply have too much to do. The best solution is to split the work up with a general manager or director of football taking on most of the administrative work. He would deal with things like players' contracts, catering for their needs off the field, overseeing the youth academy and generally knitting together the non-playing side of the club. This would leave the team manager free to concentrate on what should be his top priority – getting the best out of his players.

The problem of leaving everything to one man was

highlighted for me in a phone call I heard from a head teacher on a radio phone-in show. This man ran a school in the Northeast. He phoned the station on the day Bobby Robson took over as manager at Newcastle. His point was that Robson would not be able to solve all the problems at the club because the overall administration was not right. He then went on to describe how he had been in his study that afternoon when he saw a young couple with a baby and a child outside on the street looking in. They seemed a bit unsure of themselves so he went to see if they needed any help. They were Spanish and it took a little time to find out what was going on. Eventually, it transpired that the husband was Marcelino, who Newcastle had just bought from Real Mallorca for £5 million. The club had signed him and then left him to his own devices, to wander the streets of Newcastle looking for a school for his children. That was ridiculous. The club should deal with things like that. As soon as you sign a player, you should concern yourself with his wellbeing and happiness; it's the only way to get the best out of what are very costly and uncertain investments. I wouldn't blame Newcastle's previous manager Ruud Gullit for what happened to Marcelino. Managers now have to have such tunnel vision about the first team that they don't have time for anything else. It's the kind of thing the director of football should be able to deal with.

David Pleat at Tottenham is one of the few people with a footballing background to have been given the opportunity to play the role successfully. People opposed to the idea sometimes point out that it didn't work when Kevin Keegan and Ray Wilkins tried it at Fulham, but I think there were obvious reasons for that. Keegan seemed to find it difficult to stay out of team matters and that's bound to cause problems. The director must keep away from the footballing side. He should be appointed by the board to offer background support to the manager. He should not be seen as someone who could take over if the manager is sacked. It should be seen as a totally separate role. That way the team manager need not start feeling insecure. Quite the contrary, in fact, he should be able to rely on the director of football as someone who will help and support him, particularly in cases of political infighting at the club.

Sadly, there hasn't been much enthusiasm for this approach in English football so far. At the start of the 1999 season, I was invited by a Premier League manager to become his director of football. He wanted me to do the kind of things I've outlined above. I was quite happy to take the job on but then at the last minute the club chairman said no. He felt he could fulfil that role himself. The reality, I suspect, is that the workload simply fell back on to the shoulders of the already overstretched manager.

We can only hope for a change of attitude, although the omens are not good. In the meantime, the League Managers' Association has at least been trying to put its own house in order. We've acknowledged that one of the reasons for the high casualty rate in the past is that it has been too easy to become a manager. We see people who are players one day and then managers the next without any idea of what they are letting themselves in for. People can do a two-week course to gain their coaching licence but after that there is no way to improve their knowledge of management other than by actually doing it.

It ought to be compulsory to gain proper qualifications before you can go into management. After much lobbying from the LMA, the Football Association has joined forces with Loughborough University to set up courses for potential coaches and managers. There has been a lot of input from existing managers to make sure the courses will be as practical as possible. We do not want them to be too academically orientated.

The objective is to show people the kind of problems they will face and suggest ways in which they might deal with them. It isn't just a case of picking the team and doing a bit of coaching. There's a lot of paperwork and administration that most players don't even realise exists, yet it has to be done. We can bring home to them the enormous workload they are likely to be taking on. If nothing else, it may weed out the ones who aren't really dedicated enough to cope with the demands. There are still too many people who go into management because they can't think of anything better to do once their playing days are over. If they go on the course, they may realise they don't really fancy it and so save themselves and their prospective new employers a lot of trouble and heartache.

Those who are still unsure might try reading the next chapter in this book which gives a blow-by-blow account of an 11-day stint during my time at Nottingham Forest. It covers the manager's daily routines of training, preparing for big matches, negotiating contracts, dealing with the press and the endless other tasks that come your way once you take charge of a football club. For someone who's prepared to live and breathe football 24 hours a day it's a wonderful if pressurised life, but anyone seeking an easy time should give it a miss.

CHAPTER 8

Football Management 24/7

No two days are ever the same for a football manager, no two weeks for that matter. Patterns do emerge, however. This day-by-day account of an 11-day period from my time at Nottingham Forest covers a humiliating defeat, a tremendous win and a creditable draw. It gives a good idea of the manager's routine as I move from one game to another, agonising over team selection from a squad ravaged by injury. There's the technical coaching, the hard grind fitness training and the tactical talks. There are the demands of the press and the worries of the chairman. We have to find time to scout for new players, keep an eye on the reserves and the youth team and watch the teams we'll be playing next week. It's a 24-hours-a-day/7-days-a-week job, but then most managers wouldn't have it any other way.

On 6 November 1995, Forest beat Wimbledon 4–1 at home to establish a record unbeaten run in the Premier League of 25 games. We hoped to extend that run when we played Blackburn Rovers at Ewood Park on 18 November. We were also preparing to play Lyon in the UEFA Cup the following Tuesday, and a League match against Manchester United on the Monday after that.

Friday 17 November

I spoke to the club physio John Hazelden first thing and we agreed we couldn't put the Bryan Roy problem off any longer. He'd been carrying a knee injury all season and desperately needed a cartilage operation. The problem was that we had so many other players injured it was difficult to spare him. We decided to rest him for the Blackburn game, but then play him against Lyon and Manchester United the following week. After that, we would have to let him go for the operation. That meant him being out until after Christmas. It would be a big blow.

I had the players in for light training but nothing too strenuous. Steve Stone, Stuart Pearce, Scot Gemmill and David Phillips were back from international duty and thankfully still fit. It was good to see Stoney's England career gathering pace. He played alongside Pearce and scored in the 3–1 victory over Switzerland. He looks well on course to make Terry Venables' Euro 96 squad. Gemmill played for Scotland in their 5–0 defeat of San Marino. Phillips was on duty for Wales. I was worried they might be a bit jaded but they seemed all right.

I was at the England match watching the Swiss striker Alain Sutter. We could badly do with him, especially as Roy is going to be out, but I doubt we could raise the £1.5 million fee. I might try to get him on loan.

I wanted to get home for an hour in the afternoon but the chairman Fred Reacher wanted to finalise our submission to the Premier League tribunal on the Stan Collymore case. Stan had a clause in his contract that entitled him to five per cent of any transfer fee if he was sold at the club's request. Because he never put a transfer request in writing, he claims we owe him £425,000 from the £8.5 million we got when we sold him to Liverpool. We're compiling a dossier of press reports in which he's quoted as saying he wants to leave the club. I've got a game to prepare for tomorrow. I could do without this. Stan's left us yet his ghost remains to trouble us.

Fred and I also had a word about new contracts for Steve Stone and Colin Cooper. We felt both of them, having broken into the England squad, deserved a new deal. Both players had been quoted in the local press saying they liked the club and wanted to end their careers here, as long as the deal is acceptable. That's a good basis on which to negotiate. The first task was to find a date when we could sit down with the players and their agents to thrash out the details. That could be months away.

We met up with the players at the City Ground around 5.30, then walked up to Antonio's restaurant on Trent Bridge. It's a Forest tradition. We used to do that when I played and Brian Clough was the manager because he liked the place so much. The players still like it. We all eat there together. Mainly pasta nowadays though it tended to be steaks in Brian's day. Chairman Fred Reacher joined the staff for a glass of wine. Not the players, they stick to water and fruit juice.

We got on the team coach and drove up to Blackburn. All the way up the players remained full of themselves. And why shouldn't they be? They'd had a tremendous run and we'd got the third round of the UEFA Cup coming up against Lyon. There was a good atmosphere and I wanted them to enjoy it. We got to the hotel near Blackburn at about nine and the lads went straight to bed. The staff had a few drinks in the bar.

Saturday 18 November

On Saturday morning, we got them up at about 10.30 for a bit of a stroll and some fresh air. Some may have got up earlier for breakfast, but others prefer to stay in bed. Some don't want to get up at all, but we insist. There are limits to our pampering. At 11.45, we had a pre-match meal, mainly pasta and potato, perhaps an omelette, a little bit of chicken. Then it's back to their rooms for more rest followed by a team meeting at 1 p.m. That didn't take long. I mainly wanted to stress the need for them to put Tuesday's match against Lyon out of their minds. Blackburn was an important game for us. We had to win because at that stage we were only a few places away from qualifying for Europe again in the league, which was our main aim.

We set off to the ground and arrived at about 1.45, which is where it started to go wrong. Chettle ricked his back putting on his boots to go out for the warm-up. We were worried about whether he could play. He said he was okay but he certainly wasn't 100 per cent. We decided to risk him.

Before the game Blackburn's owner Jack Walker officially opened his newly built ground. It was nice to see the good times return to Blackburn after so long in the wilderness. That was the limit of my charitable feelings, however. I desperately wanted to win and so did the players.

Everything seemed all right to begin with, then Shearer opened the scoring after 20 minutes. It was like sounding the bugle for the cavalry charge. We lost 7–0. What a way to lose an unbeaten run. Bohinen, who'd left Forest a few weeks earlier in an acrimonious transfer deal, scored two of them. In the after-match press conference that's all the journalists wanted to talk about. Was it wise letting Bohinen go? What did I think of his performance? What were my feelings towards him now? They were obviously looking for a bit of sensationalist copy but I refused to be drawn. I just said that I didn't talk about opposition players.

The players were obviously distraught in the dressing room and no doubt expecting a real roasting from me. I didn't see any point in that. As far as I was concerned, the game was an aberration. Chettle was injured before he went out and eventually got sent off, bringing us down to ten men. Our other centre-back Colin Cooper got a knock and suffered concussion. He came off after about 20 minutes, leaving our defence depleted. The last thing you want is to face Shearer and Sutton in full flight without both centre-backs. It was just one of those games. Everything they hit went in.

I felt with the Lyon game coming up it was pointless going into any long analysis. I just told them I was disappointed that we kept going at Blackburn in a cavalry charge. Chettle was sent off at 3–0. They scored from the resulting free kick. It was 4–0 and we were down to ten men. We hadn't a hope of getting anything from the game and we should have settled for damage limitation. Instead, we kept going forward in gung-ho style and then found ourselves being caught on the break. We turned a defeat into a total humiliation. Apart from that, there was nothing to say except that we'd had a magnificent run followed by a rude awakening. Now we should look forward to setting off on another good run. Then we got on the coach and went home.

The mood was subdued at first but by the time we got to Nottingham, the players were chirpy again. They were free to go off for the night but they couldn't go wild as we had a game coming up on Tuesday. I reminded them of this as they got off the coach, but I wasn't expecting any trouble.

I went home and watched *Match of the Day*. No surprises for guessing what was the main story. I watched our humiliation again, had a few glasses of wine and tried not to mind as Alan Hansen did his customary analysis on the failings of our defence. But I was already putting Blackburn out of my mind and starting to focus on Lyon and what the team should be. Although we'd had a terrific run, there were one or two areas, especially up front, where we were having problems. Campbell was out with a long-term injury. Silenzi hadn't settled in as well as I'd hoped. There were so many question marks it was hard to settle on a team. I was wondering about

Chettle and his back problem. Cooper was a major worry because of his concussion. He'd been kept in hospital overnight.

Sunday 19 November

I had the players in for the morning. Our trainer Pete Edwards took them. Those who had played against Blackburn got a light training session, mainly just stretches and a warm-down. Those who hadn't played worked much harder and did a lot more running. We couldn't do any teamwork because half the team – Campbell, Chettle, Cooper, Roy and Lee – were injured.

At about 11.30 I had a meeting with the staff to discuss the Lyon game. I had tried to get as many people as possible to watch them play so most of us had been out there; assistant manager Alan Hill and coaches Richard Money, John Perkins and Liam O'Kane. We sat down for the first time to have a detailed chat about them. I hadn't wanted to discuss it before the Blackburn game. It may be a horrible cliché but you have to take one game at a time. When you're getting fixtures coming at you left, right and centre there is no other way to approach it.

Then I went home for lunch and to watch Queens Park Rangers play Coventry on Sky Television. It was a drab 1–1 draw and I found it difficult to concentrate. I was still wondering whether Roy would be fit; should I play Silenzi? Might I take a chance on youngsters like Bobby Howe and Paul McGregor?

Monday 20 November

Some good news to start the week. Kevin Campbell was able to join in full training. He'd missed 12 games with a back and hamstring injury. He still had a long way to go but it was good to see him on the mend.

I had formulated a team that I thought would work against Lyon, as long as everyone was fit. Morning training was light and short. Then I got the players together and told them how we thought Lyon would line up against us. We knew they would play one up the middle with two wide players, three in midfield, 4-3-3. We decided that as we were at home we would stick to our normal 4-4-2.

After training, I had a meeting with the physio John Hazelden to check on the walking wounded. It turned out that Cooper hadn't suffered concussion against Blackburn after all; he'd been struck by some strange viral infection that made him feel dizzy. He was out of hospital and able to train, but uncertain for the game. Lee was definitely out after getting a deadleg at Blackburn, but Chettle and Roy were responding well and should be OK.

At the lunchtime press conference, the Blackburn drubbing was still on everyone's minds. The reporters asked me how I was going to lift the players after such a humiliating defeat. I told them I didn't have to lift the players. They were a very resilient bunch and they were looking forward to the big game. Then they asked a different question on the state of English football. How did I feel about being the only English team left in the UEFA Cup? I didn't want to sound conceited about our success, or fall into the trap of criticising other teams. I just said I was pleased we were there but disappointed that the other sides had gone out. It showed English football still had a long way to go to catch up with the Continentals.

In the afternoon, I had a meeting with club secretary Paul White to make sure the arrangements for the away trip to Lyon were in place. I wanted to know how and when and from where we were travelling. Alan and I had sorted out the hotel while we were out in Lyon watching them play. Paul was also sorting out training facilities and I wanted to make sure that was all right. During the meeting, I got a few phone calls from agents asking if we wanted to buy anybody. Chance would be a fine thing! I told them we had no money.

By late afternoon things went a bit quiet so I went to the gym to try to do a bit of training myself. An hour on the treadmill and the cycle machines. It's a stressful job and it's important to stay fit.

On Monday evening, the Lyon team were due to train on the Forest pitch. Every away team has that facility. It would be considered bad form for any of us to go and watch them so I had a couple of spies in flat caps viewing from the top of the stand just to see if we could pick up any information. They reported back that during the training session their goalkeeper, Pascal Olmeta, had injured his ankle. He looked doubtful for the game.

That night I went home and watched the Sky game. The cameras haven't had much luck with goals this weekend. Villa won 1–0 away at Southampton in another lacklustre match. Again, I spent much of the time thinking about the next day's game. How to win it? What could go wrong? What might I say to certain people?

Tuesday 21 November

On the day of the match, morning training is optional. Most of the British players liked to do something. Pearce always did, so did Stone and Chettle. They'd do 20 minutes running round the pitch, then a few stretches and sprints. We didn't feel they needed to do it but they felt more comfortable that way. If nothing else it would break up the day for them. The continental players like Silenzi, Roy, Haaland would never come in. It's all a matter of opinion and is just the way the different sets of players are brought up. Most of the players who didn't come in to train came into the ground to have lunch. It was just to get out of the house as much as anything else.

Our spies reported back that the Lyon goalkeeper Olmeta was still doubtful for the game. They only had one replacement so they were trying to fly another over to sit on the bench.

The daily press conference was much bigger than usual. As we were the last English team in the UEFA Cup, a lot of the press big guns came down for the game. The French press were also there. They were making a big thing of the fact that many French teams seemed to have an inferiority complex about playing British sides. Apparently French and English sides had met 17 times in 35 years of European football and the French had only won twice. The French put this down to their physical and aerial frailties against 'le fighting spirit' of the English. I didn't give much credence to such theories but I was happy to let them continue to think that way. It couldn't have helped the Lyon team to have their national press writing them off as beaten before they started. With that in mind I didn't bother pointing out that one of the rare French victories against the English was carried out by our opponents that night, Lyon. They beat Tottenham in a brutal Cup Winners' Cup tie in 1967. The first leg in France was interrupted for ten minutes when a dozen players got involved in a brawl and spectators ran on to the pitch. The less said about that, I thought, the better.

After lunch, I went home to relax for a few hours. I tried to sleep in the chair but it was hard to doze off. I listened to some music and played the guitar for a while, mostly country and folk music. I'm a would-be skiffle player but I couldn't really concentrate on it that day. There was no escaping the big game. I went back to the ground at four o'clock. I like time to focus my thoughts on the game and think about what I'm going to say to the players. I checked with a few of the press to see if they had heard anything from the Lyon camp and what had been revealed at their conference the night before. Lyon were saying that Olmeta was definitely out. I thought that might unsettle them a bit, affect their confidence.

I had decided on my team by then. Roy and Silenzi would be up front. I believed experience was important. In the team talk I again stressed the importance of being patient. The last thing we wanted was a cavalry charge. It was vital that we didn't concede a goal. Nil-nil at home in Europe isn't such a bad result. I didn't want them to get carried away by the atmosphere. That was a danger because the crowd would be urging the cavalry charge, but it's important that the team don't lose discipline. I was quietly confident. I thought we could beat Lyon over two legs.

The Saturday result had been forgotten. The players

were in good heart and looking forward to it. It was a terrific occasion to have European nights at the City Ground. The crowd was very disappointing. Only 22,000. We'd had 28,000 for Auxerre.

There was real pantomime before the game with the goalkeeper. In European competitions, teams are supposed to hand the team-sheet in 45 minutes before the kick-off but it was always a shambles. The game kicked off at 7.45. At 7.30, they were still giving Olmeta a fitness test on the pitch. They hadn't handed their sheet in. We were furious. I tried not to get involved. Alan Hill was trying to deal with it. We didn't get the sheet until about ten minutes before the kick-off so we didn't give them ours either. The two teams hand them over together in the presence of the referee. It's always a case of you show me yours and I'll show you mine. It turned out Olmeta was playing.

They didn't cause us many problems and we were in control of the game but we didn't look like scoring. Roy and Silenzi weren't really doing their stuff. After an hour, I was weighing up what to do. I had two internationals on the pitch, Roy and Silenzi, and I had two kids, Howe and McGregor with only a few appearances between them, on the bench. We had to get a goal and it was a question of being brave enough to make the decision. I decided to put the kids on and give it a go. Within minutes, they transformed the game.

Olmeta was caught off his line and Howe hit a terrific volley towards an open net. Flaurent Laville was forced to handle in the box to stop a certain goal. He was sent off. Pearce took the kick but Olmeta saved it. So much for his injury slowing him down! Fortunately, McGregor reacted first and lashed it into the net. It was fairytale stuff for him. I hoped it would go down as an inspired substitution and no one would notice that I'd had my fingers crossed for luck all along. Howe and McGregor were the heroes of the night and we won the game 1–0. I was delighted with that.

There was the usual after-match press conference with radio, television and print journalists. It goes on until about 10.30. They all wanted to talk about the substitutions. In view of the result, I felt they might have thought I'd done the right thing, but apparently not. They wanted to know what possessed me to take off two experienced internationals and throw on two kids. I just said it was a gamble but one I could afford to take. I pointed out that we would have been criticised if I'd done nothing and we hadn't scored. It just reinforced my view that you can't win with the press.

After the game the staff and I stayed behind and had a few drinks with the Lyon manager Guy Stephan and his staff. They were all decent and sporting people and we got on well. Both sides fancied their chances in the next tie.

Wednesday 22 November

With no game until the following Monday I could afford to give the players all of Wednesday off. Bryan Roy's knee had got worse during the game the previous night. We decided we couldn't wait until after the Man Utd game so we sent him to hospital straightaway.

The morning papers weren't very positive about our victory. The press thought the game was low-key and that we hadn't played very well. They seem to think you should win every home game three or four nil in Europe if you're going to progress in the competition. But you can't do that. I knew that 1–0 was a terrific result that put us in the driving seat. If we could get a goal over there they would have to score three to beat us because in the case of a draw, away goals count double.

As there was no training I watched the video of the game with the rest of the staff. We talked about what could be learned to take into the next game. We came out of that discussion with our views confirmed that we could beat them over there. We didn't feel they could cause us many problems up front. They were a good all-round side. They were good technicians and they played good football but I didn't think they could hurt us. Then we had to put it out of our minds for a few weeks because we knew that on Thursday we would have to get the players in again and start preparing for the next league game which was against Manchester United.

Journalist John Lawson, who writes the Forest programme notes, came for his weekly interview. We talked about the Blackburn and Lyon games. I told him I was concerned that we were falling away from the leaders in the league, which I still considered the most important thing. We looked ahead to the Manchester United game. I talked about how Alex Ferguson had been criticised for selling players like Hughes, Ince and Kanchelskis, and not signing any big-name players to replace them. Instead, he threw in young players like Beckham, Scholes and Butt. I used that to lead into how I hoped Howe and McGregor would do something similar for us. John seemed happy enough with that and went away to write it up for the programme.

I thought about going to watch the reserves at Sheffield United but decided instead that it would be better to go to Chelsea to watch Bolton Wanderers, our opponents on the Saturday after the Manchester United game. It would also be a good opportunity to keep tabs on the Bolton winger Alan Thompson whom we rated highly. Chelsea won 3–2 but Thompson played well. It's a shame we can't afford him. I got back to Nottingham at about one o'clock.

Thursday 23 November

I had Paul McGregor in to offer him a new contract. It wasn't just because of his recent goals; he'd earned it over the last year. I told him not to be complacent though. His old contract still had eight months to run. How much he got in the new one would depend on how well he did between now and then.

We were supposed to be in London for the Premier League tribunal over the Collymore case, but it's been postponed so his representatives can assess our latest evidence. We also wanted to call independent witnesses. We were even considering whether to call Collymore's agent, Paul Stretford. It's a nuisance as it means the whole thing will drag on even longer. It's strange. The £425,000 Stan's asking for would wipe out all the revenue we got from our victory over Lyon.

We got the players in and put them through a hard training session because the Man Utd game wasn't until the Monday. I had changed things when I arrived at Forest. Under Brian Clough the players did very hard pre-season training but then didn't do a great deal once the season started. It was felt the games and a little light exercise were enough to keep the players match fit. Neither I nor my trainer Pete Edwards were sure about that. We felt fitness could easily be lost if it wasn't topped up at regular intervals, hence the occasional heavy training sessions between matches.

Reserve team coach Richard Money gave me a report on the reserve team's 3–1 victory at Sheffield United. He was delighted with their performance.

Chairman Fred Reacher called into my office for a general chat. The conversation eventually got round to our two recent big signings, Kevin Campbell and Andrea Silenzi. Fred's very supportive but he's obviously anxious about those two. He wonders whether they were worth the fees. Both cost around £2 million. Fred was worried that Campbell was too injury-prone and Silenzi just wasn't coming through for us. He was concerned that he'd been so ineffective against Lyon that I'd taken him off and substituted him with a kid. I tried to defend the two players. As Campbell had been out injured for several weeks it was hard to deflect the injury-prone criticism, but I tried to reassure Fred that Campbell would come good and would be a tremendous asset to the club. I felt Silenzi could do the same, but we had to give him time. He was the first Italian player from *Serie A* to come here and needed to settle. He too had been injured. Fred didn't seem totally convinced but he didn't pursue the matter any further.

The English and French police are worried because it seems that hundreds of Forest fans have somehow managed to buy tickets among the Lyon supporters. That's the last thing we need.

Friday 24 November

After the hard fitness training session yesterday, we let the players take it easier and do more skills work. They're much happier to train when they have a ball at their feet. I didn't keep them too long and, as there was no game the next day, I gave them the rare treat of a Saturday off. I reminded them that I didn't want anyone out on the town on Saturday night when we had the important game coming up on the Monday. It wasn't usually a problem but it was as well to stress it, especially to the younger players.

After lunch, I looked again through the scouting reports on Manchester United. As we were the home team I had made a point of watching them play away from home a couple of times to get a good idea of what to expect. We sat down with the staff to discuss how we should approach the game. We decided to play Howe a bit deeper to give us more strength in midfield where Manchester United were very strong. It sounds a negative way of looking at it but we felt it was the best way to play against them. We wanted to win and would be trying to do so, but it was finding the best way of achieving it. To attack Manchester United in a cavalier fashion means you really get hammered on the break. We decided to tackle it like a European game and play in a cagey sort of way. We didn't want to leave ourselves exposed to the counter-attack.

We finished off by working out the scouting arrangements for the coming week. We were looking at players even if we had no money to spend. Fred Reacher had made it clear there was nothing in the kitty, but you never know when things might change so you have to be ready to pounce if the chance suddenly appears. I wanted Alan

Hill to go over to France to watch a couple of the Auxerre midfielders, Moussa Saib and Corentin Martins, who had impressed during our two matches with them. If funds suddenly became available, they would be two priority targets. We were also looking at front players, because we had so many problems. We had no one in mind at this time but we had lots of people looking at games to see if anyone was worth pursuing.

An unusual development. We've had a Portuguese left-winger called Antonio Pacheco over here on trial for the last five weeks. We were going to let him go but he says he'll pay his own expenses if he can stay and extend his trial. We've agreed but I can't see it working. I don't think he can cope with the pace of English football. I decided to go to the gym or I might not be able to cope with the pace either.

Saturday 25 November

In the morning, I went to watch the youth team beat Lincoln 1–0. I don't get the chance to see them as often as I would like. It was a close game but they're coming on quite well. We could certainly do with some of them coming through. A few more graduates like Steve Stone, Steve Chettle and Scot Gemmill would be quite acceptable.

In the afternoon, I went to Manchester City to watch Aston Villa because they were coming up here soon. City won 1–0 with a great goal by the Georgian player, Georgi Kinkladze. Villa are a good side and defended well away from home. It'll be hard to break them down when they come to Forest.

I drove home in time to go out for a meal in Nottingham with my wife and some friends. It was pleasant and uneventful until a couple of fans spotted us and insisted on congratulating me on the win against Lyon. That was all right but I could sense what was coming. As soon as they got the pleasantries out of the way, they started to tell me what they thought was wrong with the side. What does Scot Gemmill actually do, they asked? And why on earth play Jason Lee? What can you do? Enter into a long explanation or just humour them? Fortunately, one of their wives came to the rescue and pulled them away while throwing us an apologetic smile.

Sunday 26 November

We brought the players in for a bit of light training. We had a chat with them and told them what the team would be and how we wanted them to play; the way I had discussed the previous Friday with the staff. I've always liked to get players doing teamwork, going on to the training field and practising the way you want them to play. It can be a good way of getting the message home, but it never used to work at Forest and I was left thinking, 'Let's hope it's all right on the night.' Fortunately, on most occasions it was. The reason was that I had an intelligent bunch of players who could assimilate what I wanted them to do just by being told. They didn't feel any need to practise. I decided therefore to stress a few points that I felt were important.

I was concerned above all that we didn't overstretch ourselves and get hit on the break. It was something I had talked to them about for the European games where it was also crucial. I wanted them to maintain their discipline and keep the shape of the team. This was particularly important when the ball is going into the opposition penalty area. The defenders must be in the right positions. It's important that they're not just thinking, 'That's a good cross. We might score from here.' They should be thinking, 'What happens if that ball comes out of there? Am I in the right position to deal with it in relation to where the opposition are?' That may sound strange but it's vital. In every incident in a game, there's a right position for all 11 players to be in; even the person furthest away from the ball. For example, if our left-winger puts a good cross into the opposition box then our furthest man away, our right-back, should be alongside the opposition's left-side striker. The right centre-back should be covering, and the left centre-back should be tight alongside the other striker. This gives us three against two.

It's important that they mark the strikers in the right way and don't just stand behind them. If they do that and the ball drops out short, they can't get there first. They must mark on the shoulder, standing alongside the opponent. Then if it comes out short we can get there first instead of letting their player get hold of it and play people in. That's why the right centre-back drops off and gives you cover. He's the one who has to worry about anything being dropped behind. The other two have got to make sure that their front players aren't allowed to pick the ball up comfortably. The work we'd been doing towards Lyon would have helped us because it would have applied there.

I was confident the players understood what I was saying

so we kept the practising to a minimum. We ran through a few things that we expected United to do at corners and free-kicks, but not too much. In the afternoon, we all went home. I watched the big match on Sky. Arsenal against Blackburn in a 0–0 draw. Seven players were booked, but the most remarkable thing for me was that Blackburn could afford to leave Chris Sutton on the bench and not even use him. He's a Nottingham lad and I wonder how he slipped through the net as a youngster. We could certainly do with him now.

Monday 27 November

The morning papers brought a useful snippet of news. The Premier League has insisted that all its games on the weekend before the Republic of Ireland's European Championship qualifying play-off against Holland on 13 December must go ahead. That means Aston Villa, who we play on the Sky match on 10 December, will be without Paul McGrath, Steve Staunton and Andy Townsend. It's tough for them but a welcome bonus for us.

My wife told me I'd made the *Daily Telegraph*'s quote of the week list. I couldn't imagine what I had said that would be so memorable. I couldn't believe it when I looked it up. It referred to the Blackburn game and Lars Bohinen. The wonderful quote? 'I never comment on opposing players.' There was obviously a dearth of memorable comments that week.

The build-up to the game was much the same as against Lyon. In fact, the build-up to any game is always the same whoever we're playing; no matter how exalted or supposedly inferior. The other thing that never seems to change is the injury problems. I'm without our four main strikers. Roy (knee), Campbell (back), Lee (thigh) and Silenzi (flu). Well, it was a great opportunity for the youngsters Howe and McGregor to do their stuff.

The press conference was a bit muted. Maybe they'd run out of big issues to explore. One reporter tried a rich man, poor man approach, asking whether it was a measure of the gulf between us and United that we were bemoaning the absence of a £250,000 striker like Jason Lee as a major loss. Yet a player like him wouldn't even get into United's multi-million-pound squad. There wasn't much to say about that except to agree. That's the world most managers live in. We can't spend fortunes and often have to shop in the bargain basement. In Lee's defence, though, I had to point out that he'd got six goals in 13 games. Even the £7 million Andy Cole would have been pleased with that.

I filled in a few hours catching up with administrative work, replying to letters from supporters, requests for public appearances by me or the players and so on. Sky matches kick off at eight, which makes it a very long day. I rang a few journalists to see if anything had come out of Manchester about what team United might play or whether they had any injury problems. That wasn't as important with United as it was with other teams because they had so many great players. Nevertheless, if Giggs or Cantona weren't playing it might make you feel a bit better. Unfortunately, they were playing.

It turned out to be a very cagey game. We played very tight because we knew how good they could be on the break, and they were careful away from home. United had most of the play and our crowd might have felt we were a bit unadventurous at times, but it was important that there wasn't a cavalry charge. The youngsters did well for us. A Bobby Howe shot was blocked by Pallister. As against Lyon, McGregor was the first to react and he opened the scoring. In the second half, they got a dubious penalty which Cantona scored. But 1–1 was a fair result. It was a good exciting game, there were 29,000 in the crowd and it was live on Sky.

The after-match press conferences were unusually positive and pleasant. Alex Ferguson was very complimentary about Forest, saying we had one of the best defences in the country and that we were lethal on the break. I responded by saying that United were probably the best team in the country at that time. Afterwards Alex and his staff came and had a drink with us. We had always had a good relationship.

I went home feeling it had been a good week for the club. We'd come out of a difficult game when we'd had a real battering. The players had re-established themselves, picked up their heads and got refocused. They'd given a good performance against one of the best teams in the country. As I drove home, however, my thoughts were already turning to our next game away at Bolton Wanderers. What would be the best way to deal with them?

CHAPTER 9

Kicking with Both Feet

I read recently about a headmaster in Northumberland who has banned parents from shouting during school matches. They should give that man a medal! If he can go a step further and find a way to ban schools football altogether, then I'll pay for his medal myself. To hear me advocating such a revolutionary step may offend some people, but there are solid reasons for it. It could help England win future World Cups and become a dominant force in international football. Sadly, we're still a long way from doing that, and schools must take a large share of the blame.

The reason is that schools football is run by people who are well meaning but not always well qualified. It has held back British football for generations. Countless numbers of players have been blighted by it. It's time this was stopped and thankfully over the last few years great steps have been made to break the stranglehold of the English Schools Football Association. To understand why that was so important, it's necessary to look at how British players compare with their European counterparts.

They lag behind when it comes to simple, basic skills. I experienced this at first hand when my Nottingham Forest side competed in the UEFA Cup in 1996. We were one of six English sides taking part in the various European competitions, yet within ten weeks of the start of the season we were the only ones left. The bigger clubs like Liverpool and Blackburn had been sent crashing out, exposing the gap in standards between Britain and the Continent. By Christmas we had got through the first three rounds, knocking out the Swedish club Malmo and then Auxerre and Lyon, both from France.

Those victories set us up with a lucrative quarter-final tie against Bayern Munich the following March. No one really expected us to win but it still meant that for three months at least, Forest could enjoy the status of being England's only standard-bearer in European competitions. This delighted our fans as each week they taunted the opposition with the chant: 'There's only one team in Europe.' Particularly sweet when sung to Manchester United, Liverpool and Blackburn.

However, I took no satisfaction in the failure of the other English clubs and although Forest had worked hard and played their hearts out in achieving their success, I was the first to admit we had also ridden our luck a little. This was certainly the case against Auxerre. We won the first leg in France 1–0 with a goal by Steve Stone, but they did most of the attacking and we had to clear off the line four times. It was a similar pattern in the second leg in

Nottingham. For much of the game our goal was under siege as the French cut through the defence. There were numerous goalmouth scrambles and desperate clearances, the most memorable being when Ian Woan tried to clear the ball off the goal line with his left foot and missed it completely. On any other night that miss would have inevitably cost a goal but that night we were leading a charmed life. Woan's horror at missing with his left foot turned to relief when by chance the ball hit his right leg and bounced away to safety. Everyone in the ground was astonished, no one more so than Woan. In most matches he played as if he didn't realise he was allowed to use his right leg. Like his team captain Stuart Pearce, he seemed to think it was just for standing on while he did the skilful stuff with his left. The game ended 0–0, which meant we went through because we won in the first leg.

After the match Pearce acknowledged that the French side had been better technically, but said Forest had won through because they had shown the British bulldog fighting spirit which kept them going when all seemed lost. It was stirring stuff and created a tremendous sense of euphoria on the night. But in the cold light of the following day, the inevitable questions had to be asked. Why were Auxerre a more skilful side than Forest? Why had the teams which had knocked out our other top clubs been so transparently more skilful?

The biggest problem we have at international level is that our defenders aren't good enough technically. Continental defenders are as skilful as some of our best forwards and midfield players. Unfortunately, if you've got a few players who aren't that good, they'll get found out at the highest level. The opposition will keep forcing them to have the ball.

Chelsea found this when they first brought Ruud Gullit over. Glenn Hoddle, the manager at the time, wanted to move to a close passing game. That was all right except they had a few players who didn't really want the ball when things started getting tight. When they got it, they couldn't wait to get rid of it. Other teams noticed this very quickly and said: 'Right, we won't let Gullit pass the ball. We'll concentrate on closing him down so he's got to lay it off to someone else, then they've got to pass it.' Of course, they made sure he was pressurised into laying it off to someone who didn't feel comfortable on the ball and couldn't do much more than boot it upfield. Then the passing movement broke down.

You couldn't really adopt that approach against top-class European sides like the Dutch or the Italians because they can all play the ball whether they're defenders, midfielders or attackers. If you spend too much time concentrating on the so-called star playmakers, you'll find a centre-back carrying the ball into the vacant space and putting you under pressure. It's very difficult to deal with and until we start producing all-round players, we're always going to struggle. Of course, within a few years Chelsea under new manager Ruud Gullit were producing those players. Unfortunately, he had to go to Italy and France to find them.

It didn't give them the edge they might have expected, though, because by that time every club was scouring Europe for talent. Soon the chairman of the Professional Footballers' Association, Gordon Taylor, was lamenting that a third of his Premier League members were from abroad. He pointed out that it was a terrible indictment of our coaching structures that we had to go cherrypicking foreign stars to make up for the dearth of talent at home. We've got to change that.

Multi-skilling has been happening in industry for years and now it's time for English football to get in on the act. We can learn a lot from the Dutch. Their forwards can defend; their defenders can attack. The average Dutch player is more comfortable receiving the ball than his English counterpart. He's more accomplished in passing it. The difference is only small but it can be enough to allow them to control and win a game.

This slight but vital difference was highlighted during the 1998 World Cup in France. No one who saw the England–Argentina game is ever likely to forget the incredible drama and tension. For me it highlighted the tremendous never-say-die attitude that we can produce in times of need. England put on a magnificent display after being reduced to ten men following David Beckham's dismissal. Tony Adams, in particular, displayed the kind of indomitable spirit that becomes an inspiration to everyone around him.

We were desperately unlucky, but England's performance that night illustrated the same point as Forest's against Auxerre: our defenders aren't good enough technically.

Throughout the World Cup the likes of Adams, Sol Campbell and Gareth Southgate were magnificent in defence with typical British strength and resolve. Unfortunately, they didn't have the skill and vision to make the kind of contribution that top defenders from other countries were making. One player and one moment illustrate this difference perfectly. In the dying minutes of the game between Holland and Argentina, Frank de Boer hit a ball 60 yards out of defence to Dennis Bergkamp. Bergkamp controlled it with the first touch, turned the defender with the second and scored with the third.

It was a sublime moment that lifted the spirit. The disappointing thing, though, is that Bergkamp would not have been able to score that goal if he had been playing for England, not because his touch would have let him down but because the ball could never have been played to him. No England defender would have even seen that 60-yard pass let alone been able to play it. Frank de Boer has no such restrictions. He has all the attributes of a typical British defender, being strong, brave and uncompromising, but unlike his British counterparts he has the technical ability of a midfielder. The opposition have to close him down straightaway as if he was a midfielder. Give him a second and he will hurt you – even from 60 yards, as the Argentinians found to their cost.

The Dutch are similar to the British in lifestyle, culture and physique, yet from a population only a third of that of England they produce a regular supply of these multi-skilled players. How? It must be something to do with their youth development schemes. In Holland, as in most of Europe, that development has been done by professional football clubs, while in England it's been left to schools. This isn't because the professionals aren't interested – quite the opposite. For years clubs tried to coach youngsters from a very early age but weren't allowed to do so because the schools had control of the game. They wouldn't let us coach youngsters under the age of 12. Even after that we were only able to have them for an hour a week.

That was a pernicious piece of legislation because it hindered the development of generations of English players. Experts in child development will tell you that between the ages of five and ten are the best years for learning skills. That's when young players should have the benefit of expert coaching, but for years it was denied to them. It was the only sport that had such restrictions. Youngsters could play rugby with a professional rugby club but they couldn't learn about football from professional football coaches.

It was ridiculous. Consider this. If you had a nine-year-old son who was a talented violinist, who would you send him to for lessons? The most highly qualified violin teacher you could afford? Or the geography teacher at the local school who played the fiddle a bit when he was younger and still fancies he can knock out a tune although he never mastered the instrument? I don't need to be a mind reader to guess that as a caring parent you would probably go for expert tuition. So why should it be any different if your son shows promise as a footballer? Why should he be entrusted to that same geography teacher who's now doubling as a football coach on the basis that he played a bit as a kid and nearly got into his college third team?

By definition, the best coaches are going to be in the professional game. So generations of children were effectively left to the mercy of amateurs – teachers or youth league managers with varying amounts of knowledge and coaching skill. I don't question the enthusiasm of those people, but I don't think they organised the game in a way that helped kids reach their full potential. They treated the children, no matter what age they were, as if they were adults.

It meant you ended up with spindly legged nine-year-olds playing 11-a-side football on a full-size pitch with a full-size ball. The emphasis was all on winning, with very little attention paid to technique. You have to ask yourself what these generations of small boys learned as they ran around an oversized pitch trying to win a pointless game of football, all the time being subjected to conflicting advice as parents and self-styled coaches shouted at them from the touchline. I don't know what it is about football but everyone seems to think they're an expert. Fathers bombard their kids with half remembered, half understood bits of clichéd advice from their own school days. It's usually to do with 'getting stuck in', 'booting it upfield' or 'getting rid of the ball' or whatever. None of it very enlightening but much of it having a damaging effect on impressionable youngsters.

It's damaging not only in terms of how to play the game, but also on the children's confidence and self-esteem. Often the shouting is abusive, even to the smallest of boys. Mistakes are criticised harshly. Anyone who's watched a schoolboy game will tell you how depressing it can be because of the parents and the pressure they place on their sons. There is very little to suggest that football is supposed to be fun.

That head teacher who banned parents from shouting is on the right track. I did the same thing ten years earlier at Leyton Orient. If parents started shouting, they were effectively sent off. It creates the wrong atmosphere in which the emphasis is all on winning. That's where we've been going wrong in the past. We've been teaching our children to compete before we've taught them how to play.

It's meant that youngsters haven't been doing enough work on technical skills at a young age when they're at their most receptive. Consequently they grow up lacking simple techniques such as knowing how to control the ball properly. Common sense will tell you that in an 11-a-side game you don't get too many touches of the ball, so how are going to practise controlling it? And if someone is yelling at you from the touchline to just boot it upfield then you're not going to learn to play intelligent passes very well. No wonder faults develop.

Take a very simple example. A player missing a chance because the ball happens to fall on his weaker foot is a familiar sight every week, even in the Premier League. Instead of shooting straightaway, they twist and turn trying to get it onto their stronger side. By the time they do, they're tackled out of it or the other side covers and the chance is lost. I can sympathise with people who say they damn well should be able to kick with both feet for the money they're getting, especially when European players don't seem to have the same problem, at least not to the same extent.

Unfortunately, there's little the players concerned can do about it. Faults like being unable to kick with both feet could be corrected quite easily at the age of nine or ten if a boy was being taught properly and given the time to practise. But it can't be corrected in a competitive match where winning is everything and there are hordes of screaming parents on the touchline. You couldn't say to a boy: 'We're going to play a game now and I want you to use only your weak foot.' Once the action starts they revert to type and play by instinct. That's what's wrong with competitive football at such an early age and that's why the weaknesses in technique persist. It's not as if the faults can easily be put right later. Once the boy is over 16 it gets more difficult to improve technique and you get to a point with senior players where it's not worth the effort. They would have to put in an enormous amount of time for only a small improvement. The time would be much better spent on other things.

The emphasis on winning football in schools has meant that youngsters very quickly develop fixed positions. Before you know it, ten-year-olds become full-backs, midfielders or strikers and that stays with them forever. That's ridiculous. At that age they should be trying out different positions in games where the result is unimportant. Dutch players don't develop fixed positions until they're about 15. Frank de Boer will have spent a lot of his childhood playing in midfield or attack before finally deciding he was best as a defender. No wonder he's an all-round player.

Hopefully, we're now addressing these problems by enabling youngsters to get proper coaching at professional clubs. It was something I was pushing for when I was running the League Managers' Association, but first we had to break the power of the English Schools Football Association. That may sound melodramatic but it was as stark as that. After years of seemingly endless meetings and negotiations, we eventually made some progress. Now clubs can start coaching boys from the age of eight. I hope English clubs will embrace the opportunity and start to develop schemes like those at the top European clubs.

We should follow the example of clubs like Ajax. They coach boys from the age of seven. It's a similar story in France and Germany. Clubs like Forest's UEFA Cup opponents Auxerre and Lyon have more than 20 teams covering all ages. They're not only professional clubs, they're also the main focal point for anyone in their area who wants to play football.

Over the last few years the game has recognised the need for change. That's why Howard Wilkinson was appointed as the Football Association's Technical Director. The Charter for Quality he produced is a blueprint for the way forward for British football. It was heavily influenced by Continental methods and incorporates some of the best practices that many English clubs were already moving towards, such as the setting up of football academies. The idea is that each club recruits 30 or 40 promising eight-year-olds each year and gives them proper coaching. This is reduced down to about 20 at the age of 12.

They'll be taught by the best coaches and in a non-competitive atmosphere. The coaches will be properly qualified and registered with the Football Association. It's hoped to keep the player–coach ratio down to ten to one. This way we'll be able to control how youngsters play. For example, the FA has banned 11-a-side football for under-tens. They'll be playing small-sided games so they'll get more touches of the ball. Each academy should employ an education liaison officer to make sure the children's schoolwork doesn't suffer.

The system needn't be elitist. We should give as many kids as possible the chance to play. That's where football in the community comes in. Most clubs now have such schemes. We should enlarge them and use them as a feeder system to the academies. This obviously means the clubs providing more facilities. We've all heard the stories about how gifted players like Jimmy Greaves developed their skills as boys by kicking a tennis ball on the streets near their homes. Those days have gone. Kids can't go out and play football in the street any more. If they kicked a ball against someone's house like we used to do, they would probably get arrested. We have to provide them with somewhere to play.

The local youth teams would remain but the best players wouldn't be playing for them. They would be training with the professional clubs. We'd tell them they can't play for us on a Saturday morning and the local youth team on Sunday morning because it isn't good for them. It's ironic that in the past some people have been opposed to professional clubs being allowed to train youngsters because they thought we would force them to play too much. The exact opposite is the case. Left to amateur control, many youngsters end up playing for their school, their local youth team and a Sunday league team. That's far too much. With us, they would only be allowed to play about 30 games a year maximum and those would only be about 60 or 70 minutes' duration. We would still play some competitive games under this new system but certainly at nine years of age it would be small-sided games, perhaps six- or seven-a-side. There would be no leagues. Once you bring leagues into it, it becomes even more competitive and that's counter-productive.

If professional coaches are given a free hand then I'm sure our young players of the future will benefit enormously. There'll be no one screaming abuse at them from the touchline and the emphasis will be on enjoyment. We'll be turning out players who are more able to compete on the world stage because their techniques will be better. We needn't worry about losing our competitive edge. We would still be competitive because as Stuart Pearce says, that's a trait of the British people.

We'll certainly need this extra technique if we're going to win major tournaments. We can't go on relying on our fighting spirit and fast pressing game. Remember, major international tournaments are held in the hot, energy-draining summer months. With games coming every three or four days, you can't always play at a hundred miles an hour, as the Republic of Ireland found in the 1994 World Cup. There will be times when games will be played at a slower tempo and that will always favour the more skilful side. They'll knock the ball around for nine or ten passes, make you chase after it and then suddenly hit you when you least expect it, often with a breathtaking long ball out of defence. We have to be able to match that. And if we make the most of the opportunities now offered to us and invest in good facilities and good coaching, then there is no reason why we shouldn't start producing much better technical players over the next five to ten years.

We could certainly have done with such players at Forest during that UEFA Cup run in 1996. After surviving the bewitching skills of Auxerre, we had to face up to the ruthless efficiency of the mighty Bayern Munich in the Olympic Stadium in Germany. Their star striker Jurgen Klinsmann, who strangely enough was still England's reigning player of the season from his time at Tottenham the year before, had scored 11 goals in Bayern's previous six UEFA Cup matches.

Nevertheless, I thought that if we could keep our discipline then our fighting qualities might see us through. Unfortunately, we didn't play well in Munich. Predictably, Klinsmann opened the scoring for Bayern; unpredictably, our centre-half Steve Chettle equalised within two minutes with a header from a free-kick. Bayern went on to score again in the second half and could have had a few more but it finished 2–1. Forest's away goal meant a 1–0 victory at the City Ground would be enough to see us through to the semi-finals. In the event of a draw on aggregate in UEFA competitions, away goals count double.

There was a sense of optimism among the fans and the players. They were encouraged by tales of discontent in the Bayern camp. They were a team of superstars, but superstars often have superegos and there was talk that the dressing room wasn't big enough to accommodate them all. For years the former German captain Lothar Matthaus had ruled the roost. He was in his mid thirties but still a major influence. He played as a sweeper and everything was said to revolve around him, both on and off the field.

There were rumours that his reign was threatened by the return to Germany of Jurgen Klinsmann. He too wanted his say about how things should be done and this apparently didn't go down very well with Matthaus. At one point, it was said he even accused Klinsmann of trying to block his return to the German national side and challenged him to a television debate on the issue. It was never clear whether any of this was true but it made encouraging speculation. The Bayern president Franz Beckenbauer refused to confirm the stories when interviewed the night before the match, but he did admit that there were certain jealousies among the players.

Tony Woodcock also had encouraging news. He had spent so long in Germany that he now spoke English with a slight German accent. He too spoke of disunity in the ranks and described the Bayern players as cold, calculating businessmen who were less a team than clinical, talented individuals. They did not pull together as a team and their resolve might be suspect if they were put under enough pressure. Woodcock thought Forest could win for this reason.

As the game kicked off there was a real air of optimism around the ground, a feeling that the pampered prima donnas might be cut down to size by a rousing display of the bulldog spirit. We decided to stick to our disciplined approach because Bayern were so good at hitting teams on the break away from home. They had been winning away matches by three- and four-goal margins. We had Phillips and Bart-Williams both playing holding midfield roles to stop them running through. It worked very well to begin with.

There were plenty of goalmouth scrambles and Bayern were a little fortunate not to concede a goal. For the first 30 minutes we produced the best football we had played at home in a European match. There was a good tempo, good passing and good movement off the ball. We had a couple of decent chances and then had a goal disallowed on a very tight offside decision. But then disaster struck and we conceded two of the kind of goals that make a mockery of any amount of preparation and tactical planning. Goalkeeper Mark Crossley let in an easy shot which he really should have saved. That was a killer. Then we lost another sloppy goal when a shot took a deflection. You can't account for that sort of thing yet, as so often happens in football, it altered the whole course of the match.

Everyone was down in the dressing room at half-time, particularly Crossley. In situations like that there's nothing you can do but try to encourage people. The last thing I wanted to do was criticise, because they had all played so well. Crossley was the first to admit he had made a mistake, yet he had been heroic throughout the European campaign and had played a huge part in getting us so far. There was no reason for him to feel ashamed. I pointed that out to him. I tried to talk them all up because they had to endure another 45 minutes no matter what.

The dilemma then, of course, is what are you going to do? At 4–1 down on aggregate the game is over because there is no way you're going to recover from a scoreline like that against Bayern Munich. You can't let the players see that, though. You have to keep them going. But what approach do you take? Go for damage limitation and try to keep the score down to 2–0, which isn't too bad? Or do you say let's go forward on a cavalry charge and at least go down with all guns blazing? I didn't have any real hope of getting a result but I told the players to continue to keep it tight to begin with because we might just sneak one and make them nervous.

They tried that and after 15 minutes it was still 2–0 on the night to Bayern. The players had kept their discipline as I had asked, but I could sense they wanted to cut loose and really have a go with all-out attack. I think the crowd wanted that as well. So I took off one of the holding midfielders, Bart-Williams, and put young Paul McGregor on instead. You wouldn't normally change your tactics to suit the expectations of the crowd, or the players for that matter, but on this occasion I thought I had nothing to lose as we were going out anyway. There might have been a miracle. Or at least we might have got a goal and made it a thrilling finish.

Unfortunately, it went the other way. As soon as Bart-Williams went off and we started to attack more, Bayern began to run right through us. They got another three classic breakaway goals in as clinical a display of finishing as you're ever likely to see. But that's what you can expect when you're up against world-class players like Klinsmann, Matthaus and Jean-Pierre Papin. Even the Forest fans had to stand up to applaud the Germans. Steve Stone scored a consolation goal just before the end, which was good because we had battled all the way.

A defeat like this at home would normally bring howls of derision from the crowd. Not that night! Everyone seemed to recognise that Forest had given it everything they'd got. As the game entered its dying moments the crowd began to sing its familiar song about being the only team left in Europe, but this time the words were slightly altered to: 'Five-one down and still in Europe.' It was a nice touch.

The crowd stayed with us and there was a good feeling between the fans and the players. I felt that was one of the most positive things we got out of the night. The spectators recognised we had kept going for 90 minutes and had a real go. If I had kept the tactics tight we could almost certainly have limited the scoreline to 2–0 which wouldn't have looked so bad, yet I'm sure the fans and the players would have left that night feeling more frustrated. There wouldn't have been the same rapport; we might even have been booed off the pitch. By bombing forward we put ourselves at risk and had to pay the price of a 5–1 hammering, but on balance on that particular night I felt it was better to go down fighting.

After the game both sides were applauded off the pitch, Bayern for their brilliance, Forest for their honesty and courage. In the post-match assessments, the supposedly arrogant German superstars proved to be very gracious in victory. Matthaus said he was delighted with the team's performance but admitted they were lucky to survive the early onslaught from Forest. Klinsmann went so far as to say the scoreline flattered Bayern and it could all have been so different if Forest had got the early goal they deserved. It was all pleasingly diplomatic but the Forest players were in no doubt that they had been outclassed. Colin Cooper summed up their feelings: 'Bayern broke our hearts.'

Against Auxerre we had been outplayed but managed to pull through because of that competitive bulldog spirit. That can't save you every time. We showed the same spirit against Bayern but were simply overrun by a side that lacked our passion but made up for it with technical efficiency. If by coaching our youngsters properly we can match that technique at the same time as maintaining our competitive edge, then we in England will be a match for anyone. It won't guarantee success, of course, but at least we might start to see our players kicking with both feet.

CHAPTER 10

Why David Keeps
Thumping Goliath

It happens several times each season yet still takes everyone by surprise. Big clubs with big reputations, multi-
million-pound players and lavish facilities get knocked
out of cup competitions by unglamorous lower division
sides surviving on a shoestring. How does it happen? I
should know, for my teams have had their fair share of
embarrassing upsets.

In the 1995–96 season Nottingham Forest were enjoying
great success in Europe. We were beating some of the
best Continental teams, yet at the same time we were
experiencing the pain of a humiliating defeat in the Coca-
Cola Cup, going out to Bradford City, at that time a Second
Division team. It wasn't as if we were going through a bad
patch. In fact, we hadn't lost during our last 19 games and
were in the process of setting that Premier League record

of 25 matches unbeaten. We were hammering top-class opponents but came unstuck against lowly Bradford.

We couldn't even claim it was a one-off, because it was a two-legged tie. We could perhaps have made an excuse that we were taken by surprise losing 3–2 away in the first leg, but there could be no excuse for the second leg when we could only manage a 2–2 draw at home. Our fans were obviously disappointed and I could understand their frustration. Bradford's whole team didn't cost as much as one Forest striker; a second- or third-choice striker at that. Manchester United fans were no doubt having similar thoughts as York City claimed their scalp that same season, and all big clubs have had similar embarrassing experiences at some point. Arsenal fans will no doubt still wince at the mere mention of Wrexham and the time a goal from the veteran Mickey Thomas sent them crashing out of the FA Cup.

Such results always infuriate the fans of the bigger club. They feel their team is a Premier League side and should have no problems against what they see as a talentless bunch from a lower division. If the team struggles it proves the players are just pampered prima donnas, or the manager hasn't got a clue what he's doing.

I understand their feelings but they're based on a widely held misconception about the difference in ability between players from different divisions. People have been given the wrong impression. Perhaps they spend too much time listening to the pundits who tell them of the huge gap that exists between the Premier League and the lower divisions. How often have we heard the likes of Alan Hansen or Andy Gray rave about Premier League players, strikers in particular, saying things like: 'You can't give a player of that quality that much time. That's the difference between the top-flight players and the rest, give them half a chance and you'll get punished. They'll bury it for sure. Absolutely first-class.'

Strangely, that class often eludes those same quality players when they come up against the likes of Bradford or Huddersfield in the drizzle on a cold, grey November afternoon. Somehow, no matter how much time those Premier League strikers are given, their quality just refuses to shine through and the ball refuses to find the back of the poorer side's net. Not only that, but the lower division strikers often seem to disregard the fact that top quality Premier League defenders won't give them any time on the ball; they go ahead and score anyway. The result is that the classy Premier League side is bundled out of the cup with a resounding thud.

At this point we're bombarded with a different set of clichés. TV commentators and former players turned pundits talk of 'the magic of the cup'. They say this quite casually yet emphatically, as if that explains it all away. They say the lower division side played above themselves, but what is that supposed to mean? No matter how psyched up you are, you still only have a certain amount of ability. You can still only run at a certain speed, tackle as hard, kick as hard, jump as high. And what does that kind of theory say about the Premier League players? That they can only play well as long as the opposition aren't psyched up and aren't trying really hard? Surely not!

No, to understand the real reason one must first understand the difference between Premier League players and those from the lower divisions. If you take away the elite group of players from the Premier League, the special

players who make up the top ten per cent, what you
have left are good solid journeymen professionals, and the
difference between them and what you see in the lower
divisions has little to do with talent. There are many lower
division players with just as much skill as the journeyman
Premier League player. Don't forget many of the players
in the lower divisions served their apprenticeships at big
clubs like Manchester United, Arsenal, Liverpool and so
on. At that stage in their careers they would have looked
just as promising as the lads who went on to make it in the
top flight.

Quite often, the reason they don't make it at the highest
level is not because of their lack of ability, but their lack of
application and consistency. Players are only human; they
can't be at their best every game and there are bound
to be peaks and troughs. With the players who make
it to Premier League standard, the gap between those
peaks and troughs is quite narrow and so they are very
consistent.

The lads who end up in the lower divisions don't have
that consistency. They can match Premiership players
sometimes but they can't do it week in, week out. Their
lows are too low. But they do have a lot of latent talent,
ready and waiting to come to the surface. Often all they
need is the spur of a cup tie against a big club. Then the
stage is set for them to really turn it on. It's their chance
to show they really are as good as the lads who made
it to the top, their chance to show the big clubs they
were wrong to have rejected them. It can be a powerful
psychological force.

Then on the day of the big match, they have all the
advantages. There's no pressure on them. They're not

expected to win, no one's going to criticise them or complain if they lose. Bradford weren't expected to beat Forest. York City weren't expected to beat Manchester United. That helps the players to relax, it gives them a kind of freedom. They can go and play like men possessed. They can pull off what the fans and the pundits regard as a shock result. But it doesn't mean they have played above themselves – it actually means they have played to their full potential.

As I've said, the problem for them is that they can't play like that every week whereas Premier League players can. You get a clue to this in the relative reactions of the two teams. Bradford beat Forest 3–2 in the first leg, a magnificent result for them. You might have thought they would be buoyed up, full of confidence and ready to go and do really well in the league. But in their next game they lost 3–0 to Peterborough, an ordinary side in their own division. Forest, however, went on to get a terrific point against an in-form Aston Villa and then a crucial victory over Malmo in the UEFA Cup. It's how teams react to these big games that shows the overall quality of the players. It was as if Bradford had used up so much of their power and mental energy, they had nothing left when they went to Peterborough. The Forest players were able to pick themselves up from a disappointing match and go on to get two great results.

Bradford played well against Forest, but that doesn't mean you could have promoted them to the Premier League at that time and expected them to survive. They couldn't produce that form every week and they would hardly get a point. Look at what happened to Bolton Wanderers in the 1994–95 campaign. They had a great cup run when they were in the First Division that year, beating two or three Premier League sides. Then they got promoted and found themselves up against the same standard every week. They couldn't cope with it and were relegated.

It can sometimes be difficult for a manager to motivate his team in a game against a lower division side. They know they are better overall players but that on their day the players from lower divisions can match them. It's important to guard against complacency. Before that first leg against Bradford, it was a case of saying: 'We've been here before. You know that if you go out feeling complacent, you'll end up with a difficult game. It's Bradford's cup final. They'll be up for it. You've got to match them for application and attitude. If you do that then your ability should see you through.'

We started so well in the first leg. For the first twenty minutes we pulverised them and should have gone 3–0 up. We did go a goal in front – and then lost our discipline totally. We let them back into the game. It became a real ding-dong match in which we were fortunate to come away with only a 3–2 defeat. I can understand the frustrations of fans when they see their supposedly better team throw away the early superiority, but again the reason is simple: you're dealing with human beings. People can lose their discipline. They indulge themselves and start playing for their own enjoyment, and you can't do that.

We're professionals; we're in the winning business. We have to go out and play football to win the game. The enjoyment comes afterwards from the knowledge and satisfaction of a job well done, and whatever rewards you reap from it, but the actual 90 minutes of the match is too important to be just enjoyed. People have to play within a team framework.

That night against Bradford we were so much on top that people started to enjoy themselves. We lost our shape, Bradford got back into it, and once you lose the initiative it's very difficult to win it back. It's better to make sure you don't lose it in the first place. Every game has a dynamic of its own. People who say 'Let's carry on from the last game' are missing the point. Each game is a self-contained unit; you have to start all over again each time the whistle blows to try to gain control of it. And if you're not doing it right in the first 20 minutes, sometimes it's too late to start.

Of course, when you look at individual results you can sometimes over-analyse things to work out what went wrong, but the answer might boil down simply to chance. The fact that someone missed an easy opportunity to score, or someone got a lucky break. We outplayed Bradford for parts of the game but just didn't take our chances. Silenzi hit the bar, we had one kicked off the line. On another day those would have gone in. How do you rationalise those kind of imponderables? It's impossible, but you still try to do it.

There can only be so much after-match analysis, however, and there inevitably comes a time when everyone has to put defeat behind them and start looking to the next game. It's part of the manager's role to lift people's spirits and restore everyone's morale as soon as possible. Just getting up the next morning and coming into work can be a therapeutic measure. You have to remind yourself that you can't afford to be down. You've got to make sure that everyone else is up, because people look to you for a lead.

The day after the Bradford cup exit, I began the process of putting a brave face on it all and trying to be philosophical. I told myself that perhaps it was a blessing in disguise that we went out. It would ease our fixture congestion. I noticed Alex Ferguson was saying much the same thing after Manchester United had gone out to York. Perhaps he was just trying to put a brave face on it too. In any case, I knew that within a few weeks when other teams would have a hard match in the next round, we would be free to concentrate on preparing for the following Saturday's league match.

It had certainly worked out for us that way before. In my first season in charge at Forest, we got to the quarter-finals of the Coca-Cola Cup. We met Tranmere when both of us were doing well in the First Division, both on the fringes of promotion. We drew at the City Ground and they beat us up there. Their victory gave them a two-legged semi-final against Aston Villa but it may also have affected their promotion drive. They hardly won another game again in the league, whereas we went the other way and hardly lost a game until the end of the season. We won automatic promotion while Tranmere stayed in the First Division.

It was perhaps ironic to think that the defeat by Bradford would ease our fixture congestion, because I think there's little doubt that fixture congestion had played a part in the defeat in the first place, even so early in the season. We had played eight matches in 27 days. That's too many and it's not surprising that some of the players were below par.

This, of course, brings us back to the complaint that has dogged British football for at least 20 years: that we play too many games in too short a time. The most notable victims of this were probably Leeds United in the early

1970s when the issue first gained prominence. Leeds under the late Don Revie were a wonderful side who seemed to be constantly getting to the finals of several competitions and then losing. The fact that they were jaded from having played so many games over a gruelling season was often quoted as the reason for the failure.

It's a concept that has never gone down too well with the fans, which is hardly surprising. People throughout the country who work hard all week so they can afford anything between £20 and £40 for a ticket to watch extravagantly paid footballers can't be expected to have a lot of sympathy with the argument about too many games.

'Two games a week?' they might say. 'So what! They get paid enough. What's the problem?' It's an attitude I can well sympathise with and let me point out that no one is complaining about the workload, but at the same time people must realise that it's bound to have an effect on a team's performance. To understand why, it's important to know what players mean when they say they are tired. In a way, 'tired' is an unfortunate word because it conjures up the image of a bunch of pampered darlings who need a lie down because they've played a game of football. People who have played football themselves, or watched their children out playing all day and still having plenty of energy, wonder what's going on.

That's not the kind of tiredness we're talking about. Footballers are very fit. They could quite happily train and play hard practice matches every day without getting tired in the ordinary meaning of the word. But there's a lot more to it than that. The difference in standard between teams in the Premiership is minute. Any side is capable of beating anyone else. As we've seen from the so-called shock results in cup matches, there's not even that much difference in standard when they meet teams from lower divisions.

What that means is that in order to have a good chance of winning a game, no matter who it's against, a team has to be as near as possible to its full potential. If the best side in the league is at 100 per cent it will probably beat anyone. If it falls even a little below that, it's in danger. So much so that if the top team in the league is only at 95 per cent and the bottom team is at 100 per cent, then the bottom team will probably win. That's the margin we're talking about. And when we talk about players being 'tired' that's usually all we mean; they've lost that five per cent edge.

How does that happen? It could be for all sorts of reasons, but the most obvious is from playing too many games. It's useful to compare football with athletics. A world class 1500 metres runner will carefully plan his training so that he is at his peak on the day of the big race. If he's prepared well he may go out and set a world record, but what would happen if you asked him to go out and equal that world record a few days later? The chances are he would not be able to do it. He could run the distance quite easily, but the previous effort would have taken a little bit out of him. He would have lost that vital edge; in footballing terms he would be 'tired'. Of course, we don't ask Olympic athletes to go out and perform to their maximum every three or four days, but we do ask that of footballers. We shouldn't be surprised if they fail to do it, because it's impossible. All we can do is keep them as near to their peak as we can.

It's not just a physical thing. Players expend an enormous amount of nervous energy. Imagine appearing in front of huge crowds in an atmosphere in which winning is everything. The pressure is enormous. It isn't very nice having abuse hurled at you, often by your own fans if you aren't doing well. You've got to be very self-disciplined because referees are cracking down on everything and there are cameras everywhere watching your every move and ready to highlight any transgression. You can't get away with anything. It is a very demanding profession. No one is complaining, it is a wonderful life – but it isn't an easy one.

There is a way to alleviate some of the problems caused by so many fixtures. Some countries in Europe play almost as many games as we do but they spread them out over a longer season incorporating a mid-winter break. The League Managers' Association is pressing for a similar system over here. We're not asking for it so we can go and have a nice holiday for a month. We're calling for it because we think it will make the game better. It wouldn't mean that the players get more time off – the season would actually become longer because we would have to add the extra month or six weeks on to the end of the season.

At the moment we have the worst of both worlds, with players being overstretched during the season and then given more time off than they need during the summer. It's bad for the game, both as a spectacle and in terms of us being able to give our best. By the time we get to Christmas, many players are starting to get a bit jaded from constantly playing two games a week. Others are carrying injuries that need more rest than their clubs can sometimes afford to give them. Both these problems could be improved if the season closed down for a month.

The players could take a few weeks' holiday which would enable them to come back refreshed, and injuries would be given a chance to heal properly. I always feel fans are being slightly short-changed when they pay out hard-earned money to see big teams and then find star players aren't in the side because they're injured. Players can be absent at any time, of course, but a mid-winter break would certainly make things better. It would enable us to compete on more equal terms with other countries in Europe. I think the Premier League is the most exciting and entertaining in the world, but that doesn't make it the best. We can't say it's the best until we start winning major tournaments on a regular basis.

The Germans have a mid-winter break and it certainly helps them. When Forest played Bayern Munich in the UEFA Cup, they were far fresher than us. From the time the quarter-final draw was made to the date of the first leg, Bayern played five matches; we played 23. The difference was amazing. After the draw was made in December they played one game then went into their six-week mid-winter break. We had to soldier on, playing two games a week and forcing players to turn out even though they were carrying injuries that would benefit from some rest. When Bayern came back from their break, we watched them and we were really struck by how fresh they looked. The benefits were obvious.

A mid-winter break would also help smaller clubs in the Premier League compete against the big-money sides. Clubs like Manchester United, Newcastle or Liverpool don't just have better players than the rest of us, they have far more of them. Most managers would kill to have a player like Blomqvist, Sheringham or Solskjaer. They would probably build their team around them. Then you see that at United these players spend a lot of their time on the subs' bench and it makes you even more envious. Imagine! It would be wonderful to select a player like Ryan Giggs, but it would be even more wonderful to be able to replace him with someone like Jesper Blomqvist if he lost a bit of form.

That's the kind of luxury most managers can only dream about, but although we can't match that strength in depth we can sometimes get 11 players together who are able to compete with the best. That's what happened when Forest finished third in the league. We were able to pick the same team every week for the last third of the season and it made us a match for anyone. The following season exactly the opposite happened. Too many of our key players carried injuries they couldn't easily overcome while having to meet the demands of a heavy season.

Bryan Roy started the campaign with damaged knee ligaments and was in a lot of discomfort for most of the year. But because he knew we relied heavily on him, he kept it to himself. Players will do that sometimes. It's bravery of sorts, but it's the wrong kind of bravery. The discomfort affected his form and he was never fully fit. Eventually he had to have an operation.

Injuries weren't the only problem. Some players were losing their edge two-thirds of the way through the season because of the heavy workload we'd had of two games a week. We'd already played 60-odd matches including the UEFA Cup run and that FA Cup game against Tottenham which went to a replay before finally being decided on penalties. At that point, I was still hoping we might put a run together and qualify for Europe again. It started well and we beat Liverpool at home 1–0, but then it all started to fizzle out.

Too many players were exhausted and had become spent forces. Stone, Bart-Williams, Lyttle, Crossley and one or two others who had been outstanding all season desperately needed to be left out of the team for a while and given a rest. At a time like that it would have been nice to turn to 'squad' players like Blomqvist, Sheringham or Solskjaer, but a club with Forest's limited resources just didn't have that kind of luxury. My team of walking wounded had to play on because there were no replacements. Not surprisingly, they weren't able to give their best and we finished ninth. Incidentally, it says a great deal about the level of expectation at a club like Forest when finishing ninth in the league and reaching the quarter-finals of both the FA Cup and the UEFA Cup is deemed disappointing. Considering that we didn't have anything like the resources of the clubs we were expected to beat, it gives a good indication of the kind of pressure the players sometimes feel.

A mid-winter break would have helped us enormously because the injured would have been given more time to recover, and the others would have stayed fresh and fitter for longer. We would have had our best 11 players available for a greater number of matches and I am sure it would have made a difference. The bigger squads would still have the advantage, of course, but the gap might be at least a little smaller.

Whatever the reason, my match-weary Forest team were certainly below par in both games against Bradford. After going out to them, I would have liked to have the players in the next morning so they could get together and the healing process could begin. But unfortunately, half the squad were away on international duty to face much grander opposition. Several countries were still trying to qualify for Euro 96 and England, who qualified automatically as the host nation, were playing a friendly as part of their preparations. It meant I wouldn't see many of our players again until nine days later on the day before our away game at Tottenham. Hardly an ideal way of preparing for a match but unavoidable in a squad containing internationals.

At least those players had another challenge to take their minds off the Bradford defeat, especially Steve Stone. He made his debut for England in the 0–0 draw against Norway. The rest of our squad had to get back to work on the training field and start concentrating on our next game.

As it happened, my faith in my players proved to be justified. Despite the defeat by Bradford and the intervening internationals, the team bounced back with a precious 1–0 away victory at Tottenham, England's Steve Stone getting the winning goal. It didn't stop there. Two days after the Tottenham game we flew out to France to take on Auxerre in the second round of the UEFA Cup. Again we won away 1–0, with Stone again scoring the winner to round off an eventful week in his career. Six days later Forest thrashed Wimbledon 4–1 to set a Premier League record of 25 games unbeaten. Not bad for a side that couldn't beat Bradford, even in two attempts.

CHAPTER 11

The Greats and the
Nearly Men

Some are born great: Pelé, George Best, Maradona. Some achieve greatness: Kevin Keegan, Stuart Pearce, Bryan Robson. But with apologies to Shakespeare, no one has greatness thrust upon them, not on a football field anyway. They have to earn it, which means there's a fourth category the great bard forgot to mention: those who could be great but throw it all away because they can't be bothered. There are a lot more of these players around than you might imagine.

So what is greatness in footballing terms? And how do we tell the difference between the genuine article and the flash pretenders of whom there are so many? Well, some spectacular performances obviously help, but there's a lot more to it than that. A young fan once showed me a video of some of the greatest goals scored by George Best. He pointed out that they weren't any more impressive than the best of Matt Le Tissier. So what was the big deal, he asked, about this legendary Sixties superstar everyone talked about? Wasn't it just a case of nostalgia with a lot of middle-aged fans looking back through rose-coloured spectacles? A kind of generation game that says the Beatles were better than Oasis, Muhammad Ali was greater than Lennox Lewis and flared trousers really were the most stylish clothes ever.

I could see his point of view. Le Tissier has a wonderful talent and to the dismay of his many admirers, he never really made it as a regular in the England team. His fans inevitably put this down to the theory that England managers through the ages never trust talented players. They cite people like Rodney Marsh, Stanley Bowles, Frank Worthington, Tony Currie and Alan Hudson as the kind of supremely gifted performers who did not win anything like the number of caps their ability deserved.

The truth is that people do not always see the downside of these players. Yes, they could win you the match with one touch of genius, but they would be just as likely to do nothing at all and so end up losing you the match. In a sport where winning is everything, few managers will want to take risks on a player who may not perform. We can't always afford to wait until the inconsistent star feels like turning on the magic – whether it's because he's in a good mood, his hair is the right length, there's a full moon that night or whatever.

There's too much at stake. Imagine you're preparing for a big game. You've got a flair player who can do just about anything on his day. You know that if you play him and he scores a spectacular goal then the fans will be deliriously happy. They'll shout and cheer. They'll sing the star's name. If you're lucky, they might even sing yours.

It sounds great and in your mind you're already uncorking the champagne to celebrate victory. But then you're brought back down to earth. You start to have doubts because you know there's another side to your inconsistent superstar. You know that having scored his wonder goal he may well sit back, fail to close someone down and conceivably cost the side a couple of goals.

Such failures on the part of the prima donna won't be noticed by most fans who were cheering only a few moments ago when he scored. Nor will they be noticed by the journalists when they come to write their match reports. They, like most spectators, tend only to see what players do on the ball; they have very little concept of what players fail to do off the ball.

Those inside the game will know what happened but the overall impression left with the public is likely to be that the rest of the team threw away the lead earned by the star. They and the manager are likely to take the blame for the defeat while the real culprit gets off scot free. This can, of course, be more than a little galling and it's hardly surprising that some managers prefer to play safe. You don't have to be a genius to work out that there's no point in playing someone who gets you one goal but gives away two. It's not exactly rocket science.

Fans the world over want to see their side play flamboyant, entertaining football and win by lots of goals. However, they know this is not possible on a regular basis and they have to prioritise. There's no doubt their overriding desire is to win, at any cost. If winning's not possible, the next best thing is not to lose. And so to go back to the hypothetical game we discussed earlier, if the inconsistent superstar hadn't been picked to play then our team may not have scored, but then they may not have thrown two goals away either. That would have left us with a 0–0 draw. That may seem a little negative but ask yourself this question: what do people want most as they walk home from the match? To have seen a goal in a game their team loses, or to have seen no goals in a game their team draws? To help you decide consider this imaginary conversation between two fans.

'My word, that was a fantastic goal our otherwise lazy superstar scored.'

'Yes. Who cares that he did nothing else and we ended up losing 7–1? That goal alone was worth the entrance fee and I for one can't wait for next week's game.'

'You're right. Isn't it great that our team plays such open, exuberant football, with our players free to express themselves instead of having to run around like mad things trying to win the match?'

'Absolutely! As if it matters who wins! No, I love this flamboyant approach where players can save their energy for doing something flash once every five matches. The manager has my full backing.'

'Mine too! I certainly shan't be screaming like a madman for him to be sacked.'

'Me neither! I tell you what. Let's phone Radio 5 Live to tell everyone how delighted we are with the wonderful carefree approach of our manager.'

'I'll race you to the phone.'

Not the most realistic of conversations, is it? The reality

is that losing, no matter how entertaining, is never acceptable. Managers ignore this at their peril. It is bound to affect their team selection.

World-class is a term thrown around a lot when describing gifted players, but the genuinely world-class performers do a lot more than produce the occasional flash of brilliance. They make sure they graft hard and meet their responsibilities to the rest of the team. They are winners. By that, I mean they have a mental toughness which enables them to get the best out of themselves in every situation. They have a hunger for success which makes them spurn the easy approach or the half measure. No matter how good they are, they constantly want to improve. They prepare properly for every match, train and perfect their skills. It enables them to battle against the odds when fainter hearts will give in. It means they have the footballing intelligence to be able to blend their individual flair into the overall pattern of the team.

Measured against these kinds of standards, most pretenders to the mantle of greatness will quickly fade away. The young fan I mentioned earlier was possibly right when he said the Le Tissier top ten goals were more spectacular than those of George Best. He was wrong, though, with his next observation that Le Tissier was therefore as good as Best. The truth is, there is no comparison. Best had a much wider range of qualities. People tend to forget these aspects of his game because they were so mesmerised by his talent and flair, but despite his playboy image off the field, Best was very thorough, workmanlike and yes, very responsible, once the game started.

Unlike so many flair players, he was prepared to close down defenders and track back on the rare occasions he lost the ball or the opposition got possession. And just to prove I'm not engaging in a generation war, let me say it's a quality shared by Ryan Giggs, the man once hailed as Manchester United's new George Best. Imagine being the full-back having to play against players like those two. In the unlikely event that you do manage to get the ball off them, you know they'll be snapping at your heels ready to chase you to the end of the earth to get it back. On the other hand, you know that if you get the ball off someone like Le Tissier, you will only face limited resistance before you're allowed to go on your way in peace!

As the Newcastle left-back I had many battles on the field with Best and he was always a handful. Despite his waif-like appearance, he was as tough as an Alan Hansen match analysis. He had to be, to contend with the physical side of the game. It was much harder in those days when crunching tackles from behind were perfectly acceptable and defenders virtually had to commit GBH to even warrant a booking.

Best had to contend with some brutal treatment from some very intimidating defenders. But Best never was intimidated. Quite the opposite! He was the one frightening others. Many defenders used to talk of giving the opposition attackers a few vicious tackles in the early minutes of the match. With some players that would be enough to frighten them out of playing their normal game. There was no way you could do that with Best. No matter how hard defenders hit him, he always came back for more, still wanting the ball and being prepared to run with it. It was an attitude which turned the tables on many Neanderthal types, who ended up being intimidated themselves by Best's refusal to be intimidated. Their problem was they couldn't stop him by fair means or foul, and that's a terrifying realisation for any defender.

Much the same could be said of Pelé, perhaps the greatest of all time. As with Best, when people think of him they think of any number of superlatives to describe his talent, flair and inventiveness. He had all those things in abundance but having played against him in a friendly match in Hong Kong, my abiding memories are of his more down-to-earth qualities. He was the hardest man I ever played against. Trying to tackle him was like trying to tackle a Chieftain tank. He was strong, and intimidating with it. No one could display that kind of talent at the top level for so long without being able to look after themselves.

Best and Pelé were without doubt the greatest footballers I ever played against. But the crucial point is that although they were extraordinarily gifted, they were both prepared to do their share of the bread-and-butter work. There have been an awful lot of hugely talented players who never became great players because they did not have the application. So far, at least, Le Tissier has fallen into this category. He got a few games for England but was overlooked for the main part by five England managers: Bobby Robson, Graham Taylor, Terry Venables, Glenn Hoddle and Kevin Keegan.

Were they all wrong? Almost certainly not. Le Tissier is a very fine player and I would have loved to have the chance to work with him. Anyone who can score as many goals as he has in a very ordinary side like Southampton has to have something special, but you have to make allowances for his weaknesses.

That means building the whole team around him. It's a major undertaking and you have to be sure it's worth the effort. At club level it probably is. Southampton certainly thought so and, for years, Le Tissier has been the centre of their universe. It meant other players had to do his share of the work. They did his running, covering and closing down. It's not a very glamorous task, but Lawrie McMenemy had this phrase about violinists and hod carriers. The hod carriers do all the grafting to give the violinist the freedom to perform.

It can work and certainly served Southampton well for several seasons. It has also happened at several other clubs to great effect. A classic example was the Tottenham side in the 1980s which David Pleat built around Glenn Hoddle and Ossie Ardiles. They were both world-class players. Hoddle didn't particularly like running up and down the field without the ball at his feet, but he was aware of his responsibilities to the team. For example, he wasn't very good at tackling but he did his share of covering. The Tottenham defence were happy as long as he made sure he got goalside of the player he was marking. The overall strategy was for the other players to win the ball and to get it to Ardiles and Hoddle as quickly as possible. They created the goals at one end while the others stopped them going in at the other.

Many other managers have made similar attempts to fashion sides around one player. The Stoke manager Tony Waddington tried it with one of the most gifted players imaginable, Alan Hudson. There was a story that when Hudson arrived at Stoke for his first training session, Waddington made him wear a different colour shirt from the other players on his side. Then he told the others: 'That's so you know who to pass to. Just get the ball to Alan and everything will be all right.' The problem with this system is that it runs into difficulties at international level. The leap in standard is one factor. Someone like Le Tissier is a giant at a small club like Southampton, but doesn't loom quite so large when rubbing shoulders in the England camp with the likes of Shearer, Beckham and Scholes. With people like that around, the argument for building the side around one player becomes far less compelling.

The other factor is the attitude of the other players. It's one thing to ask nine journeymen at a small club to work harder to compensate for the limitations of the leading star; it's quite a different thing to expect nine internationals to be so accommodating. Why should they compromise their game to suit someone who is not prepared or able to pull his weight? In fact, asking someone like Shearer to alter his game might be counter-productive. He is just as likely to score a goal as Le Tissier, yet he works twice as hard and gives the team so much more. He is always ready to close down defenders. I remember him playing for Blackburn alongside Chris Sutton against Forest. They were the most expensive strike force in the country at the time, but there was no way they were prepared to rest on their reputations. They ran themselves into the ground and gave our defenders a terrible time.

It's the same with top strikers from other countries. They don't come with much more flair than Germany's Jurgen Klinsmann. He's scored countless brilliant goals, including two for Bayern Munich which helped to knock my Nottingham Forest side out of the UEFA Cup. But again, despite all that ability, one of my abiding memories of Klinsmann is watching him run 30 yards at the City Ground to close down my right full-back Des Lyttle. He had virtually no chance of getting the ball and he didn't get it, but he panicked Lyttle into a sloppy pass and Bayern won possession. Suddenly what should have been the beginning of an attack by us and a moment for our defence to catch its breath became the beginning of an attack by them.

Managers dream of players like this. It's impossible to overstate their importance. When he was the England coach Glenn Hoddle quite rightly said that he considered the attack to be his first line of defence and the defence to be the first line of attack. I couldn't agree more, and the way Klinsmann closed down Lyttle that night was the perfect example of how it should work. I dare say various England managers have made such points to Le Tissier, but he doesn't seem to respond. He doesn't seem to have the hunger to constantly improve which marks out all great players.

Neither have a host of other mercurial talents over the years. That, of course, is entirely their decision and I wouldn't presume to criticise them, but it leaves the manager in a quandary. He may wish to use a flair player's match-winning ability, but how does he blend it into a team of internationals without losing some of their effectiveness? It's not surprising that successive England managers have decided such players can create more problems than they solve and consequently chosen not to play them.

This inevitably produces an outcry from the fans, who understandably tend to blame the manager for not getting enough out of the likes of Currie, Marsh or Bowles, and say what a waste. But I have never met a manager who would not pick a great player if he had the choice. The truth is those players wasted their talent themselves because they didn't have the drive to go out and perform at their best every week.

Sometimes luck plays a part. If players get in the right team with the right group of players when they are young, it can make a difference. Or, of course, it can go the other way. Stan Bowles was another of those 1970s mavericks. By his own admission Stan fell too easily into the world of drinking and gambling to ever be able to devote himself fully to football. He gave us some magical moments but I'm sure he could have given so much more. Even Brian Clough couldn't tame him when he brought him to Nottingham Forest, and if he couldn't sort him out then no one could.

Paul Gascoigne had all the talent to be a great player and for the main part he was until 1991 when he ruptured his cruciate ligaments in the FA Cup final against Forest. It affected his mobility and he was never the same afterwards. He no longer had the athleticism to dominate games as he used to do. People have commented that Gascoigne created his own problems by making such a reckless tackle that day on Gary Charles, but the truth is you cannot divorce the player from the personality. How you live your life off the field invariably has an effect on how you perform on it. Gascoigne is very likeable but unfortunately he is irresponsible off the field and he is irresponsible on it. He had a sense of recklessness and lack of self-discipline which cost him dearly both in his personal and professional life.

I don't wish this to sound like an attack on effortlessly gifted players, particularly Matt Le Tissier and Paul Gascoigne. I'm quite happy to acknowledge that both of them are far better footballers than I could ever have hoped to be, no matter how hard I worked. If we criticise people, I think it's important that we should also celebrate all that's good about them. For many years Le Tissier could have staged his own goal of the season competition and his countless stunning displays, which lit up many a dull afternoon, will be remembered long after the efforts of more hard-working players are forgotten.

Paul Gascoigne, too, has at times been like a breath of fresh air. He has terrific enthusiasm and a sense of humour that forces you to warm to him. It can be a joy to see him perform. The goal he scored for England in the Euro 96 game against Scotland when he flicked the ball over Colin Hendry's head and then volleyed it into the net will make most people forgive him anything. I would too, and I don't want to underestimate his achievements. Perhaps I'm just being greedy because I know he could have done more in his career. If he had pushed himself just that little bit more, taken a grip of himself a bit more, he could have joined the ranks of the greats like Johan Cruyff, Michel Platini or Lothar Matthaus.

Perhaps the supremely talented players have it all too easy. They shine right from schoolboy days when they are far more capable than anyone else and can get by without really trying. Unfortunately for them, it gets harder and harder the further you climb up the ladder. By the time you reach international level, you have to work hard no matter how talented you are. The need to go up a gear becomes a mental block that some people cannot overcome and they eventually fade out of the game, leaving their fans to lament over what might have been. Such players like Frank Worthington and Stan Bowles sometimes talk about the game being taken too seriously and how they felt they had a mission to entertain rather than a mission to win. They will say they have no regrets, but you wonder if they really mean that. How can you not regret failing to make the most of yourself and playing for your country?

I lost count of the number of times I made this point to the most talented and enigmatic player I have ever managed, Stan Collymore. When I worked with him at Nottingham Forest he had the potential to be truly world-class. He could do everything. He'd got pace and power, strength, great vision and an eye for goal. He could get tap-ins and spectacular goals. He was a wonderful player technically. On the strength of his performances at Forest he got into the England team. I saw him in the friendly international against Brazil when he came on as a sub. In ten minutes he did more than any other English front player. He got behind their defence twice, which is tremendous work at that level, and looked set to become a regular member of the squad. Sadly, it all seemed to go downhill for him after that. Despite all my best efforts to keep him, he decided to leave Forest and join Liverpool.

I could understand his desire to join one of the biggest clubs in the country but I think the move damaged his career. He was in terrific form at Forest. I had built the team around him and concentrated on giving him the right kind of platform to bring out the best of him. There was no way Liverpool were going to accommodate him in that way, not with other huge talents like Fowler, McManaman and Barnes in the team. Stan quickly found life wasn't as easy as he expected. At Forest he was an automatic first-team choice; at Liverpool he often found himself on the subs' bench.

He was Britain's most expensive player at the time and the pressure on him was enormous. He averaged almost a goal every two games at Liverpool, which has to be good by anybody's standards, but the level of expectation is so great at Liverpool that somehow it was perceived as failure.

It appeared he was often left out of the team if he failed to score. Collymore would not have been able to cope with that. He needs to feel loved and wanted.

When Liverpool didn't provide that, this affected his relationship with other players. He would find that difficult to cope with as well, and his concentration would inevitably suffer. Stan did not find it easy being a professional player. He finds it difficult to maintain sufficient self-discipline. We could never get much work out of him because he couldn't see how important it was. His biggest failing is that he doesn't think. He was never a very good trainer and sometimes he wouldn't turn up at all. If he knew we had a hard day he seemed to have an ache or something more often than most. He might have a genuine reason but often he wouldn't think to phone up to let someone know; or he'd phone in the afternoon after we'd been chasing round after him all day. He'd be very apologetic and you couldn't help but like him, but it wasn't a professional attitude.

I bumped into him in the summer of 1998 during the World Cup, shortly after he had made the headlines for attacking his girlfriend Ulrika Jonsson in a bar in Paris. I asked him how he was doing and he just said: 'Oh, pretty badly, gaffer.' He looked very down.

I said to him: 'Listen, you silly bugger. When's the penny going to drop with you, Stan? You've got to get your life in order and start showing the world what you really can do. You're in Paris brawling in a bar; you should be in Paris playing for England. The papers shouldn't be talking about you attacking people, they should be talking about whether you can do for England what Ronaldo does for Brazil.'

I didn't think the comparison was too fanciful – Stan did

have that kind of talent. Perhaps he could still do it, but temperamentally I'm not sure he'll ever be able to deal with it at the top level. I shall be very sad if he doesn't fulfil his potential. I would hate to see him end up as one of those nearly men who shone for a few moments of brilliance then faded away without ever really living up to their early promise. There have been far too many of those already.

CHAPTER 12

Death By a Thousand Cuts

There's a story that says my resignation as manager of Nottingham Forest sent shock waves through the stock market. Apparently one broker was so stunned by the news that he started panic-selling thousands of shares. He might have bankrupted his firm had his bemused colleagues not intervened. The poor man had got his wires crossed – he thought it was another Nottingham Clark who had resigned, the former Chancellor Kenneth Clarke.

I don't know whether the story's true or not, but it ought to be, because it typifies the madness surrounding my departure from the club (where, ironically, that other Mr Clarke is a big fan). The confusion was so great I tried to escape by going to a Status Quo concert. It didn't help me much. The music was blaring out but I scarcely heard a note. My mind was in turmoil, trying to make sense of the previous few days in which I had decided there was no alternative but to walk out on Nottingham Forest.

I say I walked out, but I'm not sure; maybe I was eased out by club directors. Even now it's hard to tell. There was no one fatal blow, no dramatic dismissal, but there was certainly a sense of death by a thousand cuts. The air was thick with fears of conspiracy and there was paranoia everywhere. Leading board members backed me with words but then seemed to completely undermine me with their actions. It got to a point where for my own self-respect, I felt I had to go.

So that's how I found myself in row 22 of the NEC in Birmingham trying to get into the music along with 2,000 other ageing, slightly self-conscious rock fans, my self-respect still intact but my future shot to pieces. After a traumatic event like throwing away your job, you desperately want the comfort of feeling certain that you've done the right thing. But how can you be certain, especially when the issues are so complicated? Through the wall of noise that night I found myself thinking: 'My God, what have I done?' The future looked bleak. I was out of work. I had very little money and no immediate prospects of another job.

It was ironic that I should find myself at a Status Quo concert because they reminded me of the good times at Forest. I had met the group nearly a year earlier on a flight to Hamburg. They were on a promotional tour and I was going to watch Bayern Munich, our opponents in the quarter-finals of the UEFA Cup. We had a few beers and swapped a few stories and it made for a pleasant flight. They promised to send me tickets the next time they played in England and sure enough, nine months later the tickets duly arrived. It seemed incredible to reflect on the changes those nine months had brought.

On the flight to Hamburg I was manager of one of the country's most successful clubs, the only English club still left in European competition. Forest at that time were a homely, friendly club with a terrific atmosphere. I hoped to end my career there, possibly as general manager with Stuart Pearce taking over as team manager when his ever-extending playing career finally ended. I had discussed it informally with him and my chairman at the time, Fred Reacher, and both seemed quite keen. It would probably have happened, too, if all our worlds hadn't been turned upside down by events totally beyond our control. The friendly atmosphere at the club turned sour and the reason, inevitably, was money. Forest were in the middle of a messy, protracted takeover.

There was no doubt that the club had to reform if it was to remain as a major force. For more than a hundred years it had been run along the lines of a glorified working-men's club. It was archaic and outmoded. Nobody actually owned it and no one had total control. Ultimate power rested with 209 amateur shareholders who paid just one pound each for the privilege. They came from all walks of life – shopkeepers, pub landlords, housewives. By day they sold ice cream, pulled pints of beer or looked after their children; by night they took control of the multi-million-pound business that was Nottingham Forest. For two years chairman Fred Reacher had been looking at ways of changing the constitution with a view to bringing in more finance.

There were two developments in football that made this vital. More and more clubs, even the relatively unfashionable ones, were spending fortunes on players. At the start of the 1996–97 season, Coventry had spent £18 million, Middlesbrough even more. Chelsea hadn't forked out a huge amount in transfer fees but they made up for it with the kind of wages they were paying to imported stars like Ruud Gullit, Gianfranco Zola, Gianluca Vialli, Frank Leboeuf and Roberto di Matteo. There was no way Forest under the old system of ownership were ever going to be able to compete with that.

The other major factor was the Bosman ruling. It made our bank manager feel very nervous about us running a £6 million overdraft. It hadn't been a problem before because he knew that if necessary we could sell a few star players and the books would balance. But Bosman changed all that. What if the star players waited until they were out of contract before they moved? The club would get no transfer fee at all. Suddenly, the situation didn't look so easy to control.

Fred Reacher's answer to both these problems was to look for some big-money investors to take over the club. There was no shortage of contenders. Multi-million-pound businessmen began to appear, promising untold riches in return for control. It was hard to tell how serious some of them really were or what their motives might be. The sheer love of football? Or the prospect of publicity, power and the chance to make some money? Whatever the case with different individuals, the whole process became a pantomime with some bidders emerging to make all sorts of promises, soaking up the limelight only to withdraw after a few weeks.

A video tycoon with film-star looks was the first bidder to show his hand. Grant Bovey lived in London but was born in Nottingham and boasted that he was a lifelong Forest fan.

His name was to be all over the papers a few years later for his much-publicised affair with the television presenter Anthea Turner. However, he got his first taste of the headlines when he promised to pump something like £30 million into Forest. He appeared on television and radio chat shows announcing all the great things he would do if he took over. There was talk of building a new main stand and providing me with £10 million to buy new players. He wanted to shake up the way the club was run and make it all much more professional and commercially orientated.

It all sounded very good until the media started digging further. Then it emerged that one of Mr Bovey's companies had got into financial difficulties in the past. He answered this by saying it was a mistake he had made when he was younger. He had since put everything right and the debts had all been paid. Nevertheless, it raised a question mark in people's minds over whether he really had the financial muscle to take over. A few weeks later he announced that he no longer wanted to buy the club.

The next contender was less glamorous but there was no doubting his financial acumen. Local businessman Sandy Anderson had reportedly made £30 million in less than a year. He had led a management buy-out of the Derbyshire train-leasing company Porterbrook. Seven months later it was sold to Stagecoach for £475 million, thus earning Mr Anderson his fortune. His money and the fact that he was already a Forest season-ticket holder made him the early favourite, but he was by no means going to have it all his own way.

'Tottenham, we always beat Tottenham,' was a favourite chant of the Forest crowd, reflecting the fact that we did seem to have a jinx on the north London side. Now, a former

Tottenham chairman, Irving Scholar, was about to join the fight to take over at Forest. He enlisted the help of local author and Forest fan Phil Soar to prepare the bid. For the money to bankroll the deal Scholar turned to the Monte Carlo-based millionaire Lawrie Lewis. Lewis admitted he didn't know anything about football and had never been particularly interested in it, but he was still confident his group could turn Forest into a major force in the game. Mr Lewis also enjoyed his 15 minutes of fame in the papers and on television before he, too, withdrew from the race.

This left Scholar and Soar temporarily in the lurch and out of the running, but they quickly came up with another wealthy backer, Nigel Wray, owner of Saracens rugby club and a director of Carlton Television. Together they prepared a new bid. Meanwhile, Grant Bovey said he was again back in the running, only to withdraw again a few days later. Just to confuse things even further, Lawrie Lewis popped back into the frame to offer his services to the Sandy Anderson group.

As if all this wasn't complicated enough, there were several other possible bidders waiting in the wings. There was speculation that an Indonesian billionaire called Johannes Kotjo would buy the club and flood it with money beyond our wildest dreams. Later, an American media mogul who helped organise President Clinton's election campaign joined the fray. Albert Scardino called football 'soccer' and said he wanted to 'reinvigorate the Forest family and make it healthy again.' Such would be the effect of this reinvigoration that Nottingham would become the centre of the football world and Forest would win the European Cup within two years. Heady stuff indeed!

Whatever the question marks over the various bidders and

their contact with reality, the fact remained that eventually one of them would win through. Then millions of pounds would be pumped into the club. It was a fantastic, once-in-a-lifetime opportunity to take Forest into the big league. But that was all long term. In the short term, the protracted takeover negotiations had a devastating effect.

They coincided with the team going through its worst patch of form since I arrived. We couldn't seem to win a match and were languishing near the bottom of the Premier League. The poor results and the seemingly endless saga of the takeover negotiations sent a wave of insecurity through the club and virtually paralysed it. In any situation of instability, paranoia spreads like wildfire. Everyone from the catering staff to the coaching staff feared for their jobs.

They began to see all sorts of demons. Fanciful rumours started to emerge. For example, many of my staff feared that one of the main consortiums was working behind the scenes to create a Stuart Pearce/Nigel Clough dream-ticket management team to step in once the takeover was complete. That would mean that me and my coaches would be out. The rumour was heightened when Stuart was seen coming out of the shareholders' room one night after a match. Normally players never go in the shareholders' room and everyone wanted to know what he was doing there all of a sudden. Speculation reached fever pitch a few days later when he was seen in the club car park speaking to none other than Nigel Clough, who at that time was a Manchester City player.

Let me say straightaway that I didn't believe any of this. Stuart was magnificent for me as a player and gave everything he could for me right up to the day I left. I have no axe to grind with Stuart, but the rumours typified the level of paralysing paranoia flying around at that time.

It's easy to dismiss the paranoia as nonsense but at the same time people were being given plenty of reasons to feel worried, and plenty of reasons to wonder if I was really in control of the club any more. The fact was that the takeover came to be used by the directors as an excuse to stop me managing, as our results on the pitch took a nosedive and got worse the longer the uncertainty went on.

During the previous summer, I had agreed new contracts with all my staff; that is, my senior coaches, trainers and so on. The terms were agreed verbally and everybody was happy. I then left the formalities to be sorted out by the directors and club administrators.

In October, I found to my surprise that nothing had been done. The takeover talk was in full swing and obviously the staff wanted written contracts because verbal agreements were unlikely to count for much once the new owners took over. I asked the board to formalise the contracts as agreed, but they wouldn't do it. I was amazed. I wasn't asking for anything extra for them, I just wanted them to put in writing what they had already agreed to verbally. The board said they couldn't do it because of the pending takeover. Everything would have to wait until that was complete. I was staggered and felt they were simply using the takeover as a way of stopping me from managing the club as I wanted.

It put me in an impossible situation with the staff. I needed their loyalty and commitment more than ever, but now they were looking at me and saying: 'What the hell's going on? You're the manager! You've always kept your word in the past, so what's this all about?' You can imagine the uncertainty it created. They were looking over their shoulders at each other wondering who would survive and who wouldn't. It was a very uneasy atmosphere.

I was having similar problems negotiating with players. I was told I couldn't give anyone a new contract. That was ridiculous and put us in an impossible position with Alfie Haaland. I had brought him to Forest from Norway three years earlier and he turned out to be a very good buy. He was a good utility player and had done a great job filling in for us in nearly every defence and midfield position.

He was well into the last year of his contract so I was eager to secure him for Forest. Again, the board wouldn't let me do it. I warned them that if we left it until he got into the last six months of his contract we would never get him to sign. Thanks to the Bosman ruling, he would know that he might as well let his old contract run out so he could become a free agent. I spent three months trying to get the board to realise this, but they wouldn't listen. I had to go back to Alfie and tell him that I would love to sign him but I had to wait until either the takeover was in place or it was thrown out altogether – assuming I would still be manager by then, of course. You can hardly blame him for not being impressed.

It was a similar story with Chris Bart-Williams. I had a gentlemen's agreement with Chris that if he did well for 12 months then we would discuss an improved contract for him. Well, he had done well and the 12 months was up. Unfortunately, I had to effectively go back on my word and say I couldn't give him anything after all. He took it with his typical good nature but I was upset about it. I don't like to promise something and then not deliver.

We had a totally farcical situation with some of our YTS trainees. We had four or five promising young players and I was desperately keen to re-sign them before their contracts ran out. Suddenly the board put a stop to that as well, but then, just as suddenly, they changed their minds. The reason for the about-turn? The youth team played a game on the main ground. For the first time the directors sat down to watch them and realised how good these young players were. They saw what they risked losing and authorised me to sign them.

All of this completely undermined my authority with the staff and the players. It doesn't take people long to work out when a manager isn't in total control with the complete backing of everyone at the club. Once you get in that position it's very difficult to win back people's confidence.

The rot had set in back in September when chairman Fred Reacher would tell me one thing and then his vice-chairman Irving Korn would tell me something totally different. I knew that the club was in a difficult financial situation – Reacher had told me in the summer that I might have to sell someone to raise £2 million before Christmas just to keep the bank manager happy. I said I could do that but warned him it might mean selling someone we didn't want to sell. In September he said he had seen the bank manager and had managed to put him off for a while, so everything would be all right. Then he went off on holiday to Cyprus for four weeks. As soon as he had gone, Irving Korn was coming in saying the opposite. He said the bank was getting nervous and we would have to raise the money.

I would ring around a few clubs and then go back to the board and say right, I can get £2.5 million for such and such a player. Straightaway the board would look aghast and say: 'We can't sell him. The crowd would go mad. Hang on a while!' Leeds offered £1.75 million for Alfie Haaland and I put it to the board, but again they wouldn't do it because they feared the reaction of the crowd. I accepted that but told them if the bank suddenly started asking for money and it wasn't there, not to blame me. At the AGM in October the directors voted Reacher out as chairman and replaced him with Korn. I thought that was ridiculous. The man who had done all the negotiating with the consortiums was being sidelined just as the deal was coming to a climax. I didn't have the same working relationship with Korn as I'd had with Reacher and things were never the same for me at the club after that.

The season staggered on in a similar fashion. The results got worse and the directors continued to undermine my position. Things came to a head both on and off the field just before Christmas. I went to see Korn on Monday 16 December, hoping to get some assurances that I would be allowed to manage the club as I wanted. I didn't get those assurances so I gave the directors an ultimatum: either back me or sack me. They wouldn't do either. It was ridiculous. It was as though we were all walking over a cliff and no one could do anything about it. No one would do anything positive, so I said I was thinking of resigning.

Irving Korn and others on the board tried very hard to persuade me to stay, but only with words. Words are cheap and they wouldn't back them up with action. The two main consortiums also tried to persuade me to hold on. Irving Scholar phoned me and so did Sandy Anderson. But again, all either of them could offer were words. They were both aware of my concerns and insisted they could be addressed once the takeover was in place. They both said they believed in me and wouldn't want to get rid of me once they took over.

I wasn't convinced by any of them. If they all had really wanted me to stay, they could have addressed my concerns. The directors of the club could have approached the two main consortiums and got their authority for what I wanted to do, which was renew the contracts of some of my players, authorise new contracts for the staff and so on. It would not have been that difficult, but they wouldn't do it. I interpreted that as meaning none of them was sure about me. They kept saying they wanted me to stay, but really they were just keeping their options open.

Nothing had been resolved at my meeting with Korn and I left his office wondering what to do next. It seemed inevitable that I would have to go if I was to retain any self-respect. Nevertheless, I told myself, resignation is not something to be taken lightly and I had no intention of just flinging myself on the sacrificial sword. I had always subscribed to the Brian Clough philosophy that says if you're thinking of resigning, go to bed and sleep on it. If you still feel like resigning the next morning, then go back to bed and don't get up until you've changed your mind! Well, I'd done that over and over again during the previous few weeks and kept asking, can I look myself in the face? Can I look my staff in the face?

I decided to sleep on it one more time. I went home hoping against hope that we might turn things round, we might just get a win which would put a different light on things and then maybe the board would see sense. We just needed that break. Unfortunately, football seldom gives you that break. Instead, it gives you Liverpool away. A Liverpool in rampaging form. There are no easy games in football any more, as managers say with monotonous regularity, but nevertheless, when you're struggling for survival you could do without having to face Collymore, Barnes, Fowler and McManaman. They'd just knocked five past our relegation rivals Middlesbrough with Fowler getting four of them.

Perhaps he won't be fit enough to play, I thought as I tried to lull myself off to sleep.

We set off for Anfield on a freezing Tuesday just eight days before Christmas. All the way on the coach I tried to just concentrate on the game and block out everything else. I was conscious we were playing one of the best sides in the country but I still reckoned it was possible to win. I felt I had managed to gee up the players during the last few games and got them going again. I had decided to modify our usual patient build-up play in favour of being more positive and getting the ball forward earlier. I wanted them to try to win the ball back quicker and play a more pressing, high-tempo game.

There were two reasons for this. The close passing game Forest were renowned for requires not only skill but lots of confidence. If players aren't confident and comfortable receiving the ball then they're likely to lose it and you can end up in all sorts of trouble. The other advantage of getting forward faster was that it would get the crowd behind us right from the start if we tried to dominate games immediately.

It had worked quite well in our previous three matches. We completely outplayed Wimbledon but just couldn't take our chances. We got two good draws against Blackburn and Newcastle and could have won both those games, so there was some hope if only we could keep going. It was a good theory, but it didn't work. We were murdered at Anfield. We lost 4–2 and it could have been a lot more. The result itself wasn't the end of the world – it was the way we played.

I felt that one or two of the players were ignoring my instructions on how to play. It was as if they were saying that the way I wanted them to do things wasn't working so they might as well revert to playing their own way. I think that was the final straw for me. I'm not saying there was a rebellion on the part of those players – it might even have been subconscious on their part. But it was enough.

I had always been very careful not to blame the takeover for our problems on the pitch because I didn't want to be seen to be making excuses. Initially I don't think it had anything to do with it, but the longer it went on, the more I felt it was having an effect. I could just see it rolling on and on, with me sitting there waiting to be sacked like a turkey waiting for Christmas.

The journey back from Liverpool was very difficult. I had more or less made up my mind there and then to go. The whole sorry business came down to two basic issues in my mind. My lack of authority was filtering through to the players and that meant I would almost inevitably lose them as well before long.

The other factor was the overwhelming need for the club to stay in the Premiership. That night on the way back from Liverpool, I felt we had reached a stage where they were more likely to survive with a new manager. Sometimes the arrival of a new face can give a struggling team a lift in the short term. It can help them win a few games and then before you know it, things don't look so bad. The confidence returns and you start playing better. I was still convinced that if Forest could get those couple of wins, by whatever means, it would make all the difference.

When one of the bidders, Sandy Anderson, was making his public pronouncements about how much he wanted me to stay, he reminded everyone that only a few months earlier I had been hailed as a possible England manager. He then pointed out that someone in that category doesn't just become a bad manager overnight. It was a fair comment, but in a way you *can* become a bad manager overnight; or at least, a weakened and less effective one at a particular club. A series of relatively minor incidents can destroy a manager; rows with senior players or dismissive treatment by the board can lead to a lack of confidence. It doesn't mean he can't go and manage successfully elsewhere, but it can mean he's finished at that particular club. I felt that was happening to me.

I tossed and turned on it all night but I felt no different when I woke up the next morning. I decided to ignore the final part of Brian's advice about going back to bed until I had changed my mind. Instead, I asked for a meeting with the chairman and told him I was resigning. He asked me to stay but I said it had gone too far. He then tried to make me change my mind, but again it was just words. He still wasn't prepared to do the things that would have persuaded me to stay. A board meeting was called and my resignation was 'reluctantly' accepted. I recommended that they give the job to Stuart Pearce in the short term. I knew it would be impossible to appoint a full-time manager before the takeover. I felt that under the circumstances Stuart was the best person to give the club that short-term lift.

So that was that and I went off to see Status Quo to get away from it all. I went with my assistant manager Alan Hill and our wives Janice and Pam. We went for a meal first but I didn't get much of a chance to eat. My mobile phone was ringing constantly, with both consortiums trying to persuade me to stay. They were giving me reassurances that they would keep me on once they took over, but again they didn't seem to offer what I required and again I thought that it was all just words.

The next day, the news was announced at a press conference and I said my goodbyes to everyone at the club. It was a very emotional time. All the Nottingham Forest staff had been wonderful to me during my three years. They had always supported me and it was hard to express just how much I appreciated that. I didn't get a chance to see the players because of how quickly it all happened, but I spoke to most of them on the phone afterwards. They didn't say that much, really. That's football. Players and managers come and go. You meet, establish a good working relationship and then eventually everyone moves on.

I went home to my family with the drama of it all still swirling round in my head. Resignation had been an enormous step to take. I hoped I would get another job, but I couldn't be sure what the future would hold. There had been rumours in the press a week earlier that I might be offered the vacant Manchester City job if I left Forest. I hoped there might be something in it and looked over at the phone, willing it to ring. It stayed ominously silent.

Over the next few days it remained that way, which was worrying, but at least it gave me the opportunity to enjoy something I hadn't experienced for the previous thirty years: Christmas at home with my family. I was totally out of football and had a marvellous time. For the first time in my career, I didn't have to go training and I didn't have to go to a match on Boxing Day.

I couldn't help but follow Forest's fortunes, of course. On the Saturday after I left they played Arsenal at home. Stuart Pearce led the team out for his first game in charge as player-manager. The tannoy blared out Gary Glitter's

'Leader of the Gang' and it was quite an emotional occasion by all accounts. It went just as I had hoped. Stuart couldn't make any major changes because he was dealing with the same players, but he tried one or two little things with different people which I might not have done because I had got too close to it for too long.

Stuart did have one ace up his sleeve that I didn't have – the return of Nigel Clough. Forest got him on loan from Manchester City as soon as I left. No doubt some people at the club thought the 'conspiracy' they had been envisaging earlier on was turning out to be real, but I don't think so. The fact is that Nigel's possible return had been raised with me a few days before I resigned. I got a phone call from Brian Clough. In his typical style, he said: 'I hear you're looking for a goalscorer. Well, there's a young man not too far away who's just been told he can go out on loan to any Premier League club – my son Nigel. He might just get you a goal or two.'

Had the circumstances been different, I might have brought Nigel back myself. But by then I was in turmoil about what I was going to do, so I didn't pursue it. Stuart obviously did. Nigel came on as sub against Arsenal and apparently played very well. Forest won 2–1, at last getting the crucial victory they needed to get things going. Alfie Haaland got the two goals. It was ironic really, because in the previous four games he might have had half a dozen. Against Newcastle he had a good chance and ended up hitting the post. If that had gone in, we would have won and I might still have been at Forest. But football is full of ifs and buts, and the success or failure of entire careers can depend on whether a ball hits the post and bounces in, or hits the post and bounces out.

After the match, Stuart Pearce dedicated the victory to me, saying the players owed me one. He added that he wished I was still there. It was a nice touch and much appreciated. In many ways, I wished I was still there myself.

I don't know if there was a move to get me out of the club. I probably never will know. What I do know is that the situation was even more uncertain after I left and yet the things I was told I couldn't have were suddenly granted. The staff were given new contracts, players were offered new contracts. Pearce was given a fortune to manage the club. Perhaps this shows that some of the directors wanted me out all along. Perhaps it's simply down to the fact that my resignation forced them to act and get a grip of the situation.

Whatever the case, it did them no good in the end. The Pearce revival was short-lived. After three or four good results which brought Stuart the manager of the month award, the old problems returned. The Soar-Scholar-Wray consortium finally won through and the Crystal Palace manager Dave Bassett was appointed general manager to take some of the burden off Stuart, who also had to cope with captaining the team as well as clinging on to his England career. It didn't work out and Forest were relegated.

I felt genuinely sad as I watched their decline. I still had a great affection for the club and many friends there. But as I sat in my living room that Christmas, I had more immediate problems on my mind: how to earn a living. I stared at the phone; it stared back at me. Its silence was even more deafening than Status Quo.

CHAPTER 13

The Job From Hell

Thirty thousand Manchester City fans had a message for Oasis star Noel Gallagher. 'Get your money out,' they chanted in unison, urging him to use some of his pop music millions to buy new players for the team he had supported since childhood. He declined the ad hoc invitation to splash out his hard-earned cash and buy into the club. He said he didn't want any 'scally' fans coming round to his house and putting his windows through if things didn't work out.

He's obviously got a lot of common sense. As a down-to-earth Moss Side lad and long-suffering fan of Manchester City, he would know that success is a very elusive commodity in football and the fans are very unforgiving towards managers and chairmen who fail to deliver it. City's former chairman Peter Swales would have known all about that – he was given a terrible time by the fans as the club's fortunes started to slide. Insults, abuse; they even started throwing things at him. Now his successor Francis Lee, who took over in 1994, was starting to get similar rumblings of discontent as the slump continued. No wonder Noel Gallagher didn't want to get involved.

Back in the 1960s when most footballers were spending their afternoons in the snooker halls or out chasing women, Francis Lee was getting his head round the toilet paper business. Not as glamorous as best-selling records but surprisingly lucrative. It made him a millionaire and he used some of that fortune to buy into the club and become its chairman. I had known Francis for more than 30 years, and spent a good part of that time chasing him around football fields when he was one of City's star players. I didn't catch him very often but I managed to kick him a few times. Long after he had finished playing, he was still taking knocks for the club.

They had fallen a long way since the Championship-winning days of Lee, Bell and Summerbee and by Christmas 1996 they were facing relegation to Division Two, having only just come down from the Premiership that season. They couldn't win a game and had gone through four managers since the start of the campaign. They were becoming the butt of every football fan's jokes. Even the Radio 1 DJ and Tottenham fan Simon Mayo was jumping on the bandwagon during his morning show.

'Why are the England team changing their strip?' he asked his listeners. 'So Manchester City won't be the only football outfit guaranteed to be useless after Christmas,' was the reply. Well, humour is often cruel but it was the City fans themselves who were cracking most of the jokes, and they were the cruellest of all.

The club had an unofficial Internet site run by fans which, alongside match reports and items of City news, regularly carried City jokes. The offerings were endless. For example: A City fan and a friend are in the pub when the fan's dog comes in and barks at him twice. 'Oh dear,' he says. 'We've lost the big match. My dog always barks twice when we lose.'

'That's amazing,' says the friend. 'What does he do when they win?'

'I don't know, I've only had him a year.'

Not the most original jokes in the world and certainly not the funniest, but they illustrated all too painfully how the club, and its fans, were suffering.

City's position showed just how quickly things can go wrong for a club. Only four years earlier they were an impressive outfit in the top division. They finished fourth in the league and were looking down on their rivals Manchester United. Unfortunately, the following season the fortunes of the two clubs started to move in opposite directions. United set about winning the League; City dropped into the relegation zone. They went through a succession of managers, including Peter Reid and Brian Horton. Then came Alan Ball, who had the misfortune of taking them into the First Division.

At that point things deteriorated and developed a sense of farce. After a disastrous start to the season when relegation looked more likely than instant promotion back to the Premier League, Ball was sacked. Asa Hartford took over temporarily while the club looked for a new manager. Very quickly, they appointed the ex-Manchester United and England international Steve Coppell, but just as quickly he resigned. Steve said he was ill and unable to cope with the job while his health was suffering. To be fair, it was a very difficult job at that time because the club was in turmoil. His resignation was a huge blow.

Phil Neal was then appointed as caretaker while the search went on for a long-term replacement. Unfortunately, that simply led to more embarrassment for the club. They were publicly linked to some high-profile managers who then turned them down, bringing ridicule on City. Dave Bassett was offered the job and accepted it. Then he slept on it and decided the next morning that he didn't want it after all. He decided, for reasons he couldn't quite explain, that it didn't feel right for him. He preferred to stay at Crystal Palace. Ironically, within a few months he was to take over my old job at Nottingham Forest. Even more ironically perhaps, Steve Coppell then took over Bassett's old job at Palace. No doubt his health had recovered by then, but there were still many people who saw it as another slap in the face for City.

George Graham was another big name to be offered the City job and turn it down. The club had also spoken to Howard Wilkinson, who had just been sacked by Leeds, but he too felt it wasn't quite right for him. The list of rejections was growing and with it the embarrassment. The jokers were given more ammunition. One story went that Francis Lee was going to his local supermarket when he saw an old lady struggling with five heavy bags of shopping. 'Can you manage, dear?' he asked.

'Of course I can manage,' she snapped. 'But there's no way I'm taking the City job.'

With so many public rejections, the directors wanted to be sure of their man before putting the club's reputation on the line again. I sympathised with this because sometimes managers can use such offers for their own ends. It's not unheard of for people to string a club along without ever having any intention of accepting the job. It can get them publicity and make them look more marketable. It can even help them negotiate a better deal with their existing club. I'm not saying that any of the people approached by City had done that but, nevertheless, the experiences had left the club bruised and for the sake of its morale and credibility it couldn't afford another public rejection.

It wasn't surprising, therefore, that when the phone did finally ring in my living room after leaving Forest, it wasn't anyone from Manchester City on the line. Instead, it was a journalist friend of mine who also just happened to be close to Francis Lee. He asked me tentatively how I was doing and what my plans were. I replied that I was looking forward to Christmas with my family.

'Had any job offers?' he asked.

'A few from abroad but nothing that really appealed. There's nothing in the pipeline.'

'Would you be interested in the City job if it were offered?'

'Of course. I would be interested in any job. I've got to work. I can't afford to retire.'

And that was that.

It was obvious I was being sounded out before the club would commit itself to a formal approach. Clubs will do this quite often, especially if they've had their fingers burned already as City had. Sure enough, before too long I got a call from Francis Lee offering me the job. He was on holiday in Barbados at the time and, looking at the snow outside my window, I was hoping he might invite me out to the Caribbean to negotiate the contract in the sunshine. Unfortunately, he didn't become a millionaire making gestures like that. Instead, we discussed the arrangements on the phone.

He reassured me about the backroom stability at the club. After the nightmare I had been through at Forest, that was very important to me. He told me the finances were sound and there would be a rights issue coming up within a few weeks. That would bring in several million pounds which would be made available for new players.

Lee had plans for the club which I thought were exciting. His ambition was to get back into the Premiership as quickly as possible and the resources were being made available to do it. He wanted to recapture some of the glories of the Sixties and Seventies when the club enjoyed its greatest period of success under Joe Mercer and Malcolm Allison. Their achievement was absolutely marvellous, especially winning the League back in 1968. What's more, it was all done with the kind of swashbuckling style you would expect from Malcolm Allison.

I remembered it all particularly well because I played against them on the day they clinched the title. I was playing left-back for Newcastle and a certain Francis Lee was playing on the right wing for City. We had nothing in particular to play for but they needed a win to clinch the Championship. They beat us 4–3 at St James' Park in a marvellous game of football. They won the League Cup in 1976 but there had been nothing since.

Given the position of the club – 21st in Division One – the lack of stability on the playing side and the huge expectations of the fans, managing City was described by some as the job from hell. I knew what they meant but I still saw it as a marvellous opportunity. Despite all they had been through, they were still getting an average gate of 27,000. That made them a big club with an even bigger potential, as far as I was concerned.

After leaving Forest, I would have liked to be out of work for a few months to unwind and take a complete break, but life never works out that neatly. Job offers don't come along every day. Having spoken to Lee and accepted the job in principle, I then spoke to the other directors to discuss the finer points of the contract. That all went very smoothly. I asked if I could bring in my own people if necessary and they were OK about that. I told them I wasn't going to come in and sack people just for the sake of it – I would give people the chance to work with me and we would take it from there. I also said that if they wanted to get rid of people then I would prefer them to do it before I arrived. It was all resolved very quickly. In the end, Tony Book left the club but that had nothing to do with me.

I arrived at Manchester City expecting the playing side to be in a bad way, but it turned out to be even worse than I feared. Everyone kept saying the club's lowly position was a false one and the team was better than that. The fact remained, however, that they were down there and we had to get out of trouble. Unfortunately, severe weather led to some games being postponed and so it was two weeks before I saw my new team in action. You can learn a lot about players watching them in training, you can even get a useful insight chatting to them socially, watching them play golf or relaxing in a bar, but it's only by seeing them in a first-team game that you really get to know them.

My first game was at home to Crystal Palace. Before the kick-off, I was formally introduced to the fans with as much showbiz ritual as the club could muster. The public address announcer must have been getting used to all this, having gone through it with so many managers in the previous few years, but he managed to convey an admirable amount of enthusiasm. 'This is a special day for Manchester City,' he told the crowd in dramatic tones. 'So let's give a special welcome to our new manager, Mr Frank Clark.' I walked out onto the pitch with my arms outstretched above my head in a dramatic gesture of triumph – well, as near to dramatic as I could muster anyway. It's the kind of thing Stuart Pearce loves doing but it makes me feel a little uncomfortable.

Nevertheless, I was determined to signal a new era of hope and confidence. It seemed to go down well. The reception was thunderous, disconcertingly so. They cheered so loud that for a minute I thought Noel Gallagher must have walked out behind me waving his cheque book, but when I looked round there was only me. That was a sobering thought in itself. Just me and the limitless expectations of nearly 30,000 screaming football fans desperate for success. It was a huge pressure of sorts, but a good feeling all the same. Their applause wasn't just the routine politeness you might expect on such an occasion. I felt there was a genuine sense of relief and gratitude that someone had at last agreed to manage their club.

After the hype of the introduction, however, the game was something of a disappointment. City took the lead through an own goal, but then threw it away when they failed to defend a free-kick properly. The team had thrown away several leads that season and were beginning to get something of a complex about it, so much so that instead of giving them confidence, going a goal in front tended to make them more nervous and hesitant. The same thing happened in my next game, away at Huddersfield. Again we took the lead and again we let them equalise through failing to defend a free-kick properly. There was obviously a lot of work to be done.

My assessment after seeing the side in action over two games was quite simple: we just weren't good enough. I knew that we couldn't get where we wanted to go with the squad we had. There were two ways to address this. We had to bring in new players, but while we searched for them we also had to get more out of the squad we had. There was certainly some potential. There were seven or eight players who were internationals. Steve Lomas played for Northern Ireland, Eddie McGoldrick for the Republic. Andy Dibble and Kit Symons played for Wales, Uwe Rosler was a German international and then there was the Crown Prince himself, Georgi Kinkladze. The Georgian star was possibly the most talented player ever to wear a Manchester City shirt. With that array of experience, it was understandable that people felt the club should be doing better.

It was obvious we had some good players but they had been underachieving. We hoped that was mainly because of the years of uncertainty at the club. I felt that if we could bring some stability, we could get an improvement from them. Francis Lee had obviously worked hard at getting the commercial side of the club in good condition, but very little had been done to create a professional attitude on the playing side. I sensed this as soon as I started.

Some people were playing as if they hadn't realised the gravity of the club's situation and the absolute necessity to play winning football. Too many of them were indulging themselves by playing just for their own enjoyment. Maybe it was because they had reached a point where they felt the team wasn't going to win anyway and they just wanted to make the most of their own game. Whatever the reason, I felt it was necessary to go back to basics and make Manchester City a football club again with a good club spirit. To be fair, it wasn't all the fault of the players. They weren't being treated with the respect they deserved as professional footballers. It manifested itself in all sorts of ways.

The club had very good training facilities but they were run by the council and the public had access to them at all times. That doesn't create a very professional atmosphere. The restaurant where the players were expected to eat after training was franchised out and was expected to make a profit. Consequently, it was chips with everything with no thought given to the players' nutritional needs as professional athletes. There wasn't enough training kit either. It wasn't a case of each player having his own kit with his initials on as it is at most top clubs – they had to go scratching round picking up bits and pieces wherever they could. The team bus was archaic and totally unsuitable. It was shabby and there were no facilities on it at all to occupy the players on long journeys. No food was available after the game, yet there was always beer on offer. It was ridiculous.

The joke tellers should have been using things like these for their material. They may seem trivial but most players have been around other clubs and they know how professionals should operate. If the club doesn't reach those standards and treats them in a shoddy way, it makes them feel undervalued and that shows in their performance. If they're treated like a Sunday league pub team, there's every chance they'll act like one.

I set about changing things as quickly as possible. We got them proper kit and I explored why we had such an ancient bus. It turned out we had been with the same company for 60 years. I called in their managing director and he was amazed to find we weren't happy. I reeled off our complaints and he said that was the first bit of feedback he had ever had. He gave us a better coach straightaway as a temporary measure and then set about getting one exactly as we wanted. Beer on the coach was banned and we set about providing proper food.

Another problem was the promotional demands made on the squad. Supporters and even some club officials seemed to think the players should be at everybody's disposal. Manchester City has lots of supporters' clubs all over the country, which is great. I got along to as many of them as I could. They also liked players to attend, to say a few words and answer questions. That, too, is a very good thing. It's only right that players give something back to the supporters who make the game possible. However, the timing has to be right because the game comes first. When I first arrived at the club, it was considered acceptable to send first-team players along to these meetings no matter when they were. We had occasions where players were going along to some Thursday night meetings, having a few drinks and chatting the night away with fans. We also had situations where first-team players were being made to do personal appearances on the Friday afternoon before big games.

It was ridiculous and I stopped it immediately. Apart from taking people's concentration away from the game, it sent out the wrong message. It implied that the game wasn't that important and didn't have to be taken that seriously. The other thing that struck me straightaway was the lack of team spirit and even club spirit. I felt this too was affecting people's morale and self-respect, not just the players' but that of everyone else connected with the club. Part of the problem was that everyone was spread out on three different sites. The players reported to the training ground, the commercial staff were at the ground at Maine Road and then the office staff were in a house about quarter of a mile away. It meant people saw very little of each other and there was very little sense that this was a single unit pulling together. I thought this was a weakness in the set-up and potentially damaging. You have such a huge spread of salaries at a football club that it's easy to create an 'us and them' atmosphere. I wanted to dispel that right away.

At Forest everyone was on the same site and got to know each other very well. They all ate at the same club canteen. I loved the atmosphere that created. You would have players, groundsmen and secretaries all meeting in the same place. There would always be a lot of banter between them and it created a great sense of togetherness. I often used to sit in the canteen and just soak it all up. It was a great strength of the club. I wanted to create something similar at City because it was obvious the place was crying out for it.

It turned out they hadn't had a party for 17 years. No wonder spirits were low! We decided to hold a belated Christmas party at the back of the Kippax stand. Alan Hill, who came with me to City from Forest, organised it all. We got the Beatles tribute band the Fab Four to play for us. Oasis must have already been booked.

We got everybody there, the players and their wives, the office and commercial staff, coaches, cleaners, everybody.

They all loved it. Given what we had been used to at Forest, to us it was a pleasant but quite ordinary event, but to everyone at City this was marvellous. They had never had anything like it before and thought it was one of the best things that had ever happened to the club. There obviously hadn't been too many highlights in the previous 20 years.

Having laid down standards as to how the players were treated, we were then able to lay down standards as to how they should behave. Deep down they all knew how a football club should be run and how they should train, but someone had to set the parameters. They had to learn about discipline on and off the field and about the need to play winning football as a team. The players were desperate for a lifeline. They didn't want to be losing every week, so they were eager to respond. Just by treating them properly, we were able to raise morale.

This was certainly the case with one very enigmatic player who rarely smiled when I arrived at the club. Sometimes I would catch Georgi Kinkladze looking at me out of the corner of his eye as if to say: 'Well, I'm not too sure about you.' I wanted to build the team around Kinkladze because that's the ideal way to get the best out of him. He's an incredible talent. Technically, he's excellent. He runs at people with the ball at his feet and goes past them as if they aren't there. He has excellent vision, good passing ability, great balance and control. He passes the ball into the net, he doesn't just lash it. He's a bit one-footed, but then so were Maradona and Puskas.

I felt that if we could harness his incredible talent for the benefit of the team and surround him with good players, then we would have every chance of being successful. To do that, though, we had to develop his own game and improve his relationship with the others both on and off the pitch. I talked to him a great deal about improving his decision-making. He needed to learn when to lay the ball off and use his team-mates to help himself and the rest of the side. There were occasions when he would run at people and things would open up. Another player might be in a great position to score if only Georgi could see him and pass the ball. Too often, however, Kinkladze wasn't seeing those chances or if he did, he ignored them and the opportunity was lost.

I explained to him that he was a potential matchwinner but he didn't have to do it all on his own. Great players know how to get the best out of the danger they create by using other players when the circumstances demand it. We had to play as a team. All players want to be successful, but when their side is struggling they can sometimes turn in on themselves and play for themselves rather than the good of the team. To be fair to Gio, he wasn't the only one going down that route, but because of his spectacular talent it was more obvious when he did.

Kinkladze was very responsive. He didn't resent advice and he was very professional. He wanted to be a world-class player and I think he realised that we could help him get there. Until that time, I think the adulation he had received since he arrived at City made him feel that everything was all right with his game and he didn't have to get any better.

He was a bit sloppy when we arrived. If anyone was going to be late for training, it was him. He could also be a bit lazy on the pitch. He certainly didn't like running if he didn't have the ball at his feet and I thought there was a certain amount of resentment towards him from some of the squad. It's obviously very difficult for foreign players. They don't understand English very well and it's hard for them to keep up with the dressing-room banter. They can become outsiders and then they appear stand-offish, which makes things worse.

I made it clear to the others that Gio would get no special favours. We showed that in our actions by fining him when he was late and he got his fair share of tellings-off when he'd made mistakes. He accepted it without a murmur. However, I also stressed to the others that he is a special player. He could win matches for them and for us. It was a question of pulling together. Every member of the team was bringing something of their own to the communal effort and together they could be successful. We had these conversations individually with players or as a group, whether Gio was there or not.

There didn't seem to be any major problem. Georgi made more of an effort to be a part of the group and in response the other lads started to warm to him more. After a few weeks I felt there was a sense of coming together and I hoped that would soon be reflected in our results.

The two games against Palace and Huddersfield were disappointing, but at least we hadn't lost. Now we needed to start winning a few to really get ourselves going. Our first victory arrived on cue in the third round of the FA Cup away at lowly Brentford. It wasn't a particularly memorable game except that for once we managed to take the lead and hold on to it. It was only a 1–0 victory, thanks to a Nicky Summerbee goal, but it was enough to give us a boost in confidence and we were on our way.

We got a bit of a run together and suddenly everything looked a lot brighter. The players had an extra spring in their step. People were praising them and telling them they weren't such a bad team after all. Everyone would rather be praised than criticised and they made the most of it. That made it easier for us to get them on our side and adopt our ways.

Then came a fantastic performance that sent expectations zooming. After grinding out another workmanlike draw against Sheffield United, we went to Oxford for a Sunday match in front of the Sky television cameras. With a revitalised enthusiasm, Georgi Kinkladze set about showing what a world-class performer he could be. Oxford had only conceded nine goals in their previous 14 home games but they were powerless to stop Gio that day.

He ran the match and scored two stunning goals in our 4–1 victory. We demolished Oxford and showed everyone, not least ourselves, how good we could be. Even the home fans had to applaud. Kinkladze was voted man of the match but I was just as pleased with the overall performance of the team. They had gelled together well and played for each other, which was what we had been trying to get them to do.

With the fans so desperate for success, I suppose it was inevitable that the victory, together with the fact that we were unbeaten since I arrived, set many people thinking about still making the play-offs. It meant closing a gap of 11 points with only 17 games to go. I felt that was a tall order so I tried to inject a sense of realism at the risk of sounding negative. The truth was that we weren't quite good enough and I was still more concerned with getting out of the relegation zone.

The squad lacked quality in depth. Previous managers had used youngsters who weren't really ready for first-team football but had to play because there was no one else available. I told the chairman and the directors that there were two kinds of players I would have to buy. Primarily, I would be looking for young players who could take us out of Division One but who would also be good enough to perform in the Premier League. However, I would also have to settle for a few relatively short-term buys to strengthen the squad immediately and help us gain promotion.

We couldn't afford to sit around and wait or we would be in Division Two, in spite of our mini-revival. We bought Paul Beesley from Leeds as a short-term measure. He was 30 but he did a great job for us. We also got Kevin Horlock from Swindon and Ged Brannan from Tranmere, both young players with a lot to offer. As soon as I arrived I could see the need for another quality goalkeeper, and for that I turned to my old club Nottingham Forest and signed Tommy Wright.

With the arrival of new players and the improvement in our existing squad, the results continued to go our way. We thrashed Southend and Swindon, both 3–0, and by the time we won 3–1 away at Bradford, the fans and the media were starting to hail us as the new-look City, unrecognisable from the demoralised outfit of a few months earlier. The supporters who travelled to watch us win 3–1 away at West Brom were even more impressed. 'Brazil, it's just like watching Brazil,' they chanted in a touching display of how a sense of loyalty can overcome all sense of reality.

The results picked up so well that for a time it looked as though we might indeed make the play-offs. In the end, though, it wasn't to be. We were left needing to get about 20 points from the last eight games. We had made a lot of progress in the four months we had been there, but not that much. We still didn't have enough strength in depth. We lost Beesley with an injury against Birmingham and that was a huge blow to us. He had had a tremendous impact on the team since he came in. We also lost Kinkladze through injury, which took away our main creative force for some vital games.

Then because of international matches and postponements, we ended up having to play seven games in only 20 days and we just didn't have the resources to cope with it. We faded towards the end but at least we had done enough to restore some self-respect to the club. We had silenced most of the jokers. Kinkladze was looking happy and even had a smile on his face. The fans were even happier and were queuing in their thousands to buy tickets for the following season. They were full of optimism and so was I. We were all about to be brought crashing down to earth.

CHAPTER 14

Don't Look Back in Anger

When Ruud Gullit was sacked by Chelsea, the first he knew of it was when he read the news on Teletext. Well, I think I can go one better than that. When I was sacked by Manchester City, I heard about it on the radio. It sounds callous but it was fairly typical of the club at the time. It was leaking worse than the *Titanic*, and following a similar self-destruct course to disaster.

A lot of people, including Manchester City fans, were angry on my behalf over the way the whole thing was handled. Many were kind enough to write to me and say so. But to be honest, farcical though it was, it didn't upset me that much – not nearly as much as my failure to bring those magnificent fans the success they so richly deserve. The question everybody wanted answering was why were Manchester City going from bad to worse no matter who the manager seemed to be? Why could no one stop the rot? Having seen the club closely from the inside as I did, it's not that difficult to understand.

Manchester City's fortunes during my 13 months as manager were dominated by four main elements: the sale of key players by Francis Lee and Alan Ball before I arrived; tactical errors on my part, particularly in relation to Georgi Kinkladze; the inability of players to cope with the club's level of expectation; and infighting among a divided board of directors. The first three amounted to short-term problems and could have been put right with a little time and a lot of hard work. The fourth element was far more damaging to the long-term good of the club. In fact, there was no way it could ever enjoy long-term success while the boardroom divisions existed. I don't want to be seen to be making excuses, so before I explain what was wrong inside the club, let me deal with my own failings first.

The problems I inherited were easy to recognise but difficult to solve. City had just been relegated from the Premier League. It meant a massive drop in revenue and so Francis Lee and the manager at the time, Alan Ball, tried to cut the wage bill by selling off some of the highest earners, people like Niall Quinn, Garry Flitcroft, Keith Curle and a few others.

The policy seemed to be to get rid of those on big contracts and replace them with youngsters. It was similar to the idea Alex Ferguson had at Manchester United when he sold the likes of Hughes, Kanchelskis and Sharpe and then replaced them with people like Scholes, Beckham and Butt. Unfortunately, unlike the situation across town at United, the plan had one major fault: the City youngsters weren't nearly good enough for the job.

That left the club in great difficulty on the playing side.

The most influential half of the team had gone without adequate replacements being found. If you rip the heart out of any side it will struggle, and that's what happened at City. The downward slide was then compounded by the fact that everyone involved with the club still expected instant success. This level of expectation presented me with one of my most difficult problems because too many of the players I inherited couldn't cope with it.

I'm sure many fans will find the concept of psychological factors preventing players performing as somewhat nebulous, almost offensive, seeing as they're so highly paid. Let me try to explain it further with a few examples from other areas of the game. Supporters at every club will have come across young players who emerge when someone is injured and do really well for a few matches. Everyone looks at them and thinks: 'He'll be a really good player when he gets a chance for a long stretch in the team.' Then that chance appears but somehow they don't quite make it. They get dropped and fade away and everyone wonders why. The reason is simply that they can't cope with the level of expectation placed upon them as a regular member of the team. When they're first given a chance as a replacement for an injured player, everyone makes allowances for the fact that they're young and inexperienced. No one expects them to be as good as the first-team regular and there is very little pressure on them. They respond to that sense of freedom and play well.

However, if they become a first-team regular, the level of expectation rises and allowances are no longer made. Some players can't cope with this. Most of them then drift out of the game, so it's hard to give examples that people will recognise. The classic case for me was the goalkeeper

Barry Daines. He was understudy to the great Pat Jennings when he was at Spurs. When Pat was injured and Barry replaced him, he did very well. But when Pat retired and Barry got his chance, he couldn't cope with the burden of being number one.

You get a similar situation with some utility players. They're great when they're brought in as a stopgap because injuries have robbed you of every left-back or striker or whatever. They do well for a few games until the fans forget that they're only standing in and start expecting them to perform like a regular in that position. Again, they can't cope with the level of expectation; they lose form and have to be moved to another position to get the best out of them. Tony Vaughan was a little like that for me at Manchester City, and there was a touch of it in Alfie Haaland when I was at Forest.

If you have one or two players with this kind of temperament then it's not too much of a problem. Unfortunately, when I was at City we seemed to have half a team of them. City fans will appreciate this if they cast their minds back to what happened when I first arrived at the club; suddenly we took off on a really good run. I think I can rightly claim that was partly down to the changes I introduced and the fact that I was able to give back to the players a measure of self-esteem. There was another major factor at work, however. At that time, the team had hit rock bottom and the fans had lost all hope that they would achieve anything. This gave the players a peculiar sense of freedom. There was no burden of expectation. It enabled them to put a good run together.

Winning a few games changed all that. At the start of the new season, we were suddenly expected to get automatic promotion. I knew this was happening and during the summer I worked hard to build up the players' confidence and self-belief. I stressed that we had removed all the problems they had experienced during the previous few years. They were treated properly, the club had a stable management and we had spent £8 million on new players who could give us that extra lift towards promotion. They should have every reason to feel confident and to go out and perform as they knew they could. For a while everything looked promising and in the pre-season games we were really full of ourselves. We were playing attractive, free-flowing, winning football.

I told the players I wanted to start the season with a bang: 'Let's get the crowd behind us. Instead of allowing Maine Road to be an intimidating place for us, let's make it an intimidating place for the opposition.' Their confidence seemed high and everything seemed to be going well. Unfortunately, I had not counted on their lack of resolve and it took me by surprise. I can pinpoint the moment it blew apart: our opening game at home to Portsmouth. We started off well and everything looked all right. Then after 15 minutes Portsmouth scored. The effect was amazing. It was like someone had stuck a pin in a balloon. All the confidence drained away and all that free-flowing football just disappeared. I could see the tension creeping into the players as the game wore on.

We fought back but could only manage a draw. We played another home game against Tranmere but again could only manage a draw. We lost away at Sunderland and then again at Charlton. We should have won at least two of those games and what made it particularly hard to take was that we were ahead in three of our opening matches but hadn't been able to hold onto the advantage.

So the lack of self-belief I found when I first arrived at the club was re-emerging, but this time it was more difficult to counter. I no longer had the advantage of being new. I didn't want to criticise too much because when results are going badly through lack of confidence, it can be counter-productive. Instead, I wanted to keep their spirits up. I tried to motivate them as individuals by talking to them personally, encouraging them and supporting them. I told them they were far better than the results were suggesting. I made sure they always knew as much as possible about the opposition because it's important to players that they feel they've been well prepared. I tried always to give them a solid framework so they could go out knowing that everything possible had been done to enable them to get the best out of themselves. However, I stressed that I had sorted out all the behind-the-scenes difficulties that they had previously had to endure.

I pointed out to them that they could no longer seek excuses outside of themselves. The only problems were the ones that existed inside their heads and it was up to all of us together to put that right.

We never managed to do that and it turned the crowd against us. If we weren't ahead within 20 minutes you could feel the frustration build up around the ground. Soon it would turn into outright hostility. The first bad pass, the first mistimed tackle and they would be on the players' backs straightaway. It got to the point where some of the team were almost frightened to play at home. It's perhaps unfair to single out individuals, but there were a few instances that illustrated the problem very well. In

Top players need great mental resilience. Shortly after suffering the humiliation of an early Coca-Cola Cup exit against Bradford, Steve Stone was scoring for England against Switzerland. (*Colorsport*)

Pelé, perhaps the greatest ever. He was the hardest footballer I ever played against; you couldn't stay at the top as long as he did without being able to look after yourself. (*Colorsport*)

Matt Le Tissier: the typical talented enigma. Although able to light up many a dull afternoon with his stunning efforts for Southampton, he has never made it as an England regular. (*Empics*)

Because of boardroom interference during the disruptive Forest takeover, I was forced into a position where I had to break my word to players like Chris Bart-Williams. I felt my authority was undermined and the team suffered. (*Colorsport*)

The situation came to a head just before Christmas 1996. It had been made impossible for me to manage and I could see no other option but to resign. (*Empics*)

I got a thunderous reception when I arrived at Manchester City. I could feel the limitless expectation of 30,000 screaming fans bearing down on me. *(Colorsport)*

The skilful Georgian, Georgi Kinkladze: I wanted to build the Manchester City side around him but, because of a tactical error on my part, it didn't work. (*Empics*)

Francis Lee was unfairly blamed for the problems at Manchester City, when in truth the reasons lay in the club's disunity. Colin Barlow, one of Lee's supporters, is on the left. (*Empics*)

When the crowd's expectations aren't met, they can often turn against their own players. Kit Symons got so much stick I had to take the captaincy from him to relieve the pressure. (*Colorsport*)

Ged Brannan (number 7) scored twice for Manchester City against Forest in September 1997 thanks to tactics practised on the training pitch. Sadly, our tactics weren't always so successful. (*Empics*)

Every manager prepares for a game differently. Brian Clough never bothered with tactics or worried about the other side. Don Revie discussed the opposition in minute detail. Both approaches were spectacularly successful. (*Empics/Colorsport*)

Players can make seemingly ridiculous demands. Lars Bohinen wanted about 50 clauses in his contract, including one about reflooring his house. (*Colorsport*)

The media circus can make life intolerable for players and managers. Even something as trivial as Jason Lee's hairstyle led to a frenzy of headlines and made-up stories. (*Empics*)

I would often open the papers and see false stories about Steve Stone or Georgi Kinkladze being sold for vast amounts of money. I have also been the subject of erroneous newspaper reports – once even that I was being touted as the new England manager! (*Colorsport*)

Most neutral fans were pleased to see Arsenal win the league in 1998 because it broke the monotony of Manchester United's string of successes. Big clubs are now so powerful they're in danger of making the game too predictable. (*Colorsport*)

Alex Ferguson's irrepressible desire to win provoked an outburst from Newcastle manager Kevin Keegan at the end of the 1995-96 season. My Forest team were due to play both clubs in the run-in and there had been reports in the press, supposedly emanating from Alex, that we might go easy on the Geordies because of Stuart Pearce's testimonial. (*Empics*)

four matches shortly before I was sacked, I played the same back three of Kit Symons, Murtaz Shelia and Ian Brightwell. In the two away games, Symons and Brightwell were magnificent. They gave nothing away and we won 3–0 at Portsmouth and drew 0–0 at Tranmere.

In the intervening home games, however, they were absolutely awful. The only difference was the tension they felt playing in front of demanding and hostile home fans. It wasn't just them. Richard Edghill was also feeling the pressure and his game suffered. Ged Brannan was another. He'd been used to playing in front of crowds of about 6,000 at Tranmere and found 30,000 angry City fans intimidating. There were others, too, who would hide from the ball when things started getting bad. Passes would go astray.

Many of the players were subjected to increasing hostility as the season wore on. Things got so bad with Kit Symons that I felt obliged to remove the captaincy from him. The problem came to a head when we were beaten at Stockport. Kit bore the brunt of the criticism, which was unfair because he wasn't playing that badly. He said he was happy to continue as captain but inwardly I think he was glad to be rid of it. He certainly played better afterwards. The crowd weren't on his back quite so much because he no longer had the responsibility of leading the other players.

The captaincy became something of a curse for the players who took it on. Kevin Horlock only lasted five minutes before being injured and ruled out for three months. Gerard Wiekens then took over only to suffer a similar fate and missed the next six weeks. Ian Brightwell was next up. He wasn't a great leader but he was happy to do it and at least he managed to survive.

This helps to explain why we used 32 players in 31 games during the 1997–98 season; something that understandably puzzled many City fans at the time. I had inherited a large squad of about 40 players. That sounds good but too many of them were of the same mediocre standard. I would have preferred to have just 20 outstanding players. When we made a poor start to the season, I felt I had to shuffle the pack. I was looking for the right combination of talent and mental toughness, but it was difficult to find. Some players who had the talent didn't have the character to cope with the expectations of the crowd; and those that had the character didn't always have the talent.

But looking back, I admit it's difficult to tell if the changes were the cause or the effect of our failure; were they necessary because of the bad results or did they help to cause the bad results? It's a chicken-and-egg situation, but you usually find that if a team is doing badly it tends to use a lot of different players. Maybe I did change it too much, but then if we had carried on losing with the same players we would have been criticised for that as well.

Injuries to key players were another major factor in our decline. Early on in the season we lost our two main strikers, Lee Bradbury and Uwe Rosler, to long-term injuries. This was a major blow because our main problem throughout the season was that we couldn't score enough goals. Our defensive record compared with any team in the division, but that's not enough if you aren't putting them in at the other end. The club's perilous financial situation didn't help in this respect. I had been told there was an emergency fund of £1.5 million available if we were suddenly hit by injuries. Then when I needed it I was told it wasn't there. It had been swallowed up in wages and signing-on fees.

The situation at Forest provides a good comparison. They, too, were a club with a high level of expectation. As City struggled, they got off to a great start, winning their four opening matches. Then they hit a bad patch and found it difficult to grind out results. As at City, the fans were furious and gave their players a terrible time. Kevin Campbell in particular took so much stick that manager Dave Bassett had to appeal in the local paper for people to lay off him.

There were two crucial differences between Forest and City, however. The first was the mental toughness of the players. At Forest, people like Colin Cooper were very strong and could ride out the hardest of times. That was one of the reasons I wanted to sign him for City, but Forest wouldn't sell. Campbell too had grown used to unfair treatment from the fans and had the strength of character to deal with it, while Pierre van Hooijdonk was so arrogant and laid-back the whole thing would wash over him anyway! City just didn't have players with that kind of resolve. It's no good saying they should have, for the money they're paid; if they don't have it they don't have it and that's that.

The other big difference in Forest's favour was that Campbell and van Hooijdonk remained uninjured for the whole season. Forest didn't always play well, as we've seen, yet they continued to get results because one of those two would be able to snatch a goal. It meant they were winning the tight games; it might only be 1–0 but they were winning them. For too much of the season, with

Bradbury and Rosler missing, we didn't have anyone who could get that precious goal out of nothing and it meant we ended up losing most of the tight games.

We did have a potential matchwinner, of course, in Kinkladze, but we didn't make the most of him and that was down to a tactical error on my part. When I first arrived at City I made an immediate decision about Kinkladze. I felt it was best to play him as far away from our goal and as near to the opposition's as possible. That basically meant playing 4–4–2 with Georgi as one of the two main strikers. We had played that way until the end of the season. He partnered Rosler and it proved very successful. We might have made the play-offs if the team had played that way all year.

Then, during the close season, I decided to deviate from that formation. I thought it was a limited way to play and would not be good enough to win us automatic promotion. Kinkladze tends to drift around, so if you put him up front it's often like playing with only one real striker. On many occasions I felt we were an attacker short when the ball would fall in the opposition box. At the same time I thought we could get more out of Kinkladze if we gave him a free role behind two orthodox strikers.

I felt this would make us much stronger in attack and make us real Championship contenders. In fact, it went the other way. We tied ourselves up in knots trying to accommodate Kinkladze. If you play him in midfield it means the other midfielders have to be very strong defensively because he's a liability when he loses the ball. The system suited Kinkladze perfectly because it gave him great freedom, but it didn't suit the other players and it didn't work.

It was my fault because I was trying to be too clever. If we had stuck to the original 4-4-2 with Kinkladze up front, we would have done much better. I doubt that we'd have won automatic promotion but we might have made the play-offs. Perhaps I, too, was a victim of the club's level of expectation. To have set our sights on a play-off place at the start of the season would have appeared unambitious. Indeed, to have only made the play-offs would have seemed like failure to many people, and so I suppose I felt the need to go all out for the Championship. It was a mistake and, coupled with the injuries and too many players' inability to cope with the club's level of expectation, it led to our downfall. We might have been able to deal with any one of those problems, but not all three together.

I paid the price when our failings were put on full display in a local derby match against Bury at Maine Road in February 1998. The game carried enormous symbolism for City fans. It was an embarrassment for them to be even playing Bury, a small and until recently insignificant neighbour. We played poorly and were beaten. It was more than the fans could stand. The humiliation of defeat turned to anger and their patience snapped. There were demonstrations demanding that I should be sacked and that Francis Lee should stand down as chairman.

I have no complaints about that. We had faced enormous problems but nevertheless we should have done better. I dare say City fans won't have lost too much sleep over my departure, but they ought to be concerned about the way the sacking took place. It illustrated the reason the club had suffered and would continue to suffer, irrespective of who was managing it, unless important changes were made.

It was said that the former Manchester City chairman

Peter Swales joined the board in the 1970s after over-hearing a couple of directors talking about how internal strife was damaging the club. He believed he could put it right. In his 20-year reign he went through 11 managers trying to bring the club the success it craved. None of them succeeded. Then Swales stepped down after a bitter battle to oust him. The internal strife he thought he could remove was as strong as ever.

Francis Lee was swept to power on a wave of enthusiasm after a lot of manoeuvring behind the scenes by different factions. He promised a new dawn of success and unity. It didn't work out that way. Under Lee, the club went through managers at a rate that made Swales' reign seem pedestrian. By the time Lee resigned after four turbulent years, another six managers had been appointed and the club had been relegated twice. The internal squabbling was as strong as ever. Just as it had played a major part in sweeping Lee to power, it had proceeded to sweep him out again.

When clubs do badly, it is customary to blame the manager. That may often be justified but surely it can't explain Manchester City's failure over 25 years. A club might be unlucky with one or two managers, but no club could be so cursed as to appoint 17 duffers. Don't forget many of those duffers have been successful elsewhere. Alan Ball had done well with limited resources at Southampton, Peter Reid became a hero at Sunderland, and when I was at Forest I was voted Manager of the Year by my Premier League peers.

The truth is that over any one season the manager of the time might be blamed for poor performances, but if you want to understand the long-term decline of

Manchester City you have to look much further than that. You have to look at the never-ending disunity that existed at boardroom level during those years. Different factions fought for supremacy and put their own interests above the interests of the club. While I was there, the infighting amounted to a cancer eating away at the soul of Manchester City. I have never seen anything like it.

The boardroom structure at City at that time was unusual because no one had overall control. Francis Lee was chairman but he only had a relatively small shareholding of about 10 per cent. JD Sports owned 19 per cent of the shares, while Stephen Boler of Limelight Kitchens owned 24 per cent but didn't have a direct involvement because he spent most of his time in Africa working on his game reserve.

David Bernstein was the chairman of the clothing chain, French Connection, and he too had a minority shareholding. There were a number of smaller shareholders and also some people who had been directors in the past but who had been bombed out and still carried with them a resentment about the way they had been treated. There was very little unity between the groups and they were suspicious of each other. This was hidden when we were doing well during my first season, but soon emerged when we started to struggle.

One of the most damaging ways it manifested itself was through stories being leaked to the press. Often the information leaked was only known about at boardroom level, so the leaks had to have come from one or more of the directors. There was a constant stream of stories from early on in the season that Joe Royle was being lined up to take over at City when I was eventually sacked. Even though Royle did eventually succeed me, I don't believe that Francis Lee or the majority of the board were thinking that way when the stories started to break. I think it was a rumour put about for mischievous reasons by disgruntled factions within the club who wanted to cause trouble.

It didn't bother me particularly but it caused me a lot of problems with my staff. No matter how much I tried to reassure them that our destiny lay in our own hands as long as we could get good results, they remained unconvinced. It made it more difficult for them to concentrate on their jobs. Their fears were made worse when stories appeared in the press saying that the board had supposedly decided against sacking me but were going to insist that I changed my backroom team as they were the ones letting me down. This was absolute nonsense. They weren't letting me down and there was no way I would have agreed to offering them as sacrificial lambs.

There were other stories about one of the shareholders, Raymond Donn, trying to get a financial package together to take over the club and oust Francis Lee. It was reported that his group had approached potential managers to take over from me. He was supposedly looking towards Juventus to provide us with some of their coaching skills. I have no reason to believe Mr Donn was doing any of these things and I'm sure he always had the best interests of the club at heart. However, the press were running these articles, so either journalists were making it all up or someone was feeding them information. Whether or not the information was true and Mr Donn was indeed planning something is irrelevant. The point is those stories undermined me, my coaches and, of course, the chairman.

As the tension at the club mounted, the factions became

even more concerned with protecting their interests. One of the most public examples was the way Dennis Tueart was suddenly brought in by John Wardle and David Makin of JD Sports to represent them at the club. This seemed a strange idea to me because I felt everyone involved with the club should be acting together to represent Manchester City, not different groups on the board. The appointment coincided with a reshuffle which meant some of Francis Lee's supporters, Colin Barlow, John Dunkerley and David Holt, were ousted from the board. This obviously weakened Lee's position.

I could understand how the different factions might wonder what was going on. The club averaged 30,000 gates yet still managed to lose something like £3 million. I could understand people wanting reassurance that everything was being managed as well as possible. However, the way to do that properly was for the club to be united and if necessary launch its own internal investigation on behalf of the whole board.

Tueart certainly didn't represent the whole board. His involvement was opposed by Francis Lee, who saw the move as an implicit criticism of him. Tueart didn't help matters by publicly declaring that he was going to look into every aspect of the club to find out where it was going wrong. When he had done that, he would produce a report with a list of recommendations for the board.

The move had no direct impact on me, other than the fact that other people saw him as a threat to me. I didn't see it that way at all. I knew that I would stand or fall on the results on the pitch. I didn't care where Tueart pried because I had nothing to hide. I think his intentions were good and he did some good things. He at least made the effort to turn up for some youth games, which was more than most directors did. I had known Dennis for years and got on quite well with him, but I felt his comments to the press when he was appointed were damaging to the club. When he first came to see me, he asked what he could do to help me. I told him the best thing he could do was to keep his mouth shut and just get on with his job.

I said he couldn't go making statements criticising the club because straightaway they would be seized upon and blown out of all proportion. It would perpetuate the concept of City as a joke outfit that couldn't run its own affairs. He told me he had been misquoted which, given the nature of some of the press, is quite likely. However, I felt he had been naive.

As the results got worse, the infighting escalated. A classic example was an outburst made by David Makin, who was no fan of Francis Lee or me. There was one bizarre episode when Makin called the local radio station GMR during a phone-in and started criticising us both. He sounded like a disgruntled fan as he described Lee as a dictator and called upon him to resign. It was a highly emotional outburst and as a fan he was no doubt entitled to make it. As a major shareholder, it was highly irresponsible. It can't help any organisation to wash its dirty linen in public in that way.

Factually, Makin was way off line. Francis Lee was forthright and many thought he had a massive ego, but it was totally unfair to describe him as a dictator. He could be fiercely tough, but then what successful self-made businessman isn't? He didn't ride roughshod over people and he didn't interfere in team matters. He had an opinion about it but that was understandable given his footballing background. He wasn't very popular with most of the players because of how they perceived his attitude towards them. There were times when I had to put my arms round someone's shoulder and offer a little reassurance after a disagreement with Lee, particularly during contract negotiations. His attitude wasn't always helpful, but then it wasn't particularly significant either.

It's human nature to seek scapegoats when things are going badly. We tell ourselves that if only we got rid of so-and-so then everything will be all right. It helps us to avoid having to face up to the real cause of our difficulties. I believe there was some of that mentality behind Makin's outburst. It might have made him feel better but it was too simplistic to blame Lee alone. No one person was to blame. It was the disunity.

When you understand that, it's easy to see why my dismissal turned into such an embarrassing debacle. If the club had been properly run with a unified board, they would have sacked me on Monday morning and appointed Joe Royle as my successor the same day. That would at least have given him a few days to prepare for the next game on the Wednesday night.

Because there was no cohesion, they bodged the whole thing as different groups jockeyed for position. Instead of sacking me, one faction issued a statement to the press on Monday night saying I had been told that results had to improve. I hadn't been told anything of the sort – not that I needed telling since it was obvious. I wasn't even told they were issuing the statement. Consequently, when I was contacted by the local paper asking for my reaction, I didn't know what they were talking about. It was not only embarrassing for me, it made the club look amateurish and disorganised.

It *was* disorganised, of course, for while one faction was planning my downfall another was allowing me to take Peter Beardsley on a month's loan from Bolton. The club was short of cash and Beardsley would cost more than £30,000 in wages. It was ridiculous to allow me to do this on the day that I was about to be sacked. Beardsley was a fine player but he didn't feature in the plans of my successor Joe Royle and consequently turned out to be a waste of the club's money.

There was a board meeting on Tuesday afternoon when the decision was formally taken to sack me. By this time I was driving up to Sunderland to watch them play Reading, our opponents the following week. I got a phone call from the club secretary Bernard Halford saying the chairman wanted to see me. I offered to turn round and go back. Halford checked with Lee and then told me it could wait until the next morning.

I felt it couldn't be that important and so I carried on. When I got home that night there was a message on my answerphone from a journalist friend of mine, John Richardson. He said he was sorry to have to tell me but there was a terrible story going in his paper, the *Daily Mail*, the following morning saying that I had been sacked and Joe Royle was taking over. He felt it was right that I should know about it. Well, that was obviously more than the club felt.

The following morning I got confirmation when the story was broadcast on GMR by their sports correspondent Andy Buckley. He, too, knew more than I did. About 15 minutes later I got a phone call from Francis Lee asking me to go and see him at his home. I went there and he told me officially. He seemed quite upset. It was quite amicable. He said he hoped we could still be friends and I said of course. I understood the logic of football and I didn't see any purpose in making it a personal issue.

Afterwards, journalists asked me if Lee was just trying to save his own skin by sacking me, but I don't think it was that at all. He was given an ultimatum by other factions of the board. There would have been nothing he could have done. If he had refused, they would have simply outvoted him. Dennis Tueart then met Joe Royle to discuss his appointment.

The disappointing thing from the club's point of view is that the factions on the board were unable to hold ranks for just 12 hours. Lee wanted to tell me that Tuesday night but the other directors told him to wait until the following morning. Lee warned them that the club was incapable of keeping anything secret that long, but they insisted. Sure enough, within hours of the board meeting breaking up the press had the story. The message on my answerphone proved that. The leak must have come from boardroom level. It was ridiculous. You can't run a multi-million-pound organisation that way.

There was very little I or any other manager could have done about the disunity at director level. If during that difficult period of infighting the team had suddenly won ten matches on the trot then the boardroom battles would have apparently ceased and I would probably have kept the job. We would only have been papering over the cracks, however. The factions on the board would still be hostile to each other. All that would have been needed to bring it out was a little bit of failure.

Given time and the backing of a united club, I'm sure at least a dozen of Manchester City's managers over the last 25 years could have been a huge success. The problem was that the boardroom disunity meant no one ever was given enough time. If they didn't achieve instant success, the factions of the board who weren't behind appointing them would start to cause trouble. The hapless manager would be caught in the crossfire of the different groups who were looking for reasons to do each other down. Before long the manager would be sacked to provide an uneasy compromise and the whole silly cycle would begin again. The directors got the chance to score points off each other but the club and the fans were the ultimate losers. It's hard to think of a structure more likely to encourage failure.

Within weeks of arriving at the club, I realised that what it needed to ensure stability and long-term success was for someone to come and take it over completely, not piecemeal the way Francis Lee had done. If there was one person or a united company in charge then they would have the power to clear out all the dead wood and get rid of the ex-directors and hangers-on who put very little into the club yet constantly stirred up trouble. Even more importantly, they would have the strength to stick by managers through rough periods and give them the time needed to build for success.

A club with the kind of problems Manchester City have faced needs time to get back on an even keel. When Alan Ball was sacked, he said I should be given five years to put things right. When I in turn was sacked, I was saying much the same about Joe Royle. I had no axe to grind with Joe. He was a friend and taking over my job didn't affect that in any way. I very much wanted him to succeed.

Unfortunately, in the short term at least, the task was too great. The players didn't become different players simply because a new manager took over. The underachieving continued. Joe brought in a sports psychologist, as I had considered doing before being sacked, but the results remained patchy. In the end, City were relegated.

It was a disaster for the club, but even then I knew that if just for once they kept faith with the manager, then Joe Royle could succeed. Whether that would happen depended on how long the different factions at the club could remain united. When David Bernstein took over as chairman, he quite rightly stressed the need for unity. I have a lot of admiration for him and I knew that if he succeeded in bringing that unity then the club would succeed; if he failed, the club would inevitably fail. It was as simple as that.

Anyone unsure about the folly of constantly changing managers should reflect on where Alan Ball went after his sacking. He took over at Portsmouth when they were bottom of the league. He managed to turn them round. Thanks to his efforts, his new club escaped relegation, thereby helping to send his old club down. It was one of those ironies that football throws up so often. I'm sure Ball took no satisfaction from City's demise. I certainly didn't. I wanted them to do well and still do. I would love to see them up where they belong, competing for the Premier League title. Whether that happens depends as much on the performances of the directors in the boardroom as it does on the players on the pitch.

CHAPTER 15

Behind the Scenes on Match Day

To outsiders, professional footballers may appear pampered and spoiled. Their clubs do so much for them, provide them with the best health care, the best hotels, the best food; and if there's an evening match, we send them to bed for an afternoon nap. In many ways it's an enchanted lifestyle, but don't be deceived into thinking there isn't a price. The day of reckoning comes every week when those same pampered darlings have to go out and perform in front of 25,000 screaming people, many of them hostile, all of them highly critical and some downright abusive. And that's just their own supporters, who, in all seriousness, can be far more intimidating than the opposition fans.

Managers too have to face the truth on match day, although in a way it's even worse for them because they can't go out on the pitch and compete themselves. They have to make do with exerting whatever influence they can from the touchline, and that can sometimes be limited. Imagine all the stress and tension you see on the faces of the fans during the game, then multiply it a thousand times and you might have some idea of what the manager goes through in those 90 minutes of sheer hell.

No matter what you do during the rest of the week, no matter how hard you work or what you achieve on the training pitch, those 90 minutes are all that count. They'll determine whether you'll be happy for the weekend or miserable. They may even determine whether you'll still be in a job on Monday. No wonder every minute of the working week is geared towards having those precious products the players as near to perfection as possible at the precise moment the game starts.

Everyone approaches this differently, of course. Brian Clough concentrated almost entirely on his own players. He was just as likely to take them off to lie on a beach in Spain as he was to work with them on the training pitch. He never really bothered about the opposition; never really made any notes on opposing players or made any special plans to deal with them. It was an extremely cavalier way to run a football club and might be ridiculed except for one thing – it worked brilliantly and no one can argue with success.

Don Revie, on the other hand, went to the opposite extreme at Leeds, compiling dossiers of information about the opposing side and carefully prepared plans on how to deal with them. Such meticulous attention to detail also attracted some criticism but again, who can really say it was wrong, seeing as it worked so well? I suppose I fall somewhere in the middle. It's important that a side should be confident of its own ability and concentrate on its strengths, but it does no harm to know a little about how the other side plays and make provisions to deal with them.

It may be a terrible cliché but clubs really do take one game at a time. There's no other way to do it, and as soon as we finish one game we begin thinking about the next. As with all matches, my return to Forest with my new Manchester City side in September 1997 was carefully planned in every way, from the food we would eat to the tactics we would adopt.

It was a midweek match, so the players travelled down from Manchester together on the team coach and stopped for lunch about half an hour's drive from the Forest ground. It's at lunchtime that the build-up to an evening game really gets under way. The players eat a meal which is designed to give them the greatest fitness and energy. It usually consists of things like chicken, fish, pasta, baked potato, fruit and so on.

As always, we are influenced by the latest medical and scientific opinion. When I was playing, everyone ate a huge steak before the match. Now, the nutritionists say that's the worst thing you can do because it does you no good in terms of energy and yet lies in your stomach for hours. The widely accepted opinion today is that simple carbohydrates are what's really needed, and white meat rather than red because it's easier to digest. I don't think diet makes a major difference to a footballer's performance six hours later but it does have a role to play. At this level, with teams so evenly matched, even the slightest improvement is worthwhile.

We usually hire a private room away from the public for the meal. The players need time to themselves. The conversation will be about the latest bits of gossip, television, music, girlfriends; in fact, just about anything other than the match. This is relaxation time. There will be plenty of time for tension later.

Once the players have finished their meals, they go to bed for a couple of hours' rest. They probably find it difficult to sleep but again, just the relaxation is valuable. At about five o'clock they come back down for tea and toast and then we have a pre-match team meeting at around quarter to six. By now the players are getting a bit tense and trying to focus on the game. This meeting is where we bring together all the themes we've been working on in the previous few days; all the thoughts designed to win this particular game.

The first thing to do is build up the players' confidence and self-esteem. As we've seen, this was especially important with City at that time because we had made a very poor start to the season and were hurtling towards the relegation zone. Forest on the other hand were sitting at the top of the table having won all four of their opening matches, scoring ten goals and conceding only one. The match was vital to us.

I knew I had to create a mood of optimism among the players because people were already writing us off. It may be easy to scoff at the idea of big, rough tough footballers needing building-up, but the fact is they do. Anyone who's ever worked at any job will know the negative impact of having your efforts criticised, and the positive force of a little praise and encouragement. Somebody tells you you're good at your job and suddenly there's a spring in your step, the world is a brighter place.

It's the same with footballers. The only difference is one of degree. Football takes everything to extremes. If you're losing it's all doom and gloom and everyone is very quick to criticise. Articles in the press can be savage and at times ridiculously ill-informed. The fans can be even worse. For the main part players can rise above that but there's bound to be a little bit that gets through, enough to cause a few nagging doubts about their ability, either as individuals or collectively as a team. These doubts have to be removed or they can grow like a cancer and destroy a side.

That night I was careful to bolster their self-belief. I reminded them that we had six or seven internationals in the squad. They were all good players and they didn't become bad ones overnight just because we'd had a few poor results. At the same time I was careful to debunk the myth of how good the Forest players were. I stressed that man for man they were no better than us. It was what the City players needed to hear and outwardly they responded well, but you can never tell if they really believe it until they go out onto the pitch.

Then it was time to turn our attention to the game itself and how we would approach it. We had watched Forest in their opening matches and had come up with a game plan that we thought would work. There were two aspects of their style that we thought we could concentrate on. The first was the fact that they defended quite high up the pitch with a flat back four. The other was the form of Scot Gemmill, who had run the show for Forest during their opening games. We had to deny him the time and space to run the midfield and make the kind of passes that could split our defence.

I decided that a lot of the responsibility would fall on the shoulders of Ged Brannan. I wanted him to pick up Gemmill as soon as Forest got possession. The other main strategy was to get our attackers and midfield players to run forward as soon as we got possession. It didn't matter whether they had the ball or not, I wanted them to catch the Forest defence flat-footed by getting forward as quickly as possible. Then all that remained was to get the ball to them before they were caught offside.

Our first-team coach Richard Money had worked on this during training on Monday and Tuesday. He had them playing eight against eight, with the emphasis on each side breaking quickly as soon as they got possession. The same moves would be played through time after time, with Richard constantly stopping the game to make a point or emphasise something. The key factor was stressing the need to get the ball through early to the running players. If a player makes a run five times and never receives the ball then he won't bother making the sixth run, so the early delivery was vital to keep everyone's enthusiasm alive.

After going through the match plan at the meeting, I then went on to run through the Forest team as we expected it to be and make a few points about individual players. It helped that I had been at Forest until nine months earlier and knew some of their players very well. I had brought many of them to the club, including Dean Saunders and Kevin Campbell. I reminded our defenders what a handful those two could be. For example, how Saunders was so adept at turning defenders and how important it was to be alert to that. I warned them about the power and pace of Campbell and how he too could score from apparently non-threatening situations. Forewarned isn't necessarily forearmed, of course. If players like that suddenly turn it on, they'll probably do for you anyway – but even so, it does no harm to remind people of the dangers.

As we got on the coach for the ground, the atmosphere was loud and boisterous with people talking all at once, almost for the sake of it. A lot of that is just nervous tension. Everyone has a different way of dealing with it. I tend to go very quiet but other people go the other way. It doesn't matter, as long as you can find a way of relaxing and preparing for the task in hand. I encourage them to play music on the way to games but I leave the choice up to them. If I made them listen to what I like they would probably get off the coach.

They also had a CD player in the dressing room. It's something I started at Forest. Stuart Pearce came up to me shortly after I took over and asked if it would be all right to have some 'sounds' in the dressing room. Brian Clough would never have allowed it but I didn't mind. I was prepared to do just about anything to help them relax. As soon as the serious warm-up starts, it's switched off.

As we drove to the ground that evening, I was trying to concentrate on the task ahead. I constantly question and analyse everything we do to see if there's a better way of approaching it. In the midst of all that rational analysis, however, it's not uncommon for irrational thoughts to break through. I remembered how I had signed Saunders and Campbell for Forest. Both were very good players but neither had managed to fully convince the Forest fans of their worth.

For some reason I became seized by the thought that sod's law would now prevail. Wouldn't it be a wonderful irony for them to show what they can do on the night they come up against the club managed by the man who brought them to Forest? The papers would have loved that and as we arrived at the ground, I could almost see the headlines in the next morning's papers: 'City Sunk as Clark Signings Come Good For Forest.' But that way paranoia lies and I had to put such thoughts out of my mind. The game was less than an hour away and I had to get positive.

By the time we arrive at the ground, the advance guard are already there and have sorted out some of the basics. When the players walk into the dressing room, they'll find that their kit is already laid out for them. It will have been put there by the kitman and a couple of coaches while the players were sleeping in the afternoon. I think that's important because it's good for the players to walk into the dressing room and see everything looking neat and tidy and professional. It tells them that they're important and what they're doing is important. As I've said, if you treat people as professionals then they're more likely to perform like professionals.

The players don't get changed straightaway as they usually have a few things they want to sort out. They all get complimentary tickets for the game so they'll want to make sure they get to friends and family who may have come to watch the match.

Once all the little tasks are performed they will usually go and walk on the pitch just to get a feel of it and sample the atmosphere of the stadium. Then they go back into the dressing room. The mascot might come in to meet the players and get autographs. Then it's down to business. The players start to get changed. As they're doing that, I'll be taking our team sheet to the referee and getting a copy of the opposition line-up. Against Forest, the only surprise was that they chose to play Pascolo in goal. He hadn't played for a few weeks and so I thought he might be a bit rusty.

Meanwhile the players are starting their warm-up routine with the fitness trainer. This is around five past seven, 40 minutes before kick-off. It begins with initial stretches in the dressing room and then they all go out onto the pitch to loosen up together. While they're doing this, I stay in the dressing room thinking about what I might say in the final ten minutes before kick-off.

At that point, it's just a case of geeing them up and maybe getting across one or two final points. It's not too detailed and by this time everyone starts speaking at once. Everyone has something to say. Most of it is just cliché designed to spur people on and inspire them. Lots of shouts and grunting. Things like 'get stuck in' and 'keep it tight'. Not particularly enlightening, but it makes people feel better to say something; as the tension mounts, anything is preferable to silence.

Then the players walk out onto the pitch and from that point it's all up to them. They knew the game plan, they knew the strengths of the Forest team and they had been prepared in the best way possible to shine at that particular moment. From then on, they were on their own. I sit in the directors' box for the first half because you get a better overall picture of the game from there.

I got a little bit of a reaction from the fans as I made my way to my seat. A few boos and nasty comments but nothing too serious. I was pleased about that but also aware that, despite my three and a half years at Forest, I was now no more than a footnote in the club's history. It had a new manager and a new team and the fans had come to see it win, not worry themselves about how I was doing.

That was fine by me, and I settled down to concentrate as the game kicked off. It went very well. We were very comfortable in the first half. Brannan was picking up Gemmill as planned and Forest seldom looked like being able to hurt us. At the same time, we were hurtling forward at every opportunity and causing their defence some problems. Then after about 30 minutes we got the vital breakthrough, the opening goal. Our right-back Richard Edghill collected the ball from a throw-in and lifted it over their defence for Lee Bradbury to chase. He did really well and squared the ball for Brannan to side foot it home. The Forest defence were caught completely flat-footed, just as we had hoped.

We were helped by the fact that the Forest keeper Pascolo had stayed on his line when really he should have run out and cleared the ball. Perhaps those few weeks out injured and subsequent lack of match practice had an effect on him. Whatever, he didn't react to the danger and we were able to take advantage.

It was great to score but I felt no release of tension at that point. It was far too early. We had to rally our thoughts and determination because we had gone ahead before in the season only to throw it away. It had been the same story the season before and as I mentioned earlier, some of the players and the fans were starting to get a bit of a complex about it. We had to address it at half-time to steady everyone's nerves, not least our own. During the half-time talk I stressed the need to stay positive and keep going forward.

These days, if you're 1–0 up and going well, you don't change it. You have to avoid sitting back because it's much more difficult now to close a game down than it used to be.

The great Liverpool sides of the Seventies and Eighties used to be masters of that. As soon as they got in front, the back four would start passing the ball around and eventually it would go back to the goalkeeper. He would pick it up and then roll it out to a defender and the whole thing would start all over again. Then after 90 minutes and perhaps thirty seconds of injury time, the final whistle would blow and that would be it.

The changes in the rules have put a stop to that. Nowadays you can't use the goalkeeper in the way Liverpool did because he can't pick it up. And of course, it's not uncommon to see five or six minutes of injury time being added. So it's very difficult to sit back on a lead – you're better off trying to go for another goal. We certainly felt we needed another goal that night. At 1–0 anything can still happen but at 2–0, you have a very good buffer and the other team will find it very difficult to come back.

As I spoke, however, I sensed that the players were in a quietly determined mood because they had received an awful lot of criticism for failing to hold onto a lead. I could sense that night they were determined to put it right. As they went out for the second half, I was nervous and so were the crowd, but the players showed no sign of tension. Forest upped the tempo and threw everything at us. They put us under pressure and we got a bit ragged for about ten minutes. At one point Saunders got past our defence with a brilliant turn and was unlucky to see his shot go just wide.

We weathered the onslaught and started to settle down and get back into the game. And we managed to score that vital second goal. Again, it was because of Brannan's willingness to run forward as soon as we got possession.

This time the goalkeeper did race out to clear the danger but he only succeeded in colliding with Brannan several yards outside the penalty area. The ball bounced free and Brannan managed to get up first and had the great presence of mind to lob the ball towards the goal, seeing as the keeper was way off his line. It was speculative but fortunately for us, it ended up in the back of the net.

Forest showed great strength of character and came back at us even harder. They threw everyone forward, it was real up-and-under stuff. We coped with it quite well but then conceded a bad goal when Campbell managed to get a header in the six-yard box after a corner. Our goalkeeper Martin Margetson should have come and collected it and he knew that as soon as it happened. I couldn't really complain about him because he had been deputising for the injured Tommy Wright and he had done really well. But now it's 2–1 and suddenly the fears start entering your head. Oh no, here we go again! It was going to be a nervous final ten minutes.

Forest continued to press but it was City who managed to get the next goal, making it 3–1. It came from a free-kick with only two minutes to go. Forest's marking was bad and I'm sure Dave Bassett would have been unhappy with it. The ball came across and we got a header at the far post sent back across goal to Paul Dickov, all alone on the near post. He was very calm and had loads of time to take the ball down and lash it into the net.

That was it. The whistle blew and for the first time that season I enjoyed the incredible release of tension which comes from victory. Three–one to City away from home. We had won our first game of the season. It was a really important win for so many reasons. We had gained three points, we had beaten one of the top teams in the division and we had proved to ourselves and everyone else that we could get in front and stay in front.

After a game I always go back over everything in my mind, the match itself and the build-up to it. I like to check how well we've done and whether we could have done anything differently. Sometimes you have to accept that you got it wrong or failed to adopt the right approach, but that night I felt Richard Money and I had got it exactly right. Two of our three goals came from the tactics we had rehearsed.

According to the Forest assistant manager Bobby Houghton, other teams were quick to copy our tactics when they came to the City Ground. In their first two home league matches, Forest had thumped Norwich 4–1 and then QPR 4–0. Their next visitors after us, Portsmouth and Stoke, adopted a similar approach to us. They weren't as successful and ended up losing 1–0, but they pushed Forest all the way. Tranmere went one better and forced a 2–2 draw.

I took no particular pleasure in having paved the way for other teams to thwart Forest, but I took great delight in our victory that night. After the game everyone was euphoric, as you might expect. They were all talking at once and everyone was full of it. I watched and listened and let them enjoy it for a while. I savoured the moment as well. Then after a few minutes I sat them down and tried to get their feet back on the ground. I praised them for what they had achieved and tried to reassure them that they deserved it and they really were a good side. I reminded them that I had told them that if they played as a team and concentrated, they could beat one of the best teams in the league.

I pointed out that Forest had won their four opening games comfortably, yet we had outplayed them and deserved to win. The players had to take some self-belief from that, but at the same time they couldn't sit back now and expect everything to suddenly fall into place. We had to keep working and go on from there.

After the brief post-match talk, the physio and club doctor checked on injuries to assess the damage and start treatment. Meanwhile, I had to go off to meet the press. This is an area of the manager's job that has snowballed in recent years. It's not unusual to do six or seven TV and radio interviews and then go on to do a press conference for the newspapers. In those circumstances it's hard to stay fresh and sparkling and so perhaps it's not surprising that we so often hear the same old clichés from managers about taking each game as it comes and all the rest of it.

Usually, while the press conference is going on the players will go to the players' lounge for a drink. They wouldn't be expected to have any alcohol, though, certainly not before they've had something to eat. This is a relatively new development and again it's because of our increasing scientific knowledge of the body and how it recovers after strenuous exercise.

After a game, a player's energy reserves are virtually depleted. We now know that the first two or three hours after the match are the most important in terms of beginning to recover. Having alcohol before you have had something to eat is the worst thing you can do because it inhibits the digestion of food which will help towards a quick recovery and return to normal energy levels. The best thing to do is eat soon after the game. That's why we provide lots of food on the coach for the drive back.

There are usually things like pasta, fresh fruit and loads of water to stop dehydration. Absolutely no alcohol. This is in contrast to my playing days, when it was quite usual to have a crate of lager in the dressing room for drinking straight after the game. This practice continued until fairly recently. Introducing this stricter regime hasn't caused any problems, as most players are prepared to accept anything that is likely to make them better footballers. It was simply a question of re-educating them.

So going to the players' lounge should only be a chance to unwind and meet up with old friends. Football is a very small world and players from different clubs tend to know each other well. They enjoy a quick chat to catch up on the latest gossip.

After the game I would normally get on the coach and leave with the players, but that night after the Forest game I was able to go straight home to my family in Nottingham. Before leaving, though, I went and had a drink with Dave Bassett and Liam O'Kane, the Forest coach. Most clubs usually invite the opposition manager and his staff for a drink after the game. I've certainly done that, win, lose or draw. It's usually very friendly but the talk is about anything but the game that's just been played. You might talk about football in general terms but never about the match. This is because if you've won you don't know what to say to the other manager, and if you've lost you don't want to talk about it anyway.

It was wonderful to be back at Forest that night. Not in any triumphalist way but just to be back seeing so many old friends. I have fantastic memories of the place. Everyone I met seemed to be very welcoming, from the players to the secretaries and administrative staff. I was able to have a good chat with players like Ian Woan and Mark Crossley because they were injured and so weren't playing. I had had a few run-ins with both of them when I was manager, so it was particularly nice that they sought me out and were warm and friendly. It was impossible to talk to the ones who had played but I shook hands with most of them as they came off the field, Dean Saunders, Kevin Campbell, Steve Chettle and so on. It was very emotional and I really enjoyed it, but even so, I was able to divorce it from the importance of the game, which was all about winning three points.

As I left the ground, I found the supporters were able to make the same distinction. I bumped into a few fans who, like the staff, were very welcoming and they congratulated me sincerely on our victory. But, of course, there had to be a sting in the tail. They no doubt still had painful memories of the long string of poor results we had to endure before I resigned the previous season, for as I turned to leave, one of them said, 'Congratulations again, Frank,' and then after a pause full of tension he continued: 'It's been a long time since you won here.' Even I had to smile at that one. It was a little painful, but I could afford to take it on the chin.

We had won our first game and nothing anyone could say could spoil that.

CHAPTER 16

Money, Money, Money

My accuser stomped about like a poor man's Tom Cruise fighting for justice in a dramatic courtroom battle. In true Hollywood style, he played for sympathy by casting me in the role of villain. He claimed I was trying to cheat his client, Stan Collymore, out of £425,000. Warming to his theme, he started blackening my name, making out I was some latter-day Victorian mill owner sending kids up chimneys or down the mines without breathing apparatus.

I gazed across at Collymore. His designer suit was as sharp as any film star's. He lived in a luxury home, drove a luxury car and dated glamorous women. It was hard to see him in the role of exploited street urchin, especially as he was Britain's costliest player at the time. I had always liked Stan and still do. He's a wonderful footballer, but this was getting ridiculous. It wasn't actually a courtroom, though no one seemed to have told our would-be Tom Cruise, who thundered on as if he was acting out the leading role in *A Few Good Men*. It was just a mundane Premier League tribunal designed to settle differences between clubs and players. Its role was to decide who should get the disputed £425,000.

Footballers have always tried to get as much money as possible out of the game, and understandably so. It's a short and uncertain career. But the huge sums now on offer are turning many people's heads. It's not just a case of demanding high wages. It can involve players negotiating complicated clauses into their contracts which can net them hundreds of thousands of pounds just for the sake of moving clubs.

The problem stems from the vast amounts of cash which have been flooding into the game over the last few years from television and wealthy businessmen. The fans have played their part, forking out more and more each year thanks to ever-increasing ticket prices and mushrooming football merchandise. I wonder how many parents, nagged into buying their child an expensive replica kit, would have sympathised with the 'exploited' Stan Collymore that day at the tribunal.

It could be that in his fight for the disputed money, Collymore had taken some inspiration from another great player who had left Nottingham Forest a few years earlier with a bulging bank balance. Roy Keane had pulled a masterstroke and earned himself a fortune. When I arrived at Forest, they had just been relegated. Keane was one of their star players and I hoped to persuade him to stay to help us win promotion. Within ten seconds of meeting him I knew I had no chance, and when I looked at the incredible clauses in his contract I could see why.

Forest had bought Keane for £20,000 as a fresh-faced 19-year-old from the Irish club Cobh Ramblers. He went straight into the Forest first team and ended up playing in just about every position for the club. Then after two seasons, Brian Clough got him to sign a new deal with Forest. Keane proved a shrewd operator. It was while Forest were struggling in the league and he insisted on having a get-out clause in case they were relegated. It meant he could leave if another club were prepared to pay £3 million for him. And as part of such a deal, Keane would receive more than £600,000 from Forest for himself.

I was amazed that he had ever been given such a contract, as it effectively meant it was to his advantage financially for Forest to go down. However, if you're his manager and you're faced with a situation whereby you either give him a deal like that or lose him there and then, I suppose you might feel you have no choice. It's all about player power these days. It was a tribute to Keane's professionalism that he still played his heart out to keep Forest in the Premier League.

I knew there would be nothing I could do to keep him because it was so lucrative for him to move. On my first day in charge, I was given a folder detailing the clubs interested in him. There were so many it took me 20 minutes to read through it. Keane considered offers from a number of clubs including Arsenal and Blackburn before choosing Manchester United. He continued training with Forest while the negotiations were taking place. You might have expected him to take it easy and not bother, but you would have been wrong. He was giving it everything even then, running and chasing and tackling as if his life depended on it.

A little over a year later he was back at the City Ground when United played Forest. He came on midway through the second half and the Forest fans jeered him every time he touched the ball and taunted him about being a money-grabber. I thought it a disappointing reception for a player who had run himself into the ground for Forest and then left swelling the club's bank balance by £3 million. But that's football fans; they pay a lot for their tickets and don't like to see their money being used to line the pockets of players who then desert the club. Perhaps Keane was treated harshly, but it was nothing compared to what lay in store for Stan Collymore.

I always had lots of problems with Stan. He was a wonderful player who could win you the match, but you often find that the more talented players are, the more problems they cause. Certainly as Stan's spectacular goals created more and more headlines, he began to create more and more trouble. I don't know if success went to his head. Part of his problem is that he talks well to the media. Put a microphone in front of him and he'll scarcely pause for breath. That's fine, except he's very naive and he says daft things. He caused himself a lot of problems.

He started complaining about the other Forest players not playing in the right way to suit him. That's not exactly what the other lads in the dressing room want to hear. He was probably insecure deep down.

He needed to be loved, nurtured and cherished, but no matter how much you did that, it was never enough. And for all his talent, it was bound to be difficult to maintain team morale when he complained about them. There were times when it got very close to us saying he would have to go. Fortunately, we had a very mature dressing room with one or two real leaders. I kept very close to them, people like Stuart Pearce and Colin Cooper. They kept reassuring me: 'Don't worry, as long as he's doing his stuff and scoring goals he can be a jerk and we'll deal with it. It won't be a problem.'

They did deal with it and we got by. It meant that in spite of the problems Collymore brought, I was still ready to do just about anything to keep him. That meant offering him a new contract, even though he had two years to run on his existing deal. We wanted to offer him better terms because he had done well for us and we felt he was entitled to it. Unfortunately, it was the start of all our problems and if I had known what I was letting myself in for, I might not have bothered.

The negotiations dragged on for most of the season. Then just as I thought we were getting somewhere, Stan decided he wasn't going to sign because he didn't like the way we played. The newspapers made it worse by stirring up supposed rows and speculating about where Stan might go if he left Forest. That was partly Stan's fault because he couldn't stop talking to them. It was to cost him dearly.

It got towards the end of March and we were getting close to the transfer deadline. If Stan didn't go before then, he would have to stay with us whether he liked it or not. Manchester United had said they would like him, which obviously weighed on his mind, but they never actually put a bid in and then they bought Andy Cole. With the deadline approaching and no firm offers coming in, it looked as though he would be staying and so I said to him: 'Let's put all the contract negotiations on hold. Just go out and play. That's what you do best. We're sixth in the table. Let's see if we can get a good run together and qualify for Europe. Then at the end of the season we'll look at the situation again. If you're still adamant that you want to go, then we'll let you go.'

He agreed and for the next 12 weeks he was absolutely magnificent. We never lost. We finished third behind Blackburn and Manchester United, just ahead of Liverpool. I thought that surely Stan would be happy now; surely he could see how well we'd done and how good things looked for the future. It made no difference. He was adamant that he wanted to go. He had got it into his head that he wanted to play for Liverpool.

There was no way of changing his mind. From then on it was just a case of putting a transfer fee on him and seeing who would match it. We came up with £8.5 million. It didn't surprise me that at least two clubs were prepared to pay it. He was that good. The Mersey giants Everton and Liverpool fought it out. Collymore spoke to both, but there was only ever going to be one winner. It was always Liverpool. He just used Everton as a bargaining ploy and I think Joe Royle, the manager at the time, knew that. The drama was played out for a few weeks but then, as everyone expected, Collymore signed for Liverpool. The £8.5 million fee smashed the British transfer record set only a few months earlier when Andy Cole left Newcastle in a deal worth £7 million.

There were several similarities between the two players and it's not surprising that they should both set record fees. Both were young and extremely talented; both scored goals with an arrogant ease. But perhaps the most interesting comparison between the two players lay in the relative reaction of the fans of the clubs they were leaving. Newcastle supporters were shocked and saddened by Cole's departure.

Manager Kevin Keegan, himself an idol on Tyneside, joked that he might be lynched for daring to sell the star player. In stark contrast, I didn't feel I had anything to fear from Nottingham Forest fans. Few were mourning Collymore's departure. He was one of the most talented players ever to turn out for Forest and should have been one of the most popular, but he never was. People could see the difficult side of him.

He was the same when he went to Liverpool. When he was struggling to get in the side, he started saying that Liverpool didn't play enough like Forest. Stan seems to have this notion that wherever he was before is better than where he is now, and the next place he's going to will be even better again. It was ironic listening to Stan slagging off Liverpool saying they didn't play enough like Forest. While he was at Forest he kept saying we didn't play enough like his previous club Southend! He had a period there when he played under Barry Fry, who organised the team on the basis that everyone had to get the ball to Stan as often as possible. They were happy to do it because he could win them the match. He was relatively successful, but only relatively. His goals per game ratio wasn't anything like as good at Southend as it was at Forest, even though we were in the Premier League.

I would say to him: 'You keep saying it was better at Southend. In what way was it better? You've scored more goals here.' He could never see it. He just had this memory and distance lent enchantment to it.

So Collymore departed and we thought that was the end of him, but in fact it was only the beginning. Just as the dust began to settle on the transfer deal, he dropped his bombshell. He was invoking a clause in his contract which said he was entitled to five per cent of the transfer fee if he was sold at the club's request. As he had not officially asked in writing for a transfer, he felt he was entitled to that five per cent, £425,000.

We couldn't believe it. It was ridiculous to say we wanted to sell him. We had done everything bar nail him to Trent Bridge to keep him in Nottingham. On the first day he went to talk to Liverpool, the Forest chairman Fred Reacher said to him: 'Come back and tell us what they offer you, Stan, and we'll make a better offer.' But Stan wouldn't come back and tell us. He'd made up his mind to go no matter what.

There was absolutely no way we were prepared to pay that money but Stan refused to withdraw his claim. We couldn't agree and so the dispute had to be settled by an FA tribunal. I was worried that Collymore would win, even though I thought such a decision would fly in the face of natural justice. It was true that I didn't make him put the transfer request in writing. I didn't feel it was necessary because I thought it was so well-documented that he wanted to leave. He never stopped talking about it to the newspapers. The main thing was, I didn't want to sour him at the time he was talking to Liverpool. I didn't want to say: 'You've got to put it in writing or you're not going.' I wanted relations to remain friendly because I wanted him to stay. Perhaps that was naive.

I was determined to fight it because Stan was out of order. He did ask for a move. I had 13 newspaper clippings of him saying it. I also had a recording of an interview with Radio Nottingham in which he said he had to get away from Forest to further his career. It was to take several months for the FA to rule on Collymore's claim and it hung over us like a cloud for most of the season. The £425,000 was a huge figure to a club like Forest and we couldn't afford to lose it. We were running on a £6 million overdraft as it was.

As we waited for the FA decision, I found myself embroiled in an even more bizarre saga with the Norwegian international Lars Bohinen. At least with Collymore the contract negotiations had been mainly about sensible things like money. With Bohinen they were about everything from air flights to house decorations, football tactics and just about anything else he could dream up.

It had been one of my worst weeks in charge of Forest. We had just been knocked out of the Coca-Cola Cup by Bradford and I was trying to turn my mind towards two big games for us, away to Tottenham in the league and then away to Auxerre in the UEFA Cup. It was vital to collect our thoughts and prepare for a disciplined performance in France. But the most bizarre things were getting in the way, like the woodblock flooring in Bohinen's house. The club had bought him a brand new home to keep him happy, but it seemed the fluff from the carpets was getting up his nose. He was starting to have a similar effect on me. He wanted a clause written into his new contract saying we would put down a woodblock floor to solve the problem.

I have to admit I had made a mistake. In my eagerness to sign Bohinen from his club in Norway, I had allowed him an attractive get-out clause in his contract. When we were trying to sign him we were struggling in the First Division. We were a bit of an unknown quantity to him and vice versa. He had a very good agent, a qualified lawyer, not the usual spivvy type. They were concerned about whether Lars would settle in England and whether Forest would be successful. To give them some comfort, they wanted a clause in the contract that would enable Lars to go for

£750,000 if things didn't work out. As we were only paying £450,000 for him, that meant we would still show a healthy profit. Even if we only had him for 12 months it would be better than not having him at all. I said that from a humane, man-management point of view, I would agree to it.

The way things turned out, with Forest being so successful so quickly, it became a millstone round my neck. I had thought that once he'd settled in and got to like the place it would be easy to negotiate it out of the contract. I very quickly found out I was wrong. He wanted a fortune, a massive one-off payment. I wouldn't do it so we started talking about a new contract. We were talking for about seven months. He wanted about 50 clauses written into the deal. Some of them were absolutely crazy. He wanted to always play as an offensive midfield player, and if he wasn't in the first team, he wanted the right not to have to play for the reserves. He wanted six return flights to Oslo every year and a new car for him and his wife. He also wanted us to find his wife a job and pay for her private medical insurance, something we didn't do for any other player.

Then the final clause he wanted was for the club to waive all its rights to apply UEFA and FIFA regulations in the event of a dispute. It was crazy. It would mean that if we disagreed about anything in future, there would be nothing the club could do about it. We couldn't appeal to a higher authority and would have nowhere to go. I was trying to run a football club and win matches while all this was going on, yet so much time was taken up on these ridiculous negotiations. I was constantly having to consult lawyers and accountants for advice. We stuck at it and managed to negotiate out most of the bizarre clauses and we got close to agreeing a new contract. We offered him a lot more money and agreed to retain the get-out clause until the end of the season.

It seemed all right and then someone heard about the situation and phoned Blackburn to say: 'Why don't you buy Lars Bohinen? You can get him for £750,000.' The minute Lars heard Blackburn were interested, that was it. He was gone. Not because he was unhappy at Forest; he was very happy at the club. It was because Blackburn offered him more money, but that was never the intention of the get-out clause. It was supposed to be a safeguard in case he didn't settle here, not a way to earn more money. He was legally entitled to do what he did, but it was certainly against the spirit of the agreement. I suppose I was a bit naive. I'd be very interested to see how many clauses were put into his contract with Blackburn.

The fans were disappointed to see Bohinen go. He was a stylish player, graceful and capable of scoring some spectacular goals. The occasional display of ball-juggling or improvisation often brightened up a dull patch in a hard-fought game. However, he wasn't always very popular with the other players, who regarded him as distant and aloof. I think the fans went off him too when they heard what he'd done. They went off him even more a few weeks later when he was in the Blackburn side that beat us 7–0, the worst defeat of my time at Forest.

After that game there were some suggestions that it might have been better to give in to Bohinen and offer him the money he wanted. The argument went that he had only cost Forest £450,000 and was probably worth somewhere in the region of £2 million. Didn't that mean Forest could afford to give him the money he wanted to remove the get-out clause and still be in pocket? Bohinen certainly thought so. After moving to Blackburn he said he would have settled for about £500,000. That plus the original transfer fee of £450,000 meant Forest would have paid a total of £950,000 for him. He suggested that would have been worth paying for the sake of retaining a £2 million player.

Well, I'm not sure he was a £2 million player at that time. He had been hawked around but no one wanted him except a Turkish club and he didn't want to go there. In any case, I couldn't have given Bohinen the money he wanted. It would have been bad management. It's very difficult to keep anything confidential at a football club. If it had got out that I had given Bohinen a fortune in a one-off payment, it would have put me in an impossible position with the other players.

I wouldn't buy anybody off at the risk of compromising team spirit. As a manager you have to perform a balancing act to keep everybody happy. You need the players behind you. It's vital and can help you deal with difficult situations. For example, I needed the support of the other players during that period when Collymore was slagging everybody off and causing trouble. Having got that support, I couldn't possibly give in to Bohinen's demands. How could I pay him a fortune and then expect the trust and loyalty of the others, particularly Pearce and Cooper who had been towers of strength for me? It just couldn't work like that.

Perhaps I allowed myself to make too much of the Lars Bohinen experience. It surfaced in the press and it came over as if I was accusing him of being greedy. But it was the way it was done that rankled with me. We were in the middle of long drawn-out negotiations over his new contract and all its 50 clauses. We'd bent over backwards for him. The contractors were just about to start on his new woodblock floor. Then it was literally a case of him coming up and saying, 'I've had a phone call from Blackburn. I'm going. Bye.' And that was it. He was gone without so much as a backward glance.

I accept that many players are only in it for the money and there's no such thing as loyalty in football. I would hesitate to say that I felt let down by Bohinen, mainly because if Brian Clough heard me say that, he would burst out laughing. He believed one of the first things you should expect from a player is that he'll let you down. But there are ways and means of doing things, and what Bohinen did is not the way.

The contract negotiations with Bohinen and Collymore were exceptionally difficult and neither one worked out right for Forest. But even the ones which do work out can be a headache, certainly time-consuming. The game's new-found wealth makes footballers an attractive proposition for big-time showbiz agents who wouldn't have bothered with the game ten years ago when salaries were more modest. Now they're everywhere. Even lower-division players have agents, colourful but hard-headed men like the cigar-smoking Eric Hall who struts about like a caricature of himself, flaunting his ego at anyone who'll take notice.

Eric fancies himself as a bit of a showbiz character and he's quite entertaining, but when he's negotiating contracts he's as hard as a Vinnie Jones tackle. Fortunately for me when I was at Manchester City, so was my chairman Francis Lee. I knew that when the two of them got together to thrash out a deal it was going to be difficult, if only to find a room big enough to hold both their egos.

I was grateful for Francis Lee's involvement when

Manchester City bought Lee Bradbury from Portsmouth. Bradbury was a very talented young player at the time, already an England Under-21 international. He was big, strong and fast with a good first touch, but he hadn't been in the game all that long. He had become a soldier after leaving school and so his path to professional football was somewhat unorthodox.

He had a great attitude but was very aware of the £3 million transfer fee we were paying. I knew I would have to spend time building up his confidence. That might have been more difficult if I had negotiated his contract. It's obviously harder to tell a player how wonderful you think he is if you've been telling him he's not worth the wages he's demanding. The two approaches just don't go together. That's why it's better if someone other than the manager brokers the deal.

I was in on the negotiations with Bradbury but the chairman did the talking. Things were going very smoothly until his agent Eric Hall got involved. Then it suddenly became extremely complicated. I used to read of trade unions and employers negotiating over some pay deal and wonder why it took so long. Now I know. It's a give-and-take situation and you move closer to each other inch by inch. It can drive managers to distraction. We can spend more time with players in smoke-filled rooms discussing endless contract clauses than we spend on the training pitch discussing tactics and technique.

The negotiations over the Bradbury deal became so drawn-out that eventually we sent him out of the room to prevent him from dying of boredom while Francis and Eric thrashed it out. In the end, there's no other way but to accept a little give and take. No one can win outright in these situations. It's always an honourable draw.

Without question it's good for players to have agents to negotiate contracts and look after their interests, but they're complicating matters and even setting the agenda. The Bosman ruling has opened up a whole new line of business for unscrupulous agents. They're forever ringing up managers saying they can get this player or that player, often at rock-bottom prices because they're coming out of contract with their present clubs. It's not exactly ethical, and of course every manager knows that if they're phoning him about players from other clubs, they'll also be phoning other clubs about his players.

Sometimes unscrupulous agents will contact clubs and try to sell players they don't even represent. When I was manager of Manchester City, I got a phone call at home from a good friend of mine at Wimbledon. He had been contacted by an agent saying we were looking to sell certain players. Wimbledon were interested but a bit suspicious about the agent so decided to check with me. As it was, we had no plans to sell the players mentioned and the idea had never even been discussed. It's easy to see what the agent was trying to do.

He wanted to drum up some business by creating a transfer out of nothing. He hoped that Wimbledon would be interested once they heard a certain player was supposedly for sale. Having established their interest, he would then have contacted us to say that Wimbledon fancied the player in question and would we be interested in selling? At this point he would be hoping that the chance to make some money would suddenly appeal to us and even though we had never considered selling the player, we might say yes if the price was right. Armed with this ray of hope, he's back on the phone to Wimbledon and before you know it he's suddenly negotiating a deal between the two clubs and hoping to get a nice commission into the bargain. He didn't succeed, of course, not that time anyway. There may be occasions, however, when he does.

Freedom of contract was bound to happen if football was to keep pace with modern-day business practice in the European Union, but it throws up some bizarre and uncomfortable situations. The case of Alfie Haaland at Forest is a good example. Shortly after I left the club, they tried to sell Haaland for about £2 million. He just said: 'No way. I'm not going anywhere unless I get half the fee.' He knew he could afford to say that because his contract ran out in six months' time and so he could go abroad on a free transfer, leaving him plenty of scope to get a big-money deal.

His position was strengthened even further by the fact that once he entered the last six months of his contract, he was entitled under FIFA regulations to talk to clubs outside the country where he was playing. It meant he could negotiate a new contract elsewhere while still playing for Forest. He was able to speak to three German clubs without breaking any rules. But imagine how Dave Bassett and Stuart Pearce must have felt at the time. They were working their socks off to prevent Forest being relegated and Alfie Haaland was allowed to discuss big-money deals beyond his wildest dreams with some of the top clubs in Europe. Now Alfie's the kind of lad who gives everything 100 per cent all the time, but it's easy to see how less honest players could abuse such a situation.

It's going to happen more and more, and clubs will have

to get used to it. It's a double-edged sword. As the buying club you've got to try to make it work to your advantage by signing players when they're out of contract; as the club trying to hold on to players you have to fight even harder to keep them. You have to accept that when a player signs a three-year contract then in effect it's really only a two-year deal. After that two years, you have to try like hell to get them to sign a new deal or they'll probably be looking to leave. Once they enter the final year it's difficult to hold on to them because they start getting visions of vast amounts of money elsewhere. Then instead of trying to hold on to the player, you're pushed to the other extreme of desperately trying to sell him so you at least get something back. It's very difficult.

The Bosman ruling worked in Manchester City's favour when I signed Ged Brannan from Tranmere. For some reason Brannan had a French agent who had him all set up for a move to France in the summer. This was bad news for Tranmere because they wouldn't get a fee if Brannan went abroad. It made them all the more keen to sell him to us because at least then they would get something.

The negotiations went very well to begin with. Tranmere valued Brannan at a very high figure; we valued him much lower. Gradually we moved closer and closer. Then just as the deal was about done, the agent threw a spanner in the works by saying that City would have to pay the 10 per cent agent's fee. We were stunned. We said no one in England works that way and he said: 'Well, everyone on the Continent does.' Then our secretary checked with the Football Association and it turned out we were not allowed to pay the agent's fee. Clubs throughout the rest of Europe can do it, but not in England. The deal was stuck. It was crazy. As is usually the case, the player was in the driving seat. He knew he could get the kind of money he wanted by going to France on a free transfer. No matter how much it stuck in our throats, we knew we had to match that kind of money if we wanted to sign him. And Tranmere, of course, were in an even more desperate position because they could see the deal falling apart leaving them with nothing. In the end, we had to find a way round it by giving the player a bit more to compensate him for having to pay his agent. It was either that or lose him.

When I was at Forest, we lost Bohinen because we couldn't match the wages he was offered elsewhere. Most small clubs could lose their top players in exactly the same way. Fortunately, it isn't always just about money. Not all players will leave purely for the sake of an extra £1,000 a week. If you make them a fair offer, point out how well they are doing and remind them it's a great club and a lovely city, then sometimes they will listen. If you can convince them they're likely to win something then they're even more likely to stay.

That kind of approach worked with Steve Stone at Forest. When he was a boy, Forest were the only club who would give him a trial. The other big clubs he wrote to didn't even reply. I bet they regret that now. Imagine being offered a player like Steve Stone for free and then turning him down. Steve's a tremendously loyal person and Forest's early belief in him counted for a great deal. Plus he liked Nottingham and his family were settled there. Of course, the club paid him good wages, but he still could have got better elsewhere had he taken a purely mercenary approach.

I was able to hold on to Georgi Kinkladze for similar reasons when I first arrived at Manchester City. It was asking an awful lot of a world-class player to stick out a second season in the lower divisions, but he was prepared to give it a try because he liked the city and he was grateful for the way the club and Francis Lee had looked after him.

It can work, but such examples are the exception rather than the rule and I don't think things are likely to change much in the near future. It's hard to hold on to players when you're struggling, but it's almost as difficult when you're doing well. I remember the reaction at Forest when we finished third in the Premier League after a fantastic season. I could imagine people outside the club thinking: 'I bet the manager there is going to have a fantastic summer break. The players must love it there and really want to stay.' Nothing could have been further from the truth. They were coming in saying they wanted an extra £1,000 a week or they were off.

The stars of the Sixties and Seventies must wonder what has happened. In those days, the manager would invite you into his office and offer you an extra tenner a week and you'd say, 'Wow, thanks boss,' and be out of his office as quickly as possible before he changed his mind. Thankfully, those days have gone, but perhaps we've gone from one extreme to another, which brings me back to Stan Collymore.

In spite of the best efforts of his theatrical representatives, the FA tribunal were unable to see Stan as an exploited street urchin and they ruled against him. No doubt they took into account the numerous newspaper articles in which he said he wanted to leave Forest. His liking for the media was his downfall on that occasion. He didn't get the disputed £425,000, although he did get £125,000 to which he was entitled and which wasn't in dispute, so hopefully he wasn't too disappointed.

I was careful at the time not to portray the tribunal decision as a victory. I didn't feel there were any winners. We all lost a little and in a way, the image of the game was the biggest loser of all. It was an unseemly squabble, conjuring up images of pampered stars completely removed from the lifeblood of the game, the fans.

What they made of it can be gauged from the reaction Collymore got when he returned to Nottingham later that season when Forest played Liverpool. It was the most hostile reception for a former star player I have ever seen. Remember, this was a man who had scored some of the most spectacular goals ever seen at the club. He was subjected to endless jeers and abuse, and taunts in vile language about his money-grabbing attitude. Players are used to abuse and can usually rise above it, but that night I think it got to Stan. He was substituted in the second half and I have to say I felt a little sorry for him.

For all the problems he caused me, I still regretted that Stan had left Forest. I had no reason to feel anything against him – the dispute between us was strictly business. He was a tremendous investment for Nottingham Forest. We got two great years out of him. He played a huge part in our success and scored something like 50 goals. Then we got £8.5 million for him, nearly £6 million profit. That's good business, and if Stan were to walk into the room right now, I would be the first to shake his hand. I might even invite him to the bar, although I would make sure he bought the drinks.

I think he could probably afford it.

CHAPTER 17

Lies, Damned Lies and *Sun* Exclusives

One morning on the training field, Stan Collymore landed a right hander on Alfie Haaland. I'm not sure why, maybe he overreacted because a tackle was a bit too enthusiastic. Whatever the reason, it was a totally insignificant event, the kind of heat-of-the-moment reaction that happens all the time on training grounds across the country. No harm was done and no one would have thought anything of it except for the fact that a member of the public was standing by the training ground watching what happened. He ran straight to the telephone and rang the *Sun*.

The newspaper ran a story the next day making a big deal out of it as if it was some sort of major event. Questions were raised about Stan's disciplinary record, his state of mind, internal problems at the club. It was ridiculous. Twenty years ago, a thing like that wouldn't have got a mention. It demonstrates the kind of goldfish bowl world we now inhabit, where even the most trivial action can produce damaging headlines.

As football becomes more popular, media pressure becomes more intense. It's not just the press. Every fan now has the opportunity to criticise players and managers. All they have to do is pick up a phone and they're on national radio airing their views, usually spurred on by some presenter eager to make his show as controversial as possible. If they don't want to go on radio, fans can have their say via Teletext surveys. 'Should David Beckham be forgiven?' was the big one just after his World Cup sending off. 'Was Hoddle right to send Gazza packing?' was another. Others are more mundane but still keep up the pressure on everyone in the game.

Intrusions into players' private lives are getting worse, as people like Beckham will no doubt testify. It's not enough to dissect a player's performance on the pitch, the media want to own his life off it as well. It's the same all over the world, with people closely associated with players attracting as much interest as the players themselves. Ronaldo's girlfriend is very attractive, but did we really have to see a shot of her on our television screens every five minutes during the last World Cup? She got more airtime than some of the players.

Footballers are obviously high-profile and we accept that, but for many papers, just reporting the real news isn't enough. Everyone is looking for a bit of scandal, and the public are incredibly keen to go scurrying to the papers if they see a player doing anything at all. Those papers are only too happy to pay for some bit of tittle-tattle. Then it all gets blown out of proportion.

At the end of the 1995–96 season, when I was at Forest, we took the players for a holiday in Majorca. When we got back home there was a huge big splash in the *Sun* about how they had been on a drunken rampage upsetting other guests and damaging a Spanish coach. The coach operators were supposed to have sent a £2,000 bill for the damage. I was amazed because I had been on the trip and never saw anything untoward, and neither did any of my coaching staff. But because it was all over the papers, I had to investigate. It turned out to be utter and total rubbish; it just never happened. Kevin Campbell was named as one of the troublemakers and he wasn't even on the trip, so that's an indication of how accurate the allegations were. The coach company never sent us a bill for any damage. I went to the trouble of getting a report from the company's holiday rep and it spoke in glowing terms about the players' behaviour.

There never was any problem, yet I had to waste my time checking out spurious allegations. The club's name was unfairly tarnished and there was nothing I could do about it. The papers don't bother to apologise or put the record straight once it turns out they've got it wrong. They're too busy looking for the next bit of scandal.

Whoever said there's no such thing as bad publicity had obviously never run a football club. We get bombarded with bad, unfair and damaging publicity all the time. I wouldn't complain if it were true. I could take that, but most of it is pure fabrication. The press are forever printing stories saying players are being transferred even though there's no truth in it. I had it all the time at

Manchester City when we were struggling. The papers were constantly saying that we had sold Georgi Kinkladze to someone for £7 million or whatever. There were stories quoting close but unnamed supposed 'friends' of Kinkladze saying that he had lost patience with the club and wanted to get away. It was nonsense. He was perfectly happy and spent a lot of his time stressing that to any journalist who cared to listen. Unfortunately, a true story saying he wanted to stay at City wasn't considered as interesting as a false one saying he wanted to get away. Georgi's efforts to put the record straight got little coverage.

It was the same when I was at Forest. I would wake up in the morning and read that Manchester United had put in a bid for someone like Steve Stone and I'd think, 'Well, that's the first I've heard of it.' They just make things up. Often these stories appear on big match days and you get the impression the papers are just looking for a bit of drama to create some interest. Whether there's any truth in it or not is irrelevant.

Obviously, it can be unsettling for a player to find his name linked with another club. It's upsetting for the fans too, because if they read something in the press they immediately believe it's true. They get very disgruntled, because players like Kinkladze and Stone are big heroes and the fans don't want to lose them. It also works the other way round when you've supposedly put a bid in for somebody. You can imagine the repercussions. Immediately the player who currently holds that position in the team is worried about his future and needs reassuring. The chairman wants to know what's happening. Once one paper prints the story then all the reporters from every other paper are on the phone wanting to know whether or not it's true. The story may be pure invention but the manager has to spend the next 48 hours denying it. It takes up time which could be far better spent elsewhere.

There are times, however, when you can use stupid articles in papers to your advantage. A good example is the way the French press treated our goalkeeper Mark Crossley when Forest played Auxerre in the second round of the UEFA Cup. He's always been a big, heavy lad, but as long as he keeps it to reasonable levels he's a very good goalkeeper. When we got to France, the local papers there before the game had this headline which basically said: Big Fat Goalkeeper! It was followed by an article saying he was overweight and too slow. We decided to use this to our advantage, so we made sure that Crossley knew about the article. We had it translated for him.

As we thought, he rose to it. No one was going to accuse him of being fat and slow and he responded in exactly the right way. He was absolutely outstanding, pulled off some marvellous saves and played a major part in keeping us in the tournament. So on that occasion a piece of nonsense was a motivating factor, but unfortunately examples like that are all too rare. All too often mickey-taking by the media can have a totally damaging effect, as in the case of Jason Lee. That just got completely out of control.

Jason is never going to be a technically gifted player and he certainly wasn't a typical Forest striker. We bought him from Lincoln City for £200,000. When he arrived he couldn't trap a bag of sand and a lot of people wondered what on earth we were doing. But there was method in our madness. We got him at a time when Stan Collymore was injured and our reserve striker Robert Rosario was also out with a long-term injury. We were playing small strikers like

Lee Glover and Gary Bull with five midfield players. The trouble was that every time we had to hit the ball long out of defence, it just kept coming back at us. Bull and Glover couldn't win it often enough and we kept finding ourselves back under pressure.

Jason stopped all that. He wasn't particularly skilful but he had terrific courage, gameness and honesty. He worked very hard. When the ball was hit long, he was big enough and brave enough to battle for it with anyone. Often he would win it, but even when he didn't he still caused the opposition problems. The ball would stay loose long enough for our midfield players to get onto it. He played within his limitations and I was pleasantly surprised with his progress.

In the 1995–96 season Jason was our most successful player in terms of goals per game, scoring eight league goals in 21 matches. That's not bad by anybody's standards, let alone a £200,000 striker. He had seven of those goals by New Year's Day. Then the goals started to dry up. He only got one more all season. His drop in form coincided with a drop in form in the team generally – it was a difficult time for us and a lot of players were struggling. Unfortunately, it also coincided with him becoming the butt of an endless stream of jokes by the comedians David Baddiel and Frank Skinner on the BBC 2 progamme *Fantasy Football League*.

I don't want to overstate this, and the thing was blown out of all proportion by the media at the time, but I do think it had an adverse effect on Jason; not as much as the team's overall loss of form, but it was a factor nevertheless. I don't particularly care for the kind of sneering to be found in programmes like *Fantasy Football*. It's fairly easy, cheap humour and all too often it's just insult masquerading as wit. I don't like the shallowness of the kind of people who do it, but I recognise that it can be a good way for fairly mediocre comedians to get themselves noticed and I accept you have to deal with them. Most of the time it's relatively harmless and it can be funny – as long as you're not the person on the end of the sneering, of course. But the Jason Lee thing went over the top. It started off as just a bit of nonsense with them calling him Pineapple Head because of his hairstyle.

That wasn't a problem. What concerned me more was the denigration of him as a player. That started to get nasty. What made it worse is that it was very successful in their terms. It became a talking point. It was an insignificant, minority programme but the Lee thing propelled it into the headlines. I asked Jason what he thought and he said it didn't bother him, but I sensed all along that it affected his confidence, certainly by the end of the season. If the team had been playing well and he'd been knocking a few goals in it might not have mattered, but we were struggling as a team.

He was battling away on his own up front, with team-mates who were struggling to find top form themselves. He began to take more than his fair share of the blame when the team wasn't playing well. It might not have been so bad if he had been an established international or even a regular first-team player, but he was neither. He was just a young lad trying to make his way in the game, stepping up from a lower division and trying to establish himself in the Premier League. At first, he became a bit of a cult hero with our fans, who recognised his limitations but also admired his gameness. But by the end of the season they had turned from laughing with him to laughing at him. There's a world of difference. It couldn't have been very pleasant to be walking down the street listening to the public shouting abuse picked up from this programme.

Having said all that, it still wasn't a major issue at the club and would have been forgotten if the *Sun* and the rest of the pack hadn't decided to blow it out of all proportion. The furore blew up because at the end of the season Jason was put on the transfer list through mutual consent. That decision had nothing to do with the *Fantasy Football* nonsense. It was down to money.

Jason was in the last year of his contract and was experiencing some financial difficulties. Having moved clubs twice within a few years, he had accumulated three houses which he was having difficulty selling. Nothing more sinister than that. He needed a big payday but I couldn't offer him one. We felt that the best way out of everything was for him to go on the transfer list and see if he could get a decent signing-on fee.

The next thing I know, there's a big article in the *Sun* saying I had put Jason on the transfer list because of the nonsense over the *Fantasy Football* show. It was utter rubbish. They made it look as if I had given them an exclusive interview, but I had never even spoken to them. It all blew up over a comment I made at a presentation dinner in Guernsey.

I was asked by a friend there to present some prizes and then do a question and answer session at the end. It went very well and then one of the audience asked me what I thought of Jason Lee and *Fantasy Football*. I answered in much the same way that I outlined above. Then someone in the audience rang the *Sun* to give them 'the big story'. That I had blamed *Fantasy Football* for ruining his career and that's why he was on the transfer list. That's not what I said at all. Either the informant in the audience had misinterpreted what I said or the *Sun* did.

The story appeared and I got slaughtered for it. Jason got slaughtered. It made us appear as if we couldn't take a bit of fun and were getting things out of all proportion, which just was not the case. It was a scandalous piece of journalism. What the *Sun* did was more damaging to me than what *Fantasy Football* did. It damaged my reputation and standing as a manager.

The problem is that once something gets into the papers, no matter how untrue or nonsensical it is, you can't stop it. It builds up a momentum and unfortunately all too often it's the tabloids that set the agenda. When a story like that appears in the *Sun* then for the next seven days the so-called quality papers chew the bones off it. They all picked it up. I got hammered, with them saying how ridiculous it was that a manager should put a player on the transfer list because of some trivial mickey-taking about his hairstyle.

I agree. It would have been ridiculous if it had been true, but it wasn't. The facts get overlooked and the papers quite happily blunder on regardless. It's very frustrating but there's little you can do about it. The more you protest about it, the bigger you make it, so sometimes all you can do is ignore it.

Even if you do try to complain and set the record straight, you're unlikely to get much satisfaction. I was particularly upset by an article in the *Daily Telegraph* reiterating the allegations about the Forest team's alleged behaviour in Majorca. Again, it was an example of the so-called quality press letting the tabloids set the agenda. The columnist Robert Philip followed up the story that had appeared in the *Sun* and did a piece on it. I complained to the paper, saying how disappointed I was that they should perpetuate a story that was completely untrue. They acknowledged my point but didn't do anything about it. There was no follow-up article the next day saying the allegations were unfounded.

The media can hit you when you least expect it with a story that has no grain of truth in it at all, even though you half wish it had. I was amazed to wake up one morning and read that I was about to become the new England manager. The *Sunday Express* had this big back page story by Richard Bott saying the whole thing had all been worked out. It said that having been turned down by the likes of Kevin Keegan and Bryan Robson, the FA had decided to turn to me. Apparently they were very impressed by the quiet, no-nonsense way I had taken over from Brian Clough and set about rebuilding Nottingham Forest. The article pointed out how I had got the team promoted at the first attempt and then taken it to third place in the Premier League.

The good men of the FA were also very impressed by the way I had masterminded Forest's impressive run in the UEFA Cup. Then I read about how I would be ready to quit Forest if we lost to Bayern Munich in the quarter-final. Apparently I felt there was no more I could achieve at the club, given its limited resources. I was ready for a fresh challenge and I was ready to take over the England side.

It was certainly fascinating reading, some of it very flattering. There was only one thing wrong with it: it was completely untrue. The FA never approached me. It was just a total embarrassment and I had to reassure people at the club. Fortunately, my chairman Fred Reacher knew that if I was approached by anybody, he'd be the first to know. Richard Bott wrote to me afterwards and said he was sorry to have embarrassed me, which was good of him. He said his sources were impeccable. Well, not too impeccable really. I don't think there was anything malicious in it. I think he genuinely thought it was true, and although it was a bit awkward for me, at least it did no real harm for once.

Success is the thing we all crave and strive for, but it can bring its own particular problems; problems which inevitably end up in the media. Our run to the quarter-finals of the UEFA Cup and that tie against Bayern Munich were obviously great for the club but they also put the media spotlight on us. Our performances had brought us a lot of well-earned praise. I was pleased because I wanted the players to enjoy their success and the attention it brought. Unfortunately, a few of them let it go to their heads.

It's the kind of thing that's difficult to put your finger on, but you know it's there. People start thinking they're better than they really are. I suppose it's the same in all organisations, everyone wants to own a piece of the credit. The problems arise when people start believing they're a bigger part of the success than everyone else. During that UEFA Cup run it manifested itself in different ways.

Some players stopped firing on all cylinders. They started believing the publicity and began to feel they could coast along. One or two others were getting a bit Johnny Big Potatoes about it all. I would go down to the training ground to find someone had invited a cameraman along for a photo session without getting permission. Then a TV crew turned up to interview someone else without letting anyone know. I heard a few unfortunate comments in the dressing room. There was a cockiness about the place which wasn't very helpful in enabling us to get on with our basic task of winning league points.

I decided to talk it through with the players before it got out of hand. I stressed how well we had done to get so far in the UEFA Cup and how it was great that we could look forward to playing a big glamour club like Bayern Munich. It would be a great occasion, but for now we had to put it out of our minds and keep our feet on the floor. The important thing was to concentrate on winning league matches. They seemed to appreciate that, everyone went away happy and it seemed the problem had been nipped in the bud.

Unfortunately, footballers tend to be very naive in dealing with the press. At the same time as the UEFA Cup run, I was having long-running negotiations with Ian Woan over his new contract. In the middle of it all we were due to play Aston Villa at home. The match had been chosen by Sky and so had been switched to Sunday. I got up in the morning feeling great. I had sorted out all the problems with the players, I was looking forward to the game and I fancied our chances. Then I picked up the Sunday papers and saw a big article on Woan that brought me right down to earth with a bump.

He was quoted as saying that because he was having such a good season, he could hold the club to ransom over his contract. It also said he thought we had no chance of winning the UEFA Cup – he thought we had done well to get so far but he didn't think we could beat Bayern Munich. I couldn't believe it. I spoke to him about it when we got to the ground. He said his comments about the Bayern game had been exaggerated, but it turned out that the quotes about his contract were basically true. I told him I wasn't happy about things like contract negotiations being made public; and after the talk we had all had, it was particularly disappointing to hear him saying he could hold the club to ransom.

I think he had just been naive, but unfortunately for him it came just at the wrong time. If it had happened a month or so earlier and had been an isolated incident, I might have ignored it on the day and had a quiet word with him later. But as there had been so many other problems, I felt I had to stamp on it before it got out of hand. I sent him home and he missed the game. He didn't like it very much but he accepted it. The other players responded well to it. They didn't like to see someone punished in that way but they recognised I had to do something.

At least it brought the matter of Ian's contract to a head and he signed a few days later. To his credit, he got straight back down to work and went on to put in some magnificent performances for us. We drew the game with Villa. Who knows, if Ian had been playing we might have won, but sometimes you have to make difficult decisions for the overall good of the club.

Another problem managers face with the media is the need for instant comments at moments when you're least able to give them. The after-match press conference, or press mauling as it should be called, is a good example. Ten years ago, you might only have had to do one interview with one reporter. Now, with the proliferation of papers and TV and radio stations, it can be half a dozen rapid-fire interrogations, one after another.

It means that within minutes of a match when you're still pumped up, still under stress, still reeling from the unfair decision or the missed open goal or whatever, you're being bombarded with questions by reporters ready to pounce on every little word you say. It's like being arrested by the police: you don't have to say anything but what you do say may be taken down and used in evidence against you. But with the press there's no judge to ensure justice is done.

Towards the end of my time at Forest, we were going through a terrible time on the pitch. In the midst of it all came a nightmare performance which was incredibly depressing even by our standards. West Ham had just knocked us out of the Coca-Cola Cup. It wasn't the defeat so much that hurt, it was the way we played.

We were absolutely abysmal and I felt totally desolate. I had tried to remain positive throughout our bad run and had done as much as I could to lift the players. We had changed the training routines, changed the formation; I had done everything I could think of and it had come to nothing. Then in the heat of the moment after the West Ham debacle, it was hard to see where to go next – and unfortunately that's the view I let slip at the press conference.

The game ended just before ten o'clock and by five past I'm being questioned by a pack of reporters wanting instant answers to all our problems. Normally in those situations you have to box a little clever, be diplomatic and put a brave face on things. Managers tend to try to put out an image of omnipotence, suggesting they always know what needs to be done to put things right. You see it during a match when they make a substitution. Everyone likes to give the impression that they have some wonderful master plan to save the match, when often they have no idea and are just clutching at straws. Sometimes it succeeds, most times it doesn't.

That night I was so down I let the mask slip. Some reporter asked: 'Where do we go from here?' I just answered honestly, saying that there was so much wrong that I didn't know where to begin. Bang! The charade of omnipotence was blown apart. It was one of those things you say and then instantly regret. I knew I would be made to pay.

I was immediately questioned about my health and I admitted that I hadn't been sleeping very well. There was nothing particularly sinister about that, it was nothing to do with my health. It was just that I was lying awake trying to work out where we were going wrong. The thoughts were constantly swirling around in my mind, as I'm sure they do with most people when they're facing a difficult problem at work. I'm not sure where all that thinking gets you, but you can't help doing it. Lying awake at night is hardly going to influence whether your striker scores that open goal or misses it, but nevertheless, no matter what you tell yourself, there's no escaping it.

As I expected, I got slaughtered in the press the next day with headlines saying things like 'Clark says he doesn't know what to do' and so on. The sleepless nights were mentioned and comments were made about my health. The impression given was that I was like the captain of the *Titanic* steering my ship towards the iceberg with no idea how to stop it. There were innuendos that it was all getting too much for me. That was nonsense, of course. I was simply giving a gut reaction at that moment because I felt so down.

An hour or so later I was starting to get over it and see how we might improve things. But, of course, the press have gone by then, they've got their story and the damage is done. As is so often the case, your one moment of desperation is frozen in time and held up for everyone to see and pass judgement. Your hundred moments of optimism afterwards count for nothing.

But then I have always been disappointed by the inability of the press to welcome anything which is good and positive. Bad news means big banner headlines whereas good news means nothing at all. One of the happiest occasions of my time at Forest was the Stuart Pearce testimonial match against Newcastle.

I've been involved in a lot of testimonials over the years and they've become a bit hackneyed. A lot of them aren't very good games and sometimes you almost feel that the supporters have been short-changed. But that was just an incredible night. The rapport between Pearce and the supporters was great. Twenty-four thousand of them paid their respects by turning out. They chanted Pearce's name but were also quick to take the mickey out of him when, uncharacteristically, he miskicked, sending the ball high into the stands. Pearce then did something even more uncharacteristic: he smiled on a football pitch.

The way Kevin Keegan and his team and their supporters conducted themselves was magnificent. They had just lost the Championship and had a real kick in the teeth, but their attitude that night was superb. They brought the whole squad down including Ginola, Asprilla, Ferdinand, Albert and Beardsley.

It was just the right kind of game, serious enough to be a contest but slack enough to produce lots of goals without becoming a farce. It was a wonderful spectacle which ended up 6–5. Pearce, fittingly, scored the winning goal. Keegan and his assistant Terry McDermott came on to play the last ten minutes and that put the icing on the cake. When they saw that, our supporters even started chanting for me to turn out – but I thought that would be going too far, even for a testimonial.

Our supporters really appreciated Newcastle. About a thousand of their supporters came down and I'm sure they enjoyed it too. There was a great atmosphere between the two sets of fans. We even had the Newcastle contingent chanting, 'There's only one Stuart Pearce.' Little did they think then that he would eventually end up on Tyneside. I think it was a wonderful night for football. I tried like hell to get something in the papers about it but it never got a mention. They just didn't want to know. You can bet your life if there had been any trouble, any whiff of controversy, they would have descended upon us like a pack of wolves.

Looking back over this chapter, I realise it may appear a little vitriolic at times. I don't mean to be, but when you have to endure the endless nonsense the media comes up with it's hard to remain calm all the time. But just to make sure I can't be accused of hypocrisy by producing an unbalanced report myself, let me say I have several friends among the gentlemen of the press and I know that most of them are honest and try to be fair most of the time. It's without doubt a small minority who cause the problems.

Should any of that small minority feel I have been unfair then I would be delighted to hear from them so I can put the record straight. They'll have to forgive me, though, if I can't refrain from smiling should they have the gall to say they've been misquoted, taken out of context or, heaven forbid, the victim of a totally inaccurate story.

CHAPTER 18

Man Utd, Murdoch and the Chattering Classes

A few years ago it would have seemed inconceivable that the whole nation could celebrate Arsenal winning the League and Cup double. Arsenal were the team everybody loved to hate, so what could have made them so popular all of a sudden? The answer is simple: in 1998 they stopped Manchester United winning the Premiership yet again. Football desperately needed the title to leave Old Trafford – United were in danger of making the game boring.

This is not a criticism, quite the contrary. It's the ultimate compliment. It wasn't the way United played that was boring, it was the fact that they were winning everything. It was taking the excitement and uncertainty out of the game. Manager Alex Ferguson and chairman Martin Edwards have done a brilliant job in taking Manchester United to unparalleled heights. Unfortunately, in doing so they've also created a monster. It's growing at such a pace it may soon devour us all.

During his highly successful reign, Alex Ferguson has shown an irrepressible will to win. You can only admire that, although it has led him to say some outrageous things on the rare occasions when his team has been beaten. That was especially the case in his earlier days at the club when he wasn't quite so secure in his position.

I was on the receiving end of some of his outbursts when I was manager of Nottingham Forest. The most public was towards the end of the 1995–96 season when we found ourselves about to play Manchester United and Newcastle within the space of a week. They were the two main contenders for the title so it meant we would play a major part in determining who won the race. By pure coincidence, the Newcastle manager Kevin Keegan had already agreed to bring his team down to play Forest in the testimonial match for Stuart Pearce at the end of the season.

At that time, we had only three games left to play and I was hoping we would take maximum points and qualify for Europe. However, our preparation for the final run-in took a dramatic turn when I got a phone call from a journalist on the *Sun* called Neil Custis. He asked if I wanted to reply to some comments he claimed Alex had made; apparently he'd been saying he thought Forest might go easy on Newcastle because of Pearce's testimonial. His reasoning was that Newcastle coming down as champions rather than as runners-up would help to ensure a bumper crowd for the testimonial.

I thought the idea was ridiculous and outrageous. I told

Neil I didn't want to comment until I had seen it in print; but apparently the comments were so strong the *Sun*'s lawyers were uneasy about them and the paper didn't publish the article. I thought that would be the end of it, but then gradually bits of the story began to appear in other newspapers. Various reporters started to embellish it, pointing out that I had played for Newcastle for most of my career. They honed in on the fact that some of our players were Geordies, that I'm a Geordie and still president of the London branch of the Newcastle fan club.

The whole thing started to snowball. Some of our players did some interviews and made some careless remarks. Ian Woan was quoted as saying he would prefer anyone rather than Manchester United win the title. Mark Crossley was similarly quoted. They weren't being nasty, just naive. Both were good professionals who would be doing their best against United and Newcastle. They were only echoing what most football fans throughout the country would have been saying. If there's one thing that unites the supporters of Arsenal, Liverpool, Newcastle and every other club, it's a dislike of Manchester United. Everyone wants to see them beaten no matter who they're playing. There's nothing sinister in that. It happens in all sports and is the price you pay for being spectacularly successful. It's partly envy, but it's mainly boredom at seeing the same side winning all the time.

Unfortunately, the comments by our players were used to prolong the argument. Then it got worse with the Newcastle players getting involved. Winger Keith Gillespie was quoted in the *Mirror* commenting on how Forest could do them a favour by beating United. He pointed out that we could still qualify for Europe and followed up by saying what a good record we had at Old Trafford.

That much was true. Forest did have a tremendous record against United at that time. In 1995, my newly promoted team went up there and beat them 2–1. Alex was very ungracious in defeat and accused Forest of playing dirty. I think he was trying to take the gloss off our victory, and so rather than explain why they had lost 2–1, he tried to criticise us instead. Alex is a very bad loser, but then to be fair he doesn't get much practice. It was the same with the great Liverpool sides of the Seventies and Eighties. They were diabolical losers, but again, they didn't do it enough to get good at it.

United were losers that year, though. They missed out on the League title, pipped at the post on the final day of the season by Blackburn. No single result determines the league, of course, yet the fact remains that if United had won against Forest they could also have won the title.

Much the same had happened in 1992 when Forest were managed by Brian Clough. They went up to Manchester with a makeshift team that had been ravaged by injuries. They were so desperate they had to play striker Nigel Clough at centre-half. Even Forest's most fervent fans thought they would be thrashed, yet they managed to pull off a 2–1 victory. It was good to win, obviously, but otherwise the result had no particular significance for Forest. It had an enormous significance for United, however. They were beaten to the League title that season too, this time by Leeds. Again, if they had won that day they would have won the Championship.

No wonder Ferguson was getting a little twitchy at the thought of playing us again. Forest had already played a major part in denying United two League titles. Maybe a touch of *déjà vu* was setting in and he could see history repeating itself. However, his reported remarks about the testimonial and Forest giving Newcastle an easy ride were unhelpful. Kevin Keegan looked furious when he was asked about it on television. He got very angry and emotional and said Ferguson had certainly gone down in his estimation. It didn't bother me that much, but I had to get involved to put the record straight. I ended up in the strange position of stating the obvious, that Forest would be doing their best to beat Newcastle.

In the end, the match at Old Trafford was a huge disappointment for us as United exacted a cruel revenge for our impertinence in denying them the title the previous year. We produced one of our worst performances of the season and were thrashed 5–0. Ironically, in view of what Ferguson had said, we played much better at home to Newcastle and the game ended up a 1–1 draw. It virtually put an end to their title hopes, so as it turned out we did play a major part in determining the fate of the Championship, but in exactly the opposite way to what had been suggested.

Afterwards people asked me if I thought it had all been a crafty ploy by Ferguson, a sort of psychological game to wind us up and get the best out of us when we played Newcastle. There may be some truth in this. He does seem to cultivate an attitude among his players that everyone is out to do them down, so it's them against the world. It no doubt helps to galvanise them and motivate them as a team. Nevertheless, he does tend to speak as he thinks, regardless of the consequences. He's paranoid as far as Manchester United are concerned and he would easily see images of a conspiracy forming. After a tough game against Leeds, he lambasted the Leeds players because they had played so well and tried so hard. He accused them of cheating their manager by not playing like that every week against other teams. He was the same in 1992 when United blew their chance of winning the title by losing 1–0 away at West Ham, who were relegated that year. Again, he laid into the West Ham players, saying it was 'obscene', if they played like that every week they would win the title.

You would think that by now he would have come to terms with the fact that everyone wants to beat United. Everyone gets psyched up to play them because they are the biggest and the best. He should take it as a compliment.

While Alex Ferguson has been busy making Manchester United invincible on the field, chairman Martin Edwards has been busy making them unassailable off it. He has been so successful that it now seems strange to think he tried to sell the club for a mere £10 million in 1989. The deal fell through. Edwards was no doubt disappointed at the time but he's been laughing all the way to the bank ever since. By 1998 the club's value had soared to over £600 million and Martin Edwards still owned a large slice of it. According to a survey carried out by the accountancy firm Deloitte and Touche in 1999, Manchester United are the richest club in the world in terms of annual turnover.

The catalyst that allowed Edwards and Manchester United to achieve such amazing success was the emergence of satellite television. Media magnate Rupert Murdoch needed a big exclusive attraction to persuade people to subscribe to his new stations, and, football provided the answer. It now attracts 70 per cent of BSkyB's audience. In return, Murdoch is pumping millions of pounds a year into the game.

As far as I know he has never even kicked a football, yet he is responsible for some of the greatest play ever seen in this country. For it's his millions which have helped to make the Premier League the richest in the world, even surpassing the Italian *Serie A*. It's his money that has enabled Premier League clubs to afford the wages of such stars as Gianfranco Zola, Dennis Bergkamp, Juninho and a host of others. The public has lapped it up and the game has become more popular than ever.

It's meant the image of the game has changed. It's no longer seen as the ballet of the working classes. Now it's becoming the plaything of the chattering classes. Businessmen, academics, even politicians are using it as a way of casting off a stuffy image and showing they have a bit of street cred. We've had former Prime Minister John Major attending matches and proudly proclaiming his interest in the game. His successor Tony Blair thought it would be a good photo opportunity to do some head tennis with Kevin Keegan.

Politicians who once found it fashionable to criticise football for its hooligan element are now more likely to be calling for a better deal for the fans. There seems to be no end to it. Former cabinet ministers used to write their memoirs or become something in the City once they left government. Now, like David Mellor, they're more likely to host football phone-in shows on radio and parade themselves as the people's champion by heading football task forces. The game has been going upmarket at an amazing pace, helped enormously by Sky Television. Just because a few rough-looking pubs show Sky matches, don't imagine the average Sky football subscriber is a lager-swilling boot boy. Murdoch's BSkyB has a much more affluent audience than ITV. Its percentage of the AB viewers much beloved by advertisers is much higher.

All clubs have benefited enormously from Murdoch's money and the game's higher profile, but no one has benefited as much as Manchester United. It was perhaps inevitable then that Murdoch's BSkyB should make a takeover bid for the club. It was easy to see the mutual attraction. Murdoch's money could make United even more powerful, while the club's worldwide popularity would help BSkyB open up new markets in the football-mad countries of the Far East. But with or without BSkyB it was obvious that Manchester United would continue to thrive as the country's glamour club and favourite team of the non-committed fan. They now cast a shadow over everybody. As teams like Liverpool, Arsenal, Newcastle and Chelsea battle it out with United for the League title, it's easy to imagine that they're all pretty much on a par. Nothing could be further from the truth. United are light years ahead. A comparison with Newcastle helps put the difference into perspective. The Geordie giants are a big club by anybody's standards. In 1999 when the cable TV company NTL was trying to buy Newcastle United, they valued it at £160m. That seems colossal until you remember that at the same time Manchester United was valued at four times that amount when Rupert Murdoch made his failed attempt to buy the club for BSkyB. And that was before United won the treble!

United's financial muscle isn't based purely on their ability to get people through the turnstiles. In 1999, gate receipts of £41.9m only accounted for about two fifths of their annual turnover of £110.7m. Television income, boosted by the Champions League revenue to £22.5m, provided another fifth. The remaining two fifths was made up of things like sponsorship, catering and the much-criticised sale of replica kits.

A comparison with a medium-sized club like Sheffield United might also help put things into perspective. Their turnover that same year was £6.4m, less than a fifteenth of Manchester United's. The turnover of Manchester United's catering department was nearly double what Sheffield United took in gate receipts.

You don't need to pore over company reports to appreciate the difference. A stroll through the big high street stores rams the message home. WH Smith in Nottingham city centre is barely a mile away from the Forest ground. Bear in mind that Forest are no small fry and have a track record that bears comparison with most top clubs – not many teams have won two European Cups, even Manchester United can't better that. Yet that WH Smith store in the heart of Forest territory has at least five times as many videos and books on sale about United as it does about Forest.

United's commercial strength is growing so fast even the big Continental clubs are being left behind. The commercial managers of clubs like Juventus and AC Milan look on with envy as they see grown men walking around towns in England wearing United football shirts. The same thing just doesn't happen in Italy. It's the land of style, of course, and style for them does not consist of a football shirt, even among football fans. AC Milan's merchandising manager Frederico Barbaro was amazed to see people wearing United shirts in a Manchester night club. He said he would love to see fans in Italy wearing his team's shirt in the same way but was forced to find other ways of merchandising the club's name. He was working on cakes and pastries in the team colours, but so far they haven't really taken off. As a result Milan's merchandising revenue is only 20 per cent of Manchester United's and shows little sign of catching up.

United's financial muscle is setting them apart from the rest of the Premier League. But clubs like Newcastle, Arsenal, Liverpool, Chelsea and perhaps one or two others form a second wave who are also pulling further away from the rest of the pack. Their wealth means it's likely that these teams will get stronger and go on to dominate the game even more than they do now.

There have always been wealthy clubs, of course, and the difference today is only one of degree. However, that small degree is crucial, for the big clubs are even stronger now than they were only five or ten years ago and their increasing wealth has come at a time when they can use it to greater effect than ever before. It's not just that they can pay ever-higher transfer fees; they have also been helped enormously by changes in contract law which enables them to accumulate more and more of the top players.

The first change was the freedom of contract ruling introduced in the 1980s. Before then, football clubs wielded enormous power over their players. They could virtually hold onto them for their entire careers if they wanted. Some clubs did that. All they had to do was offer a new contract when the old one ran out and the player had little option but to accept it. He could ask for a transfer, but if the club refused there was little he could do.

Freedom of contract quite rightly changed all that by allowing a player to leave his club if he wanted to. The only saving grace from the club's point of view was that his new club would still have to pay a transfer fee. On its own, freedom of contract didn't have a major effect on the game, but it was a time bomb waiting to explode. All it needed was one bright spark to cause the detonation and, in 1995, a little-known Belgian midfielder stepped into the limelight to do the honours.

Jean-Marc Bosman was never more than a journeyman footballer but he's had a bigger impact on the game than any other player in history. When he went to the European Court of Justice to challenge the existing transfer system, it was to change our industry forever. He won the all-important ruling which meant players could change clubs when their contracts expired without a transfer fee having to be paid. This inevitably means that the best players will gravitate to the bigger clubs which can pay the highest wages. This has always tended to be the case but now it's happening more and more, because players are so mobile and the rewards for moving are so much greater.

The high wages on offer because of the ruling have led to a change of attitude among players. Until Bosman, top-flight stars would expect an almost automatic right to a first-team place. If they didn't get it they would be asking for a transfer. Now it's quite common to see internationals sitting on the subs bench or not even featuring at all. Think of Jesper Blomqvist and Ole Gunnar Solskjaer at Manchester United, Patrik Berger at Liverpool and Tore Andre Flo at Chelsea.

It's frequently said that money can't guarantee success and that's true, of course, but it certainly helps. If anyone is in any doubt about that then I suggest they check out the top five places in the Premiership over the last five years and write down how many names appear other than Manchester United, Arsenal, Chelsea, Newcastle and Liverpool. They'll be in no danger of suffering from writer's cramp. If they wanted to continue the exercise, they could write down the names of all the Premier League clubs, starting with the richest and finishing with the poorest. They'll find the list bears an uncanny resemblance to the league table at the end of the season. Money is talking louder and louder.

Some might say the situation today isn't all that different from the Seventies and Eighties when Liverpool were dominant. The truth is, there's a world of difference. In those days, when Liverpool slipped up it was still possible for clubs like Nottingham Forest, Aston Villa and Everton to win the league. They're all fairly sizeable clubs but it's hard to see them winning the league today. Another difference is that even when Liverpool were winning the title, they were challenged by a much wider range of teams. Even small clubs like Ipswich and Queens Park Rangers were able to run them close.

It could be argued that Newcastle paying £15 million for Shearer is no different from Forest paying £1 million in 1979 for Trevor Francis, the first player to break the million-pound barrier. There is a crucial difference, however. When Trevor Francis was the most expensive player around, it was still possible for a relatively modest club like Nottingham Forest to afford him. He could have gone to any one of a dozen clubs. There's no way they could afford the inflated price for his modern-day equivalent, Alan Shearer.

I was a member of the Nottingham Forest side that won the League title in 1978 under Brian Clough. The proceeds from that great year provided the money to buy Francis. He paid most of that money back when he scored the winning goal in the 1979 European Cup final. We were European champions, and it was a tremendous achievement for such a small club. A few years later Aston Villa did the same thing.

It summed up the romance and glorious unpredictability of football at that time. What would be the chances of a medium-sized club doing the same today? Someone like West Ham, Queens Park Rangers or Bolton Wanderers – the very idea seems laughable. Even if another manager with the genius of Brian Clough emerged, I doubt whether he could pull it off. The gulf in resources has become too great.

Does this really matter? I think it must, because it's robbing the game of its most precious commodity, uncertainty. In most businesses, if you can see off the opposition and create a monopoly then you've got it made. You can sit back like Microsoft's Bill Gates and watch the profits roll in. In football, however, you may be doing no more than cutting your own throat, certainly in the long run. What is the good of Manchester United and a few other select clubs disappearing into the stratosphere only to find there's nobody up there who can give them a decent game?

Uncertainty really is the lifeblood of football. It needs as much evenly balanced competition as possible. If the game is to remain exciting, we need to find it difficult to forecast who will win the major competitions. Yet with the rich getting richer and the poor getting poorer, all the uncertainty of the past is disappearing. We're now getting to a situation where we're pretty sure at the start of the season that the richest three or four clubs will share out all the top prizes. Similarly, we have a pretty fair idea which four or five weaker clubs will provide the three for relegation.

Can the game afford for this to happen if it's to hold on to its present level of popularity? It depends on whether the public of the future want to watch a sport where the outcome is virtually certain before the season starts. Some of them will, of course: the genuine hard-core fans – the people prepared to stand in the rain queuing for tickets for their favourite team, travel 300 miles to see them lose and still come back next week. But what about the less committed, those who've hardly ever attended a match but who've been part of the armchair revolution that has made television football such a great success? I'm not at all sure about them. Their interest might vanish just as quickly as it emerged.

The chattering classes could quickly move their fickle attention elsewhere and the boom of the last ten years could come to an abrupt end. This could have a dramatic impact. I can't foresee a time when football fades so much from the public's eye that no one will want to televise it. But I can easily foresee a situation where a dip in viewing figures will mean a big drop in the amount of money the TV moguls are prepared to pay for it. They may well decide the time has come to reduce their investment and pump some of their millions into another sport such as American football, basketball or whatever.

A drop in the television money paid to football wouldn't have to be that great to have a major impact. If it's enough to mean we're no longer richer than the Italian and Spanish leagues, then we could find that the foreign legion who've brightened up our afternoons over the last few years could abandon us for a sunnier and more lucrative climate. We might even find that instead of importing star players, we'll be exporting them. It's a mercenary business and the Gascoignes, Platts and Linekers of the future may once again be tempted abroad by the lure of the lira or the pull of the peseta.

We could then find ourselves in a vicious circle where the game, already wounded by its predictability, becomes even less attractive when it loses its glamour players. That would inevitably lead to falling attendances and even lower TV revenues. When that happens, we need to be sure we haven't cut ourselves off from the genuine fans at the grass roots of the game. Not the chattering classes, but the kind who sustained us 20 years ago and will still sustain us in 20 years' time if we treat them with the respect they deserve. Unfortunately, I think our eyes have been so dazzled by visions of cash registers and pound signs that we've been neglecting them. I fear too many of them are being priced out of our stadiums. This should not be allowed to happen.

We can learn something here from the experience of baseball in America. It fell victim to its own greed during the Seventies and Eighties. Fuelled by television and huge merchandising operations, its popularity seemed invincible. Then as the ticket prices went up to accommodate the ever-increasing wage bills, the fans eventually decided enough was enough. They resented having their loyalty taken for granted and they stayed away in droves. Once slighted, it took years of effort to woo them back. They are returning, but in nothing like the same numbers and it will be some time before the game rediscovers its former glories.

Like baseball, football over here has become so popular that the ticket prices have skyrocketed. The laws of the market make this inevitable but surely something can be done to protect the committed but less well-off fans. I would like to see more variation in seating prices. The expensive seats, especially those used in corporate hospitality, should be far more expensive. Big businesses seem perfectly willing to pay at the moment, but we shouldn't be fooled into thinking they'll do this forever. Most people attending such functions aren't particularly interested in football anyway. It's just a novelty and many of them don't even watch the game.

Soon the whole thing will become passé and businessmen will find some other way to impress clients or reward high-flying executives. Flights to Paris, tickets to rock concerts, a private audience with a TV star or whatever. The football bandwagon certainly won't keep rolling forever, so we may as well take the money while it's on offer, but we should use it to subsidise a large area of much cheaper seats for the ordinary fans who are being priced out.

At the moment, most big clubs aren't all that keen to offer cheaper prices. The commercial managers point to a simple case of supply and demand. They say they're selling out every week so why should they cut the prices? Well, I hope they're right because public taste can change overnight. When you're on a roll, it's very easy to think that the good times will last forever and business will just keep getting better and better. That never really happens. Ask the baseball players.

The pendulum always starts to swing backwards. When that happens to football, we need to be sure the game still has a solid foundation. We must treat the genuine fans with the respect they deserve. The time will come again when we need them. In the meantime, the game could do itself a power of good by denting the domination of Manchester United and the other big clubs. Short of kidnapping their players there is no easy solution, yet we've got to keep trying. Hopefully someone will do it. There are about 90 league managers all hoping it will be them. It will take time, determination and an endless amount of hard work. And if anyone has about £50 million to spare, that would help as well.

INDEX

Note: 'FC' denotes Frank Clark.